English Collocations in Use

How words
work together
for fluent and
natural English

Self-study and
classroom use

Felicity O'Dell

Michael McCarthy

CAMBRIDGE
UNIVERSITY PRESS

CAMBRIDGE UNIVERSITY PRESS
Cambridge, New York, Melbourne, Madrid, Cape Town,
Singapore, São Paulo, Delhi, Mexico City

Cambridge University Press
The Edinburgh Building, Cambridge CB2 8RU, UK

www.cambridge.org
Information on this title: www.cambridge.org/9780521707800

First published 2008
7th printing 2013

Printed in Italy by L.E.G.O. S.p.A.

A catalogue record for this publication is available from the British Library

ISBN 978-0-521-70780-0 Edition with answers

Contents

Topics: the modern world

Topics: people

Basic concepts

Functions

Acknowledgements

The authors wish above all to thank their editors at Cambridge University Press, especially Caroline Thiriau and Frances Disken whose expertise and unfailing guidance and encouragement have supported the project from beginning to end. We also thank Alyson Maskell for all her professional skills in steering the book through its final stages. Linda Matthews, too, deserves our thanks for organising the production schedules for the book.

We must also thank the Corpus team at Cambridge University Press for their help in providing lists of frequent collocation errors made by learners taking advanced exams. Special thanks also must go to Liz Walter for her invaluable feedback and suggestions while we were compiling the lists of collocations.

Also, as always, we thank our domestic partners for their patience and support during the writing of this book.

We have also received invaluable feedback from both students and teachers. Their comments have had a great influence on the final manuscript and we are very grateful to them. In particular, we would like to thank the following teachers from all over the world who have reviewed the material throughout its development:

Garan Holcombe, UK
Terry Nelson, Korea
Brendan Ó Sé, Ireland
Paul Pauwels, Belgium
Artur Polit, UK
Mark Tondeur, UK

The authors and publishers acknowledge the following sources of copyright material and are grateful for the permissions granted. While every effort has been made, it has not always been possible to identify the sources of all the material used, or to trace all copyright holders. If any omissions are brought to our notice, we will be happy to include the appropriate acknowledgements on reprinting.

p12, A-: extract from *Cambridge Advanced Learner's Dictionary* (third edition 2008), reproduced by permission of Cambridge University Press; p14, A, first text: adapted extract of 'I need help with my homework' by Rebecca O'Connor from *The Times*, 24 March 2007, © NI Syndication; p14, A, second text: adapted extract of 'Movie review: The Interpreter' by Angus Wolfe Murray from www.eyeforfilm.co.uk/reviews.php?film_id=10698, reproduced by permission of Eye for Film; p54, C: adapted extract of 'The Sideways Bike' from BBC News at bbc.co.uk/news reproduced by permission of the BBC; p56, B second text: adapted extract of 'A Selection of Great European Train Routes, London – Tangiers' from http://www.hostelbookers.com/content/train-travel/europe, © HostelBookers.com Ltd.

Produced by Kamae Design, Oxford

Illustrations by Kathy Baxendale, Jo Blake, Robert Calow, David Mostyn and Sam Thompson

Using this book

What is a collocation?

Collocation means a natural combination of words; it refers to the way English words are closely associated with each other. For example, *pay* and *attention* go together, as do *commit* and *crime*; *blond* goes with *hair* and *heavy* with *rain*.

Why learn collocations?

You need to learn collocations because they will help you to speak and write English in a more natural and accurate way. People will probably understand what you mean if you talk about *making a crime* or say *there was very hard rain this morning*, but your language will sound unnatural and might perhaps confuse. Did you mean that there was a lot of rain or perhaps that there was a hailstorm?

Learning collocations will also help you to increase your range of English vocabulary. For example, you'll find it easier to avoid words like *very* or *nice* or *beautiful* or *get* by choosing a word that fits the context better and has a more precise meaning. This is particularly useful if you are taking a written exam in English and want to make a good impression on the examiners. In advanced level exams, marks are often specifically awarded for the appropriate handling of collocation.

At an advanced level an appreciation of collocation can also be helpful in terms of appreciating other writers' use of language. Skilled users of the language may choose to create effects by varying the normal patterns of collocation, with the aim of either startling or amusing their audience. This technique is particularly popular with poets, journalists and advertisers. From an appreciation of the way in which creative writers play with language, you may then even want to move on to use words in more original ways yourself. You are more likely to be able to do this effectively if you have assimilated the standard patterns of language use presented in this book.

How were the collocations in this book selected?

The collocations presented in this book were all selected from those identified as significant by the CANCODE corpus of spoken English, developed at the University of Nottingham in association with Cambridge University Press, and the *Cambridge International Corpus* of written and spoken English. We also made extensive use of the *Cambridge Learner Corpus*, a corpus of student language which showed us what kind of collocation errors learners tend to make.

These corpora show that there are many thousands of collocations in English. So how could we select which ones would be most useful for you to work on in this book?

Firstly, of course, we wanted to choose ones that you might want to use in your own written and spoken English. So, in the unit *Health and medicine* we include, for example, **shake off a cold** and **respond well to treatment** but not **grumbling appendix**, which is a strong collocation, but one which – we hope – most of you will not feel the need for.

Secondly, we decided it would be most useful for you if we focused on those collocations which are not immediately obvious. **A pretty girl**, **a modern car** or **to buy a ticket** are all collocations, but they are combinations which you can easily understand and produce yourself without any problems. So we deal here with less obvious word combinations, for instance, **flatly contradict** (not ~~strongly~~ contradict) and **bitter enemies** (not ~~serious~~ enemies).

Some of you may have already used our *English Collocations in Use Intermediate*. In general, we have tried to avoid focusing on collocations that we dealt with in that book. The one exception is with collocations that the *Cambridge Learner Corpus* highlighted as causing frequent problems for students, even in advanced level exams. We felt that it would be useful to draw attention to such collocations again, even if we had dealt with them previously.

Idioms can be seen as one type of collocation. We deal with them separately in *English Idioms in Use*, and so do not focus on them here.

How is the book organised?

The book has 60 two-page units. The left-hand page presents the collocations that are focused on in the unit. You will usually find examples of collocations in typical contexts with, where appropriate, any special notes about their meaning and their usage. The right-hand page checks that you have understood the information on the left-hand page by giving you a series of exercises that practise the material just presented.

The units are organised into different sections. First we start with important information relating to learning about collocations in general. Then there is a section focusing on different types of collocation. The rest of the book deals with collocations that relate to particular topics such as *Student life* and *Film and book reviews*, concepts such as *Sound* or *Difficulty* and functions such as *Cause and effect* or *Comparing and contrasting*.

The book has a key to all the exercises and an index which lists all the collocations we deal with, and indicates the units where they can be found.

How should I use this book?

It is strongly recommended that you work through the six introductory units first, so that you become familiar with the nature of collocations and with how best to study them. After that, you may work on the units in any order that suits you.

What else do I need in order to work with this book?

You need a notebook or file in which you can write down the collocations that you study in this book, as well as any others that you come across elsewhere.

You also need to have access to a good dictionary. At this level we strongly recommend the *Cambridge Advanced Learner's Dictionary* as this gives exactly the kind of information that you need to have about collocations. It does this both through the examples provided for each word entry and through special collocations boxes or mini-panels. Your teacher, however, may also be able to recommend other dictionaries that you will find useful. If you have access to the Internet, you will also find this a useful source of information about language use and we occasionally suggest possible activities using the web.

So, a study of collocation is **highly recommended** (*Unit 8*) if you want to impress people with your natural and accurate use of language and to **gain more marks** (*Unit 1*) in English exams. Above all, we **sincerely hope** (*Unit 57*) both that this book will help you **acquire the knowledge** (*Unit 17*) you need about English collocations and also that you will **thoroughly enjoy** (*Unit 8*) working through the units in *English Collocations in Use Advanced*.

1 Introducing collocations

A What are collocations?

A collocation is a combination of two or more words which frequently occur together. If someone says, 'She's got *yellow hair*', they would probably be understood, but it is not what would ordinarily be said in English. We'd say, 'She's got **blond hair**'. In other words, *yellow* doesn't collocate with *hair* in everyday English. *Yellow* collocates with, say, *flowers* or *paint*.

Collocations are not just a matter of how adjectives combine with nouns. They can refer to any kind of typical word combination, for example verb + noun (e.g. **arouse someone's interest, lead a seminar**), adverb + adjective (e.g. **fundamentally different**), adverb + verb (e.g. **flatly contradict**), noun + noun (e.g. **a lick of paint, a team of experts, words of wisdom**). There is much more about different grammatical types of collocation in Unit 3.

Phrasal verbs (e.g. *come up with, run up, adhere to*) and compound nouns (e.g. *economy drive, stock market*) are sometimes described as types of collocations. However, in this book we consider them as individual lexical items and so include them here only in combination with something else, e.g. **come up with a suggestion, run up a bill, adhere to your principles, go on an economy drive, play the stock market**.

It can be difficult for learners of English to know which words collocate, as natural collocations are not always logical or guessable. There is, for example, no obvious reason why we say **making friends** rather than *getting friends* or **heavy rain**, not *strong rain*.

Learners also need to know when specific collocations are appropriate. This is usually referred to by linguists as knowing which register to use. **Alight from a bus** is a formal collocation used in notices and other official contexts. In everyday situations we would, of course, always talk about **getting off a bus**. There is more about register and collocation in Unit 6.

B Why is it important to learn collocations?

An appreciation of collocation will help you to:
- use the words you know more accurately
  In other words, you'll **make** (NOT do) fewer **mistakes**.

- sound more natural when you speak and write
  By saying, for example, **of great importance**, rather than *of big* or *high importance*, you won't just be understood, you will – quite rightly – sound like a fluent user of English.

- vary your speech and, probably more importantly, your writing
  Instead of repeating everyday words like *very*, *good* or *nice*, you will be able to exploit a wider range of language. You would gain more marks in an exam, for instance, for writing *We had a blissfully happy holiday in a picturesque little village surrounded by spectacular mountains* than for *We had a very happy holiday in a nice little village surrounded by beautiful mountains*, even though both sentences are perfectly correct.

- understand when a skilful writer departs from normal patterns of collocation
  A journalist, poet, advertiser or other inventive user of language often creates an effect by not choosing the expected collocation. For example, a travel article about the Italian capital might be entitled *No place like Rome*, a reference to the popular expression **There's no place like home**.

Exercises

1.1   **Match the two parts of these collocations.**

1	adhere to	rain
2	arouse	different
3	blond	of wisdom
4	come up with	your principles
5	flatly	an economy drive
6	fundamentally	a seminar
7	go on	someone's interest
8	heavy	contradict
9	lead	hair
10	a lick	the stock market
11	play	of paint
12	words	a suggestion

1.2   **Correct the underlined collocation errors with words from B. Be careful, you will find the words in the *text*, not in the examples.**

1 Exam candidates often make <u>faults</u> in their use of verbs like *do*, *make*, *go* and *get*.
2 Try to use a <u>longer</u> range of language when you write.
3 Exam candidates who use collocations well <u>gather</u> better marks.
4 You have to know what normal collocation patterns are before you can <u>lose</u> them.
5 The writer used colloquial language to <u>form</u> an effect.

1.3   **Look at these sentences from a hotel brochure. Improve the style by replacing the words in italics with the word in brackets that forms the best collocation. (Use each word only once.)**

1 Our new family hotel is set in a *nice* location and all the rooms have *nice* furnishings and *nice* views over the surrounding countryside. (stylish / secluded / breathtaking)
2 Visitors will enjoy the *good* atmosphere in either of our *good* dining rooms, both serving *good* food to both residents and non-residents. (delicious / relaxing / spacious)
3 We organise tours to *beautiful* surrounding villages where you'll have the opportunity to take some *beautiful* photographs and sample the *beautiful* local cuisine. (mouth watering / picturesque / stunning)

1.4   **Write F (formal), I (informal) or N (neutral) in the brackets at the end of each sentence. In each pair of sentences, there is one neutral sentence and one formal or informal sentence. Underline the collocations that are noticeably formal or informal.**

1 a Passengers must not alight from the bus while it is in motion. ( )
   b Passengers must not get off the bus while it is moving. ( )
2 a Let's grab a bite before we get down to work. ( )
   b Let's have something to eat before we start work. ( )
3 a SFTS has the right to bring the agreement to an end with three months' notice. ( )
   b SFTS reserves the right to terminate the agreement with three months' notice. ( )
4 a She thinks her boyfriend is planning to pop the question tonight. ( )
   b She thinks her boyfriend is planning to ask her to marry him tonight. ( )

1.5   **Correct the four collocation errors in this paragraph.**

The yellow-haired boy said he had joined the English class to get some new friends. He also said that he wanted to learn about collocations because it would be of big importance in helping him to do fewer mistakes when writing in English.

2 Strong, fixed and weak collocations

A Strong collocations

A strong collocation is one in which the words are very closely associated with each other. For example, the adjective **mitigating** almost always collocates with **circumstances** or **factors**; it rarely collocates with any other word. *Although she was found guilty, the jury felt there were mitigating circumstances*. [factors or circumstances that lessen the blame]
Here are some other examples of strong collocations.

collocation	comment
Inclement weather was expected.	(very formal) = unpleasant weather *Inclement* collocates almost exclusively with *weather*.
She has **auburn hair**.	*Auburn* only collocates with words connected with hair (e.g. *curls, tresses, locks*).
I felt **deliriously happy**.	= extremely happy Strongly associated with *happy*. Not used with *glad, content, sad*, etc.
The chairperson **adjourned the meeting**.	= have a pause or rest during a meeting/trial *Adjourn* is very strongly associated with *meeting* and *trial*.

B Fixed collocations

Fixed collocations are collocations so strong that they cannot be changed in any way. For example, you can say *I was walking to and fro* (meaning I was walking in one direction and then in the opposite direction, a repeated number of times). No other words can replace *to* or *fro* or *and* in this collocation. It is completely fixed. The meaning of some fixed collocations cannot be guessed from the individual words. These collocations are called idioms and are focused on in the book *English Idioms in Use*.

C Weak collocations

Weak collocations are made up of words that collocate with a wide range of other words. For example, you can say you are **in broad agreement** with someone [generally in agreement with them]. However, *broad* can also be used with a number of other words – **a broad avenue, a broad smile, broad shoulders, a broad accent** [a strong accent], **a broad hint** [a strong hint] and so on. These are weak collocations, in the sense that *broad* collocates with **a broad range** of different nouns.

Strong collocations and weak collocations form a continuum, with stronger ones at one end and weaker ones at the other. Most collocations lie somewhere between the two. For example, the (formal) adjective *picturesque* collocates with *village, location* and *town*, and so appears near the middle of the continuum.

stronger ← ——————————————————————— → weaker
inclement weather   *picturesque village*   *broad hint*
                             picturesque location   *broad accent*
                                                             broad smile

D Types of collocations in this book

The collocations in this book are all frequently used in modern English. We used a corpus (a database of language) to check this. We have also selected the collocations which will be useful to you as an advanced learner. We pay most attention to those that are not predictable. *A broad avenue*, for example, would be predicted by any student who knows *broad* and *avenue*. However, the use of *broad* to mean *strong* as in **a broad accent** is more difficult to predict.

Exercises

2.1 Complete the collocations using the words in the box. You will need to use some words more than once.

adjourn	auburn	broad	deliriously	inclement	mitigating	picturesque

1 a .... accent
2 in .... agreement
3 .... circumstances
4 .... factors
5 .... hair
6 .... happy
7 a .... smile
8 a .... location
9 .... a meeting
10 a .... town
11 .... a trial
12 .... weather

2.2 Rewrite each sentence using a collocation from 2.1.

1 Melissa has quite a strong Scottish accent.
2 Bad weather led to the cancellation of the President's garden party.
3 We were all very happy when we heard we'd won the award.
4 Their new home was in a very pretty location.
5 Because there were circumstances that made the theft less serious, the judge let him off with a warning.
6 I think we should stop the meeting now and continue it tomorrow.
7 She had a big smile on her face when she arrived.
8 She has lovely reddish-brown hair.
9 I think we're generally in agreement as to what should be done.

2.3 Think of as many collocations as you can for each word. Then look in a dictionary for other suitable words. Write W (weak) or S (strong) next to each group depending on how many words you found.

1 extremely ....
2 .... an effort
3 cancel ....
4 deliver ....
5 .... a living

2.4 How useful do you think the collocations you have worked on in 2.2 and 2.3 are for you personally? Choose which collocations are most important to you personally and make sentences with them.

FOLLOW UP Choose an English-language text that you have worked on recently. Underline five collocations in it. Are these collocations weak, strong or fixed?

3 Grammatical categories of collocation

A Verb + noun

verb	noun	example	meaning of verb
draw up	a list a contract	Our lawyer **drew up a contract** for us to sign.	prepare something, usually official, in writing
pass up	a chance an opportunity	I didn't want to **pass up the chance** of seeing Hong Kong, so I agreed to go on the trip.	fail to take advantage of
withstand	pressure the impact	The police officer's vest **can withstand the impact** of a bullet.	bear

B Noun + verb

noun	verb	example
opportunity	arise	An **opportunity arose** for me to work in China, so I went and spent a year there.
standards	slip	People feel educational **standards slipped** when the government cut finances.

C Noun + noun

- Noun + noun collocations used to describe groups or sets:
  There's been **a spate of attacks/thefts** in our area recently. [unusually large number happening in close succession]
  The minister had to put up with **a barrage of questions/insults** from the angry audience. [unusually large number, happening at the same time]
- Noun + noun collocations used with uncountable nouns:
  By **a stroke of luck** I found my keys in the rubbish bin! [sudden, unexpected piece of luck]
  She gave me **a snippet of information** which is top secret. [small piece of information]

D Adjective + noun

This is not an **idle threat**; I will call the police if this happens again! [simply a threat]
He waited in the **vain hope** that the Minister would meet him. [unlikely to be fulfilled hope]
There is **mounting concern/criticism/fury** over the decision. [growing concern etc.]
The **simple/plain truth** is that no one was aware of the problem.

E Adverb + adjective

The article provides an **intensely personal** account of the writer's relationship with his sons.
Joe's sister was a **stunningly attractive** woman.

F Verb + adverb or prepositional phrase

The teenager tried to persuade his mother that he was innocent but he **failed miserably**.
I don't like to travel with my brother because he **drives recklessly**. [wildly, without care]
As soon as the singer came on stage she **burst into song**.
If your dog starts to **foam at the mouth**, you should take it to the vet immediately.

G More complex collocations

Mary was looking forward to retiring and **taking it easy for a while**.
It's time you **put the past behind you** and started focusing on the future.

Exercises

3.1 Match a word from each box to form collocations. Not all the collocations appear on the opposite page, so use a dictionary to help you if necessary.

A disease	evidence	opportunity	smoke	**B** arises	chatter	howls	pressure
standards	teeth	wind	withstand	rises	slip	spreads	suggests

1 .... 5 ....
2 .... 6 ....
3 .... 7 ....
4 .... 8 ....

3.2 Complete each sentence using a collocation from 3.1 in the appropriate form.

1 The scientific .... human beings first emerged in Africa.
2 The .... was .... all night and it was raining, so I couldn't sleep.
3 The machine has to be made of materials that can .... a lot of ....
4 Oh, no! There's a fire. Look at the .... from those buildings.
5 It was so cold I couldn't stop my .... from ....
6 Our survey shows that parents believe .... have .... at the school.
7 You must accompany Bob on one of his business trips to Asia, if the .... ever ....
8 An alarming new .... is .... among cattle in the south of the country.

3.3 Rewrite the underlined part of each sentence using a collocation from the opposite page.

1 I don't want to <u>say no to</u> the chance of meeting such a famous person.
2 We'll have to <u>write</u> a contract before you start work, as it's a new position.
3 You're working too hard. You should try to <u>relax for a short period of</u> time.
4 This new bullet-proof car can <u>take</u> the impact of a rocket-propelled grenade.
5 Do you have any interesting <u>little bits</u> of information about our new boss to tell us?
6 The Minister faced a <u>large number</u> of questions from reporters.
7 I had <u>some</u> luck last week. The police found my stolen wallet and nothing was missing.
8 There's been a <u>number</u> of violent attacks in the area recently.
9 After her divorce Mandy was determined to <u>forget the past</u> and build a new life.

3.4 Answer these questions.

1 Who do you think is the most stunningly attractive person you have ever seen?
2 What should you do if you are in a car with someone who is driving recklessly?
3 Do you prefer walking in the country if there is a gentle breeze or a strong wind?
4 Would you write your most intensely personal thoughts and feelings in your diary?

3.5 Choose the correct collocation.

1 He said he would throw us out, but it was just a(n) *vain / idle / lazy* threat.
2 They rushed the victim to hospital, in the *idle / simple / vain* hope of saving her life.
3 The government is encountering *mounting / climbing / rising* criticism of its policies.
4 There is *raising / mounting / vain* concern across the world about climate change.
5 The horse was *fuming / foaming / fainting* at the mouth, so we called the vet.
6 Suddenly, without warning, Marjorie *busted / bustled / burst* into song.
7 The *right / straight / plain* truth is that I hate my job.
8 I tried to persuade her but I'm afraid I failed *desperately / miserably / wholeheartedly*.

4 Using your dictionary and other resources

A Using dictionaries

Good modern learners' dictionaries include example sentences which make a point of illustrating each word's most frequent collocations. Enormous databases of language, known as corpora, are used to analyse speech and text to identify which words collocate most frequently. Look up the word

> **abject** /'æb.dʒekt/ *adjective* FORMAL **EXTREME** **1 abject misery/poverty/terror, etc.** when someone is extremely unhappy, poor, frightened, etc: *They live in abject poverty.* ○ *This policy has turned out to be an abject failure.* **NOT PROUD** **2** showing no PRIDE or respect for yourself: *an abject apology* ○ *He is almost abject in his respect for his boss.* ● **abjectly** /'æb.dʒekt.li/ *adverb*

abject in the *Cambridge Advanced Learner's Dictionary* and you will find the entry above. Notice how frequent collocations are used in the example sentences.

Remember that dictionaries today are not only available on paper; you can also access them on CD-ROM and online. These can be particularly helpful when you are exploring collocations, as they make it quick and easy to search for items in different ways and to jump from one entry to another. Online dictionaries give you easy access to an enormous amount of information relating to meaning, collocation and register, for which there is not enough space in a book. In whatever form, a dictionary is an invaluable tool for developing your knowledge of collocation.

B Using other resources

The Internet enables you to explore collocations in other ways too. A search engine can be very helpful. Although it is almost impossible to come up with a word combination that a search engine will be unable to find examples of, the number of results can give you a good idea of whether a combination is a true collocation or not. For example, compare the results below for "abject failure" and "abject success". (You need to use inverted commas so that the search covers only instances where the words occur consecutively.)

> Results **1–10** of about **104** for "abject success". (**0.14** seconds)
>
> Results **1–10** of about **283,000** for "abject failure". (**0.04** seconds)

To be sure that a word combination is a normal collocation you would expect a search engine to find thousands of instances of it.

It is often useful to consult a corpus to find out how words are commonly used. Here is an example of how a corpus presents information:

> s he came from a domestic situation of **abject** poverty, it was a radical chang
> despite their efforts, the project was an **abject** failure, and all involved were
> many years the population had suffered **abject** terror as a result of the policie
> vast majority of this tiny country live in **abject** poverty, despite the immense
> ir living conditions can be described as **abject** misery, such was the state of t

The site www.webcorp.org.uk lets you use the web as a corpus. It will search the web for words of your choice and display samples of text containing those words. You can make various choices about how you wish the web to be searched and how you would like the information to be presented to you.

The problem with using the web as a corpus is, of course, that the Internet includes a certain amount of language that is not accurate or standard. You may prefer to do a search of the British National Corpus at www.natcorp.ox.ac.uk which is a real corpus, so should produce a more accurate result. Both these sites should prove useful resources if you want to do your own in-depth investigation of specific collocations.

Exercises

4.1 Use your dictionary (book, CD-ROM or online version) to find three collocations for each of these words.

1 cast (as verb with basic meaning of throw) ....
2 application ....
3 utter (as adjective) ....
4 absolutely ....
5 release (as verb) ....

4.2 Rewrite the underlined part of each sentence using the word in brackets. Use a dictionary to help you.

1 His opponent <u>made critical and damaging remarks about</u> his honesty. (ASPERSIONS)
2 The point you're making <u>is quite unrelated to</u> our topic. (RELEVANCE)
3 The speaker <u>praised</u> Janice's contribution to the project. (TRIBUTE)
4 As soon as she got home Kay <u>started working</u>. (SET)
5 His rudeness <u>made</u> us all <u>fall silent</u>. (RENDERED)
6 <u>It is uncertain how many</u> workers will be affected by the changes. (INDETERMINATE)
7 The marketing campaign <u>was better than we had expected</u>. (EXCEEDED)
8 <u>I'm slightly unsure</u> about these sales figures. (NIGGLING)

4.3 Type these phrases into a search engine. Don't forget to use inverted commas. How many results do you get for each? What does this suggest about whether these phrases are collocations or not?

| cast a concert | cast a groan | cast a play | cast a smile |

4.4 Go to www.natcorp.ox.ac.uk. Type in the words below. Note the number of times the words appear in the same collocations as in the sentences in 4.2. Do they often collocate with any other words?

| aspersions | indeterminate | niggling | tribute |

4.5 a) Answer these questions.

1 What field do you work in, or plan to work in?
2 What do you enjoy doing at the weekend?
3 What is, or was, your favourite subject at school or college?
4 How did you spend your last holiday?
5 What did you have to eat yesterday?
6 What was the last book you read?

b) Now use a dictionary to find three collocations that relate to each of your answers to 1–6.

Find the collocations by looking up key words relating to your answer. For example, if your answer to question 1 was *medicine*, you could look up key words such as *medication*, *ill* and *surgical* to find such collocations as *to prescribe medication*, *terminally ill*, *a surgical procedure*.

c) Now write example sentences using the collocations you have found.

> **TIP** Be careful when using corpora to check or find new collocations. Corpora include many types of text, some of which are technical. Check the sources of the texts where the collocations appear to see if the collocations are used in a variety of situations.

5 Finding and working on collocations in texts

A Finding collocations

You can expand your collocation vocabulary by training yourself to notice collocations whenever you read. Note the collocations in these three examples of texts from different sources – a newspaper feature, a film review and a website for London tourists.

> As a **newly qualified** teacher at a comprehensive school in Wiltshire, every day Joe **faces the challenge** of **gaining the respect** of a class of 15-year-olds. Joe, 26, admits it is a **tough challenge** but thinks he is **winning the battle**. Joe, who teaches English and media studies and coaches a school football team, will **qualify fully** in July, **pending the results**[1] of his lesson assessments. With this **milestone passed**[2], and the increased financial stability it will bring, Joe will **turn his thoughts to** buying his first home.

[1] (formal) as long as he achieves successful results   [2] major life event behind him

> ### ★★★ *The Interpreter*
>
> She has a **gift for languages**, which brings her to the UN. She wants to **make a difference**. She is idealistic in that single-minded, dedicated manner associated with freedom fighters. Silvia (Nicole Kidman) remains an enigma. When Tobin Keller (Sean Penn) begins to investigate her, he is faced with a blank sheet. She is beautiful, blonde, lissom and lithe. She lives alone, has no lover, rides a Vespa throughout New York and works all day, **providing simultaneous translation** for delegates. She has an odd accent, which, like everything else about her, is **difficult to pin down**[3].

[3] hard to fix or place

> **Entertaining children in London**
> Covent Garden's buskers and jugglers **provide** no-cost **entertainment** in a car-free setting, and you've always **got the chance** of being plucked from the crowd to help out with a trick. Don't **underestimate the value of** London's public transport as a **source of fun**, either. The #11 double-decker from Victoria, for instance, will trundle you past the Houses of Parliament, Trafalgar Square and the Strand on its way to St Paul's Cathedral for a modest sum. The driverless Docklands Light Railway is another guaranteed **source of amusement** – **grab a seat**[4] at the front of the train and pretend to be the driver, then **take a boat** back to the centre of town from Greenwich.

[4] (informal) take a seat

Remember you will also hear collocations in conversations, lectures, songs and films. Try to get into the habit of recording any interesting collocations that you notice.

B Recording collocations

When working on collocations in a text, use your dictionary to find more relating to one or both parts of the original collocation. You can record strong collocations effectively in collocation forks:

simultaneous < translation / equation   **pending** < the outcome / the results / the response

and weak ones in collocation bubbles (because there are so many more of them):

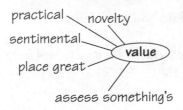

practical, novelty, sentimental, place great, assess something's — **value**

reliable, valuable, cheap, rich — **source** — of funding, of income, of entertainment

Exercises

5.1 Complete each sentence using a collocation from A.

1 Tania has always had a .... so I'm not surprised she wants to study Chinese at university.

2 At high tide the sea covers the causeway and the only way to get to the island is to
....

3 It's very crowded in this café. You .... and I'll get our drinks.

4 Once my exams are over I'll .... planning a holiday.

5 Far more people these days manage to ....
against cancer.

6 Most politicians say they enter politics because they want to ....

7 Try not to .... having good friends. Ultimately, friendship is far more important than work.

8 He's got the job – .... a successful .... in his driving test tomorrow.

9 Although they lack experience, ... doctors are often very enthusiastic and passionate about their work.

5.2 Complete the collocations. The first letters are given to help you. Use a dictionary if necessary.

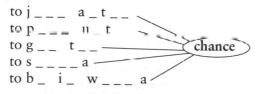
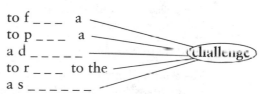

to j _ _ _ a _ t _ _
to p _ _ _ u _ t
to g _ _ t _ _
to s _ _ _ _ a
to b _ i _ w _ _ _ a
→ chance

to f _ _ _ a
to p _ _ _ a
a d _ _ _ _ _
to r _ _ _ to the
a s _ _ _ _ _ _
→ challenge

5.3 Check these expressions (a) in a good dictionary and (b) using a search engine. Which two are collocations and which two are not?

1 learn by head   2 learn by heart   3 lose a chance   4 miss a chance

5.4 Answer these questions.

1 Name three milestones in your life that you have already passed.
2 Are you already fully qualifed? If so, as what? If not, when will you be?
3 What are some typical sources of income?
4 What is the toughest challenge you have ever faced?
5 What qualities would be needed by someone providing simultaneous translation?
6 What are some examples of things that have sentimental value for you?

5.5 Here is one student's plan for work on collocations. Complete the gaps, using a dictionary if necessary. Then tick the ideas you can use yourself.

- (1) .... an effort to notice collocations in any English text I read.
- (2) .... hold of a good dictionary to check other collocations for words that I want to learn.
- Write down at least three collocations for each new word I want to (3) .... to memory.
- Look back over old homework to see where I have (4) .... mistakes with collocations and (5) .... my best to (6) .... those mistakes in future.
- (7) .... a point of using good collocations when I have to write or speak in English.
- Read and listen to as much English as (8) .... because that will expose me to natural collocations.
- Every week revise the collocations I have (9) .... a note of in my vocabulary file.

6 Register

A What is register?

Our use of language changes according to the situation that we are in. If your close friend hosts a party, you could say, 'Thanks for the party. It was a blast.'(very informal) However, if your boss was the host, you would probably say, 'Thanks for the party. I really enjoyed it.' (neutral) In this example, *neutral* and *very informal* are both examples of register.

The register of most language is neutral (it can be used in any situation). However, register can also be formal, informal, characteristic of a certain professional field (e.g. legal, journalistic or media) or specific to official notices and forms.

Our choice of register depends on **what** we are talking about (business, the news, the neighbours), **who** we are talking to (friends, strangers, figures of authority) and **how** we are talking to them (in a letter, in an email, in public, in private). Study the table below and notice how different words and phrases are used to describe the same situation.

example	register	comment
The police are **investigating / looking into** the arms deal.	neutral	Either version would not seem out of place in any spoken or written contexts.
The cops are trying to **dig out info about** the arms deal.	informal	Phrasal verbs are often an informal alternative – although some are neutral.
The police are **conducting an investigation into** the arms deal.	formal	Longer words of Latin or Greek origin often indicate more formal language.
Police to **probe** arms deal	neutral, journalistic	*Probe* is typical of newspaper headline style.
The arms deal may be **subject to police investigation**.	formal, legal and official	*Subject to investigation* is typical of a bureaucratic or legal style.

Be careful not to think of formal language as written and informal language as spoken. There is a lot of overlap. For example, markedly formal language is most typical of official or academic writing and official legal or bureaucratic speech. Informal language is typical of conversation, personal letters and emails, and some journalism.

B Formal versus neutral collocations

formal (from official documents)	neutral (spoken)
Students must **submit** their **assignments** by 1 May.	'You have to **hand in** your **assignments** by 1 May.'
Students may **request an extension** after **consulting their tutor**.	'You can **ask for an extension** after you've talked to / **had a word with** your tutor.'

C Informal versus neutral collocations

That film was **totally awesome**! (mainly used by teenagers, predominantly US) [neutral equivalent: absolutely amazing/fantastic]
That party was **well good**! (*Well* used to mean 'very'/'really', mainly by younger speakers.)
I **haven't a clue / the foggiest idea** what you mean. [neutral equivalent: I have no idea]
We can **grab a snack** before the meeting if you're hungry. [neutral equivalent: have a snack]

 Make a note in your notebook if a collocation is very formal or informal in register.

Exercises

6.1 Write F (formal), I (informal) or N (neutral) in the brackets at the end of each sentence. Underline the collocations which indicate the register. Then rewrite the formal and informal sentences to make them neutral.

Example: Do not alight from the bus until it stops. (F)   *Do not get off the bus until it stops.*
1 I feel dead tired all the time. ( )
2 We were all bored stupid by the poetry reading. ( )
3 Currency exchange offices are located in the arrivals lounge. ( )
4 She conducted a study of single-parent family units. ( )
5 She did her degree in London and found work there in 2001. ( )
6 I just got the latest software so my computer is bang up-to-date. ( )
7 Affix a passport-size photograph to the application form. ( )
8 Jake asked his tutor for an extension to complete his dissertation. ( )

6.2 Match the beginning of each sentence with its ending. Then label each sentence with the appropriate register from the list below. Underline the collocations which indicate the register.

Registers: informal conversation (IC)   journalism/news (J)   entertainment (E)
technical (T)   legal (L)   notices (N)

1 This is breaking	a ring after dinner.
2 These are the songs that are climbing	according to model and road conditions.
3 There are tons of good reasons	blockbuster from Star Studios.
4 Visitors must keep to the designated	news here on Global TV Extra.
5 In any such case, customers shall forfeit	electronic circuit.
6 Fuel consumption may vary	of the fitness machines to 20 minutes.
7 I'll give you	to win support for the plan.
8 The Minister will tour Asia in a bid	the charts this week.
9 Joss Engold stars in the latest	for not studying law.
10 A microchip is a miniaturised	testify for a second time.
11 Please restrict your use	areas at all times.
12 A witness may be asked to	the right to compensation.

6.3 Complete this conversation between a doctor and a patient, using the verbs in the box in the appropriate form. The language is quite informal, without technical medical terms.

come	clear	do	feel	get	run	take	write

Doctor: What can I (1)...................... for you, Mr Wilson?
Patient: Well, Doctor, I've been (2) .... a temperature for the last couple of days and I've (3) .... out in a rash on my neck. Do you see? These red spots here.
Doctor: Hmm. Let's (4) .... a look.
Patient: It's very irritating and I have trouble (5) .... off to sleep at night. Then I (6) .... down all day and can't concentrate on my work.
Doctor: Right. I don't think it's anything serious. I'll (7) .... you out a prescription for some lotion which should help to (8) .... up the rash.

6.4 Look at how the doctor describes the case in his records using more technical language. Choose the correct word from the choice provided. Use a dictionary to help if necessary.

A patient (1) *presented / represented* this morning with an (2) *elevating / elevated* temperature. He was also (3) *exposing / exhibiting* a neck rash. He further (4) *complained / grumbled* of an (5) *inability / impossibility* to concentrate.

7 Metaphor

When we speak metaphorically, we use words in a non-literal sense. For example, when we say a writer **casts light on a situation**, we mean that the writer helps us understand it more clearly, in the same way that putting a light on in a dark room helps us see more clearly.

A Metaphors based on the body

collocation	example	meaning
face (up to) the facts	You're never going to run in the Olympics. It's time you **faced (up to) the facts**.	accepted reality
shoulder the blame	Although others were also responsible for the problem, Sue decided to **shoulder the blame**.	take responsibility for something bad
foot the bill	Choose what you like from the menu – the company is **footing the bill**.	paying
head a team	Jo **heads a team** working on crime prevention.	leads a project group
keep someone on their toes	Having three sons under the age of five **keeps** Jana **on her toes**.	makes her stay active and concentrated
have an eye for	Gina **has an eye for** detail, so ask her to check the report.	is good at noticing
go hand in hand with	Unemployment **goes hand in hand with** social unrest.	happens at the same time or as a result of

B Metaphors based on weight

Heavy can be used to mean serious or difficult, as in **heavy responsibility. A heavy burden** can be either something heavy to carry or a difficult responsibility to deal with, while a **heavy book** can be either one that weighs a lot or one with difficult content. A **weighty tome**, however, would only be used to mean a book with difficult content. Similarly in **weighty matters** or **weighty problems**, *weighty* means difficult and serious.

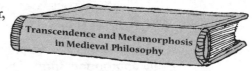

Light, the opposite of *heavy*, can also be used metaphorically to mean carefree or lacking in seriousness. So **light reading** is reading material that is not serious. If you do something with a **light heart**, you feel carefree and happy.

If someone has a **slim chance** of doing something, there is a chance, but it is small. **Fat chance** (very informal) means almost no chance.

C Metaphors based on movement

James did a lot of partying in his final year and **ran into difficulties** with his course. His father was **hopping mad**[1] when he only just managed to get his degree. However, when he left university he **walked straight into a job**[2] in an excellent company. Some people **jumped to the conclusion** that this was because he'd started going out with the Managing Director's daughter. His mother worried that, if their relationship **hit the rocks**[3], he would **run into trouble** at work too.

[1] (informal) extremely angry [3] ended (metaphor based on a boat being destroyed on rocks)
[2] got a job very easily

Exercises

7.1 Rewrite the underlined part of each sentence using a metaphor from A.

1 The presidential visit <u>meant no one had time to relax</u>.
2 Rosetta <u>took full responsibility</u> for the failure of the project.
3 I don't think Greg will ever win Rosie's heart; it's time he <u>accepted that</u>.
4 The company had done so well that year that it agreed to <u>pay</u> for a staff night out.
5 I'm glad I'm not <u>in charge of</u> this team.
6 Carola <u>is very good at finding</u> a bargain.

7.2 Answer these questions about the metaphors on the opposite page.

1 What usually goes hand in hand with inflation, an increase or a decrease in savings?
2 If a relationship hits the rocks, is it the end or the beginning of that relationship?
3 If you say that someone is hopping mad, do you mean that they are good at athletics or that they are very angry?
4 If you run into difficulties or trouble, does that mean that they happen quickly?
5 Would you be more likely to call a magazine publishing gossip about celebrities light reading or a weighty tome?
6 If you talk about facing the facts, are the facts more likely to be pleasant or unpleasant?

7.3 Explain the difference in meaning between the sentences in each pair.

1a Jill walked into a well-paid job in the City.   1b Jill got a well-paid job in the City.
2a Pat is heading the project team.   2b Pat is backing the project team.
3a Dad jumped to the wrong conclusion.   3b Dad came to the wrong conclusion.
4a Rod left the room with a light heart.   4b Rod left the room with a heavy heart.
5a Fat chance I've got of winning!   5b I've got a slim chance of winning.

7.4 Choose the correct collocation.

1 Kieran's constant whistling is *riding / getting / driving* me crazy.
2 Sylvia is a first-class designer as she has a good *eye / nose / hand* for detail.
3 You mustn't shoulder the heavy *weight / burden / task* of redecorating the house all by yourself.
4 There is just a *thin / slim / skinny* chance that Marek might pop in today.
5 The committee has some *fat / weighty / heavy* matters to discuss on today's agenda.
6 When the results came out, Marco was thrilled to see his name *footing / facing / heading* the list of successful candidates.

7.5 Explain what the play on words is based on in each of these headlines.

1
ATHLETE RUNS INTO TROUBLE

4
SHOEWORLD CO. TO FOOT THE BILL

2
DIET PILLS HAVE FAT CHANCE OF SUCCESS

5
NEW LAW MAKES RABBIT OWNERS HOPPING MAD

3
NEW DIRECTOR KEEPS ROYAL BALLET ON ITS TOES

TIP You may find it useful to draw little pictures in your vocabulary notebook – or imagine them in your mind – to help you remember some collocations.

8 Intensifying and softening adverbs

Adverbs are often used before adjectives and verbs either to strengthen their meaning (intensifying adverbs) or to weaken it (softening adverbs).
Her comments were **deeply offensive**. (intensifier – very/extremely)
Her comments were **slightly offensive**. (softener – a little bit)

A Intensifying adverbs

Notice how intensifying adverbs are used to mean 'extremely' or 'completely' in the sentences below. The expressions marked with * are very informal.

Jane really enjoys doing housework. You should see her flat – it's always **spotlessly clean**.
It was **downright rude** of Antonio to tell Paula that she looked older than her own mother. I hope he feels **thoroughly ashamed**.
It's **blatantly obvious** that Olga is only interested in Richard because he's **stinking rich***.
I wonder what she'll do when she finds out he's **wildly exaggerated** how rich he really is!
I don't know what I was worrying about! The exam turned out to be **dead easy***!
This celebrity website is good fun but most of the information is **wildly inaccurate**.

B Softening adverbs

Note the softening adverbs used in these sentences from newspapers.

The spokesperson said the new insurance scheme was only **slightly different** from the old one. [weak collocation; *slightly* can be used with a wide range of adjectives]
The Chief Executive said he was **mildly surprised** by the public interest in the firm's plans. [*mildly* also collocates with *amusing/ed, irritating/ed, offensive*]
Alfredo Scaluzzi's new film is **loosely based on** a nineteenth century novel. [*loosely* also collocates with *centred, structured, related, connected*]
Ms Giroa said she regarded reports that she was about to seek a divorce as **faintly ridiculous**. [fairly formal; *faintly* also collocates with *amused, surprised, patronising, absurd*]

C Alternatives to very

There are a variety of words that you can use as alternatives to *very* which collocate with most adjectives, for example: *really, extremely, terribly, incredibly* and *awfully*. Other adverbs collocate with certain adjectives and verbs but not with others.

alternatives to very	✓	NOT
highly	unlikely, educated, recommended	~~appreciate, influence, interesting~~
strongly	influence	~~appreciate~~
greatly	appreciate, influence	
utterly	absurd, ridiculous	~~sorry, busy, glad, lonely~~
completely/totally/entirely	different, dependent, separate	
thoroughly	enjoy	

Absolutely only collocates with adjectives which have strong meanings, e.g. **absolutely** (NOT ~~very~~) **delighted**, **very** (NOT ~~absolutely~~) **happy**.

Exercises

8.1 Match a word from each box to form collocations.

| blatantly downright spotlessly | ashamed clean inaccurate |
| stinking thoroughly wildly | obvious rich rude |

8.2 Complete each sentence using a collocation from 8.1.

1 He's just bought a 200,000 dollar yacht – he must be .... !
2 I'm amazed you didn't realise she was lying! It was......................... .... to me!
3 It was .... of him not to say hello to the secretary.
4 I've been hoovering and dusting all day, so now my flat is ....
5 Most of the facts were wrong in that news report. It was ....
6 You should be .... of yourself. Your behaviour was appalling!

8.3 Rewrite the underlined part of each sentence using a collocation from the opposite page.

1 The American writer Mark Twain is famous for commenting that reports of his death had been <u>over-exaggerated</u>.
2 This restaurant is <u>recommended by many different people</u>.
3 The exam was <u>extremely easy</u>; everyone got high marks. (make this informal)
4 The musical *West Side Story* is <u>kind of based on</u> the plot of Shakespeare's play *Romeo and Juliet*. (make this less informal)
5 The idea of the boss singing *Happy Birthday* to me struck me as <u>a little bit ridiculous</u>.
6 The success of the Wimbledon tennis tournament is <u>100% dependent</u> on the weather. (give two answers)
7 I <u>really enjoyed</u> the days I spent at your lovely house in the country.
8 I was <u>just a little surprised</u> by her decision to quit her job so soon.
9 I was <u>really delighted</u> when they told me I'd got the job.
10 The new model of this camera is <u>a little bit different</u> from the old one.

8.4 Add intensifying adverbs from the opposite page to these sentences to make the words in bold stronger.

1 I **appreciate** the fact that you have given me so much of your time.
2 Sometimes Tony says **ridiculous** things.
3 The crossword in today's newspaper is **difficult**. I can't even start it!
4 It's **sweet** of you to offer to help.
5 I found his remarks **offensive**; he should apologise.
6 She leads a **lonely** life in a tiny house on a remote island.
7 We should try to keep the two groups **separate** from each other.
8 She is an **educated** person.
9 I've been **busy** all week.
10 That meal was **expensive**! I'm not eating there again.

8.5 Are the adverb collocations correct or not? If they are incorrect, correct them using collocations from C opposite.

1 I thoroughly enjoyed the film.
2 Your help would be strongly appreciated.
3 The song is highly influenced by Brazilian folk rhythms.
4 I find the situation utterly absurd.

TIP Look out for more collocations with these words as you listen and read, and record them in collocation bubbles indicating what they do, and do not collocate with.

9 Make and verbs that mean make

A Common errors with make

The *Cambridge Learner Corpus* shows that some of the most frequent collocation errors made by candidates in advanced English exams relate to the use of *make*. Here are some typical errors and their corrections.

I would like to ~~do/give~~ some suggestions – **make some suggestions**
I think that I could ~~have/give~~ a contribution to the project – **make a contribution**
I expect you to ~~give~~ a formal apology – **make a** formal **apology**
There is still some way to go and lots of improvements to ~~do~~ – **improvements to make**
Thank you very much for ~~doing~~ these arrangements – **making these arrangements**

Sometimes candidates use *make* where another verb is required. For example:
We're going to ~~make a party~~ on Saturday – **have a party**
Lana ~~made some interesting research~~ into her family roots – **did ... research**

B Other expressions with make

It's a good idea to **make a habit of** switching off the lights when you leave a room.
If you always say exactly what you think, you'll **make** a lot of **enemies**.
The team **made** several **attempts** to climb the mountain before they finally succeeded.
I hope that they'll **make a success of** their new restaurant business.
I have to go to a party for a colleague after work but I will try and **make an** early **escape**.
Our research team has **made** an important **discovery** about how whales communicate.
When doing your accounts, try to ensure you **make** all the **calculations** correctly.
If we move the sofa closer to the window, it'll **make room for** the piano.
I first **made his acquaintance** when he moved in next door. [formal: got to know him]
The house we looked at is just what we want and we've decided to **make an offer** on it.
As no one else has any ideas, I'd like to **make a proposal**. [make a formal suggestion]
We must **make a stand against** the casino they propose to build here. [protest about]

C Other verbs that mean make

collocation	example	comment
create a good/bad impression	Wear your grey suit to the interview if you want to **create a good impression**.	slightly more formal than **make an impression**
create a (+ adj.) atmosphere	The lanterns in the garden **create a** romantic **atmosphere**.	more formal than **make for a romantic atmosphere**
stage a protest	The students **staged a protest** against rising tuition fees.	= make a formal protest
lodge a complaint	Several people have **lodged a complaint** about the bank manager's rudeness.	= make a formal complaint
rustle up a meal	It took Sam ten minutes to **rustle up a meal**.	(informal) = make a meal very quickly
run up curtains	This weekend I'm going to **run up** some **curtains** for my new room.	= make quickly using a sewing machine
turn in a profit	This month our company should **turn in a profit** for the first time.	slightly more informal than **make a profit**
coin a phrase	I wonder who **coined the term** 'blogging'.	= invent / make up a new phrase

Exercises

9.1 Are these sentences correct or incorrect? If they are incorrect, correct them.

1 Have you any suggestions to make about how to celebrate the school's anniversary?
2 We are planning to have a party next Saturday.
3 The company director gave a formal apology for his earlier comments.
4 The manager had to make a number of changes to office procedures in order to do all the improvements he had planned for the company.
5 My sister did all the arrangements for the party.

9.2 Complete each sentence using a word from the box.

acquaintance	attempt	calculations	discovery	enemies
habit	offer	room	stand	success

1 Try to make a .... of noticing good collocations in any text you read.
2 A railway official asked us to move our luggage to make .... for the boy's bike.
3 The new CEO has made a lot of .... by being so autocratic.
4 If Pauline makes a .... of this project, she'll probably get promoted.
5 The old gentleman said he was delighted to make my ....
6 Do you think you'll make an .... on the flat you viewed yesterday?
7 Every young scientist dreams of making a .... that will change the world.
8 Rachel made no .... to contact me when she was over here last year.
9 We tried to make a .... against the new housing development but to no avail: the contractors started work this morning.
10 The .... that you made contained a few inaccuracies.

9.3 Replace *make* in each sentence with an alternative word. Then say whether you have made the sentence more or less formal.

1 The Green Party plans to make a major protest against the government's new farming policy.
2 Tessa helped me to make some lovely cushion covers for my new flat.
3 I regret to inform you that several clients have made complaints about your conduct.
4 You won't make a good first impression if you arrive late for your interview.
5 It won't take me long to make a meal for the children.
6 Do you expect your business to make a profit this year?

9.4 Rewrite each sentence using the word in brackets.

1 At the meeting the chairman proposed something rather interesting. (PROPOSAL)
2 I hope we can leave soon as I'm terribly tired. (ESCAPE)
3 I'm reading a fascinating book about the invention of new words and phrases to express new social and technical needs. (COINED)
4 We changed the layout of the hall to make it more relaxed for the yoga class. (ATMOSPHERE)
5 I tried to phone the company several times at the weekend. (ATTEMPTS)
6 Kim contributed very positively to the discussion. (CONTRIBUTION)
7 The service was poor but I wouldn't go so far as to formally complain. (LODGE)
8 I first got talking to Roger on a train. (ACQUAINTANCE)

> **FOLLOW UP**
>
> **Make a point of** looking back through any pieces of your writing that a teacher has corrected. Have you ever **made any mistakes** involving collocations with *make*? If so, **make an effort** to use those expressions correctly in your next assignment.

10 Communicating

A Collocations with *say*, *speak*, *talk* and *tell*

I **wouldn't say no to** a nice cup of tea. [informal: I'd really like]
Needless to say / It goes without saying that the workers voted in favour of the wage increase.
Jana **didn't say a word** when I told her I was leaving.
Generally speaking, people are aware of the environmental consequences of their actions.
Strictly speaking, a tomato is a fruit and not a vegetable because it contains seeds.
She always **speaks very highly** of you. [says good things about you]
Charlie, stop mumbling and **speak properly**. I can't understand a word you're saying.
(generally used by parents or teachers to children, not between adults)
Now we've got to know each other, I think it's time we **talked business**.
At first, Andrew appears to be **talking nonsense** but
after a while you realise he's actually **talking a lot of sense**.
I'll **tell** you **a secret** but please don't tell anyone else.
The old woman looked at Glen's palm and began to
tell his fortune. [predict his future life]

B Collocations meaning communicate

example	comment
I asked why she didn't trust him but she wouldn't **give** me **a reason**.	NOT ~~say~~ a reason
The charity **states its aim** as being to help underprivileged children.	(formal) also **state your purpose/goal**
The staff on reception required each visitor to **state their business** before issuing them with an entry permit.	(formal) = say what their intentions are
In her lecture Lucia **gave an account of** her trip to the Andes.	used about both speech and writing
The speech **got** the **message** about the policy changes **across**.	(informal) = conveyed the idea
I **declare** Hiroshi Yamamoto **the winner of** the gold medal.	(formal) statement made at the time of the win
He was **pronounced dead** at 1.10.	(formal) used when making an official statement of death
The old man tried to **impart** his **knowledge** to his sons.	(formal) = transfer knowledge; also **impart wisdom**
That journalist gets amazing stories but he won't **divulge** his **sources**.	(formal) = make something secret known; also **divulge a secret**
The Internet is a powerful means of **disseminating information**.	(formal) = spreading information to a lot of people
We **notified the police** of the burglary.	(formal) = officially informed
Although found guilty, Robson continued to **protest his innocence**.	(formal) = insist he was not guilty
He **professed ignorance** of the dent to the car but I think he was lying.	(formal) = claimed – perhaps insincerely – that he did not know
Did you **break the news** to her that her mother is in prison?	used for news that is very upsetting

Exercises

10.1 Complete each sentence with the appropriate form of *say*, *speak*, *talk* or *tell*.

1 Strictly .... , you shouldn't be here.
2 Ilya .... me a secret and made me promise not to pass it on to anyone else.
3 It goes without .... that we'll invite you to our wedding.
4 I spend most days with my three-year-old son, so forgive me if I start .... nonsense.
5 The teachers always .... very highly of my son's abilities.
6 I had my fortune .... at the fair yesterday.
7 It's so hot. I wouldn't .... no to an ice cream, would you?
8 Shall we have lunch first and then sit down to .... business?
9 I think that, generally .... , it's better to use public transport than drive yourself.

10.2 Rewrite the underlined part of each sentence to make it more formal.

1 The victim was asked why he had not <u>told</u> the police sooner about the mugging.
2 The older generation has always attempted to <u>pass its wisdom on</u> to young people.
3 Stockman has always <u>insisted that he is innocent</u>.
4 Robert <u>claimed that he knew nothing</u> of the damage to the car.
5 The reporter had no option but to <u>explain where he had got his information from</u>.
6 The doctors <u>said he was</u> dead when they arrived at the scene of the accident.
7 The judges <u>said that Magda Karlson had won</u> the competition.
8 The charity does a great deal to <u>inform people</u> about its activities.

10.3 Are these sentences correct or incorrect? If they are incorrect, correct them.

1 Do you think I managed to give the message across in my speech?
2 Needless to say, he didn't tell a word to his parents about what had happened.
3 You can't chew gum and say properly at the same time.
4 He refused to say his reasons for turning down our invitation.
5 She was devastated when we dropped the news to her.
6 In your report we would like you to give a detailed account of what happened.
7 I really like this documentary maker, he tells a lot of sense.
8 At the beginning of your dissertation you must say your goals clearly.

10.4 Use a dictionary to find nouns to complete these phrases based on collocations in B.

1 .... of innocence in the face of evidence to the contrary
2 a company's .... of aims
3 .... of information among the population
4 .... of a crime to the police
5 .... of the winner of a competition

10.5 Use a dictionary to complete these collocation forks.

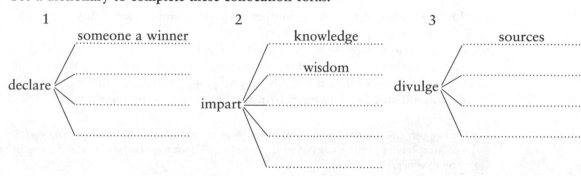

11 Collocations with phrasal verbs

A News items

The Justice Minister said he would **abide by the decision**[1] of the High Court to free the prisoner.

The police, **acting on a tip-off**[3], arrested the thieves as they left the building.

Hollywood star Glenda Nixon has **filed for divorce**[4]. She and her husband Kevin Lomax have lived apart for the last six months.

The new Regional Governor will **take up office**[2] on 1 March, following his party's recent election victory. The Education Commission has been asked by the government to **come up with an alternative** to the present schools examination system.

The police intend to **come down heavily on**[5] anyone causing trouble at tomorrow's football final.

[1] (formal) accept the decision
[2] (formal) start work in an official position
[3] a secret warning
[4] made an official request for a divorce
[5] punish very strongly

B Everyday conversation

Note how B uses a collocation with a phrasal verb to repeat A's ideas.

A: It was great just sitting in the town square and enjoying the feel of the place, wasn't it?
B: Yes, it was nice to just sit there **soaking up the atmosphere**.

A: I think we should both arrange our work schedules so we don't have to work in May.
B: Yes, I'll try to **free up some time** so we can go away together.

A: I'm finding it hard to find time to practise the French I learnt at school.
B: Yes, I have a similar problem **keeping up my Spanish**.

A: Well, all that gardening has made me hungry.
B: Yes, it certainly helps to **work up an appetite**.

A: It'd suit my arrangements if we could meet up at lunch-time.
B: Yes, that would **fit in** perfectly **with my plans** too.

A: The hotel wasn't as good as I thought it would be.
B: No, it didn't **live up to my expectations** either.

C Other phrasal verbs with strong collocations

burst into laughter/tears [suddenly start to laugh/cry]
 When she saw the damage the floods had done to her house, she **burst into tears**.
dip into savings/funds [spend part of some money which was being saved]
 The club had to **dip into** their emergency **funds** to pay for the repairs to the roof.
jot down an address / a phone number / a room number [write down quickly]
 Can I **jot down** your email **address**?
see off an intruder/opponent [get rid of, defeat]
 He's a tough guy. He **saw off several intruders** who were trying to break into his house.
adhere to principles / beliefs / ideals / a philosophy [formal: continue to maintain a belief]
 It's difficult to **adhere to one's beliefs** when one is being constantly attacked.

> **TIP** It is often difficult to remember the meanings of phrasal verbs. When a phrasal verb has a set of collocations as in the examples in C, write them down together. This is a good way of remembering the meaning.

Exercises

11.1 Complete the collocations using prepositions from the box.

by	down	for	in with	to	up	up to	up with

1 file .... divorce
2 come .... an alternative
3 take .... office
4 adhere .... a philosophy

5 live .... expectations
6 abide .... a decision
7 jot .... someone's address
8 fit .... plans

11.2 Complete each sentence using a collocation from 11.1 in the appropriate form.

1 I'd been looking forward to the course but unfortunately it .... my expectations.
2 Has anyone .... a good alternative to the petrol- or diesel-fuelled car yet?
3 I should .... your address in case I forget it.
4 The new president of our club is due to .... office next week.
5 We have to .... the decision of the committee; we have no choice.
6 Most members of the group .... a common philosopy.
7 I don't have any special arrangements, so can easily .... your plans.
8 Hilda Bragg has .... divorce in a New York court.

11.3 Answer these questions using collocations from the opposite page.

1 What can you do with savings or funds in an emergency?
2 What can you do with principles or ideals?
3 What can you try to do with a language if you don't want to lose it?
4 What can guard dogs help you to do if you have intruders?

11.4 Correct the collocation errors in these sentences.

1 Everyone broke into laughter when she told the story.
2 We had a run along the beach to work in an appetite before lunch.
3 The police have said they intend to go down heavily on anyone carrying an offensive weapon at the match.
4 Do you think you could free out some time to have a quick meeting this afternoon?
5 The police acted on a rip-off and managed to avert a possible disaster.
6 I hope the party will live on to your expectations.
7 We sat on our hotel balcony, soaking through the atmosphere of the carnival.
8 Tanya quickly saw out her opponent in the semi-final and now goes on to the final.

11.5 Answer these questions. Write full sentences using the word in brackets in a collocation from the opposite page.

1 What do you plan to do in future to make sure you don't lose your English? (KEEP)
2 What film or gig or sports event have you been to that wasn't as good as you expected? (LIVE)
3 What sort of thing might tempt you to use some of your savings? (DIP)
4 Your best friend is getting married 100 miles away tomorrow and all the trains have been cancelled. What would you try to do? (COME)
5 At short notice some friends have invited you to stay for the weekend. They've already made some plans for the weekend. What would you do your best to do? (FIT)
6 How easy do you find it always to act according to your principles? (ADHERE)

12 Working life

A Fiona

In my mid-twenties I **joined the staff** of a language school. The pay wasn't brilliant but I could **make a living**[1] and there were many **aspects of the job** that I enjoyed. The other **members of staff** were nice and I enjoyed teaching the students. A few years later, after returning from **maternity leave**, I decided to **go part-time**. Luckily I was able to **do a job-share**[2] with another woman who had a small child. Then the school began to go through a difficult period and had to **lay off staff**[3]. I decided to **go freelance**[4]. I had managed to build up a **network of contacts** and this gave me a good start. I soon had a substantial **volume of work** – private students and marking exams – and was able to **earn a good living**.

[1] earn enough to live (can also be used just to refer to one's job and how one earns one's money: *She makes a living as a hairdresser*)
[2] situation where two people share equal parts of the same job
[3] dismiss staff because there is no work for them to do
[4] work for several different organisations rather than working full-time for one organisation

 ERROR WARNING People usually **do work**, NOT ~~make~~ work. If we talk about people **making work**, it means that they create work for other people to do, e.g. *A baby **makes** a lot of **work** for its parents – but it's worth it.*

B Ben

After graduating, I **practised medicine**[1] for a number of years in London. I managed to **carve a niche for myself**[2] as a specialist in dermatology. Then I realised I needed some fresh challenges and so I did a job swap for a year with my **opposite number**[3] in a clinic in Vancouver. When I returned, I went back to my old job and also **took up** the **post**[4] of editor of a leading medical journal. I **held that position** for a number of years. I'm now hoping to go abroad again and so am letting everyone know that I **am open to offers**.

[1] worked as a doctor
[2] make a special position for myself
[3] someone doing the same job in a different location
[4] started work

C Julia

After graduating in economics, I did the usual thing of **putting together my CV**[1] and applying for jobs. I got a very **tempting offer** from an investment bank and accepted it. It was a high pressure environment but I felt motivated and I did very well. I was put on a **fast-track scheme**[2] and was **moving up the ladder**[3] fast. However, one day I **had a change of heart**[4]. I realised I'd stopped enjoying the excitement. I felt I needed to **get my priorities right**[5]. I decided that other aspects of my life should **take priority over**[6] my work. I **handed in my resignation** and moved to the country.

[1] CV = *curriculum vitae*, a written description of your education, qualifications, skills and career
[2] system for rapid training and promotion of talented staff
[3] being promoted
[4] my attitude or mood changed
[5] give importance to the right aspects of life
[6] be more important to me than

 ERROR WARNING We say someone is **under a lot of / considerable pressure**, NOT under ~~high~~ pressure.

Exercises

12.1 Match the beginning of each sentence with its ending.

1 My husband and I do	of contacts.
2 Circulate the report to all members	the staff in our company.
3 Kazuki has been happier since he went	of work this month.
4 I hope it won't be necessary to lay	of staff.
5 It's not easy to make	part-time.
6 Meeting people is the best aspect	a job-share.
7 Marian was the last person to join	off many of our staff.
8 Anna will be going on maternity	of the job.
9 Try to build up a good network	a living as an actor.
10 We've had a ridiculous volume	leave next month.

12.2 Complete the conversation using words from the opposite page.

Meg: Did you know my son's in Australia at the moment? He's doing a job swap with his opposite (1) .... , the person who (2) .... a similar position to his in the company's Sydney office.

José: Wow, that's good! But I thought he wanted to go to the States this year?

Meg: Well, yes. He did have a very tempting (3) .... from a company in New York and he was about to accept, but then he had a (4) .... of heart.

José: So, have you met the exchange person from Sydney?

Meg: Yes, he's been to dinner a couple of times. He'd like to settle here in fact and has asked us to tell everyone he's (5) .... to offers from any companies that might be interested. Maybe your firm might be interested?

José: Perhaps. We could do with someone with good Australian contacts. But we could really do with someone who could (6) .... a post before the end of the year.

Meg: That could work out perhaps. He certainly seems very nice. And he'd be motivated to do well for you because he's so keen to stay here.

José: And do you think your son will stay in Australia?

Meg: I hope not. I've told him to get his priorities (7) .... Being near his mum should (8) .... priority over Australian beaches and sunshine!

12.3 Rewrite each sentence using the word in brackets.

1 The recession meant that the company had to make some workers redundant. (LAY)
2 Your family should really be more important to you than your work. (PRIORITY)
3 Nita soon gained several promotions at work. (LADDER)
4 Bill hates his new boss so much that I think he'll soon leave. (RESIGNATION)
5 Vic earns good money as a freelance journalist. (LIVING)
6 I need to write down all my qualifications and experience before I apply for jobs. (CV)
7 My father always wanted to work as a doctor in a rural community. (PRACTISE)

12.4 Correct the seven collocation errors in this paragraph.

George makes a life as a sports reporter on a local newspaper but he is under high pressure at work at the moment. He's had far too much work to make recently. He's been put on a fast-train scheme for promotion and they're really pushing him. It's so hard that he's thinking of handing over his resignation and going freelancing. It wouldn't be easy but I'm sure he'd soon work a niche for himself as a sports journalist.

13 New employment

A Discussing job applicants

Guy: So which of these applicants do you think we should interview? They all seem to **fit the job description** quite well to me. It's quite a **daunting task** to **narrow the list down** to just one person.

Julia: I agree. So, lets start by **taking up references** for these ten people.

Guy: OK. So why did you pick these ten out of the fifty who applied?

Julia: Well, these ten all seem to be people who realise the importance of **working as a team**. They've all shown that they are capable of **mastering new skills**. And they're all clearly comfortable with **taking on responsibility**.

Guy: Did you automatically eliminate the two who'd previously **taken industrial action**[1]?

Julia: One of them – I'd also heard rumours about his involvement in a **professional misconduct** case. He was certainly **relieved of his duties**[2] at ARG under mysterious circumstances. But the other was standing up for a woman who'd been **wrongfully dismissed**[3], even though he knew he might lose his own job. So he sounded good to me.

Guy: Fair enough. He must have strength of character to risk **losing his** own **livelihood**.

Julia: That's right. So could we **pencil in a meeting** for considering the references? And then I'd better leave you and go and **clear my desk**[4] before I go home.

Guy: Yes, sure. How about Friday at 10?

[1] gone on strike
[2] (formal) dismissed
[3] (formal, legal) unfairly dismissed
[4] deal with all the papers on one's desk (also used when someone is clearing their desk because they are leaving their job)

> **ERROR WARNING**
> If workers refuse to work, they **go on strike** or **stage a strike**, NOT ~~make~~ a strike.

B Conversation about a new job

Jenny: I hear your brother's **landed a** fantastic **new job**[1].

Ali: Actually it's not as good as he hoped. He's got a terribly **heavy workload** and that means working some very **unsocial hours**. He also complains about having to do lots of **menial tasks** around the office, **running errands** for his boss.

Jenny: But he's paid well?

Ali: Not really. He just about gets a **living wage**[2]. And all the **overtime** is **unpaid**.

Jenny: He'll just have to **throw a sickie**[3] from time to time.

Ali: Yes, I suggested he did that too, but he says he's afraid of **getting the sack**[4] if he does. He feels there might **be** some **prospects for** him there eventually, even if he is just being used as **sweated labour**[5] at the moment.

Jenny: Well, with any luck he'll eventually find that he can **realise his potential**[6] there.

Ali: I hope so. But they have a very **high turnover of staff** and it won't be easy for him to **stay the course**[7].

Jenny: No, but he's very determined, isn't he? So let's hope it all works out.

[1] (informal) got a new (and usually a good) job
[2] enough money to live on
[3] (informal) take a day off work pretending to be sick
[4] (informal) being dismissed
[5] workers who are paid very little and work in very bad conditions
[6] achieve all that he is capable of
[7] remain there until he is successful

Exercises

13.1 Find a collocation in A that matches each definition.

1 to make a provisional date for a meeting
2 an alarmingly difficult task
3 to become skilled at doing new things
4 to request statements from referees
5 to have the skills required for a job
6 unfairly sacked
7 to be deprived of your source of income
8 behaviour unacceptable for someone in a particular job

13.2 Complete this paragraph using words from the box in the appropriate form.

be	fit	land	run	sweat	take

Mel was surprised but happy to (1) .... a job on her local newspaper as soon as she left university. She was surprised because she didn't feel that she (2) .... the job description, but she was happy because she had always dreamt of working as a journalist. So she didn't really mind when she found that she was spending much of her time (3) .... errands for the editor. Her brother said she was just being used as (4) .... labour but she felt confident that there (5) .... good prospects for her there. She was sure she would soon have the chance to (6) .... on more responsibility.

13.3 Complete each conversation using a collocation from the opposite page to make B agree with what A says.

1 A: I think that Mick will leave his new job before the year is out.
   B: Yes, I agree. I don't think he'll .... either.
2 A: Had you heard that they may fire some members of staff?
   B: Yes, I did hear a rumour that some people might ....
3 A: Inflation is so high that I don't seem to earn enough to live on any more.
   B: No. I don't feel I earn .... myself.
4 A: Has the HR Manager been removed from his job?
   B: Yes, he was .... yesterday.
5 A: I hope the workers don't decide to go on strike.
   B: Yes, it would be very unfortunate if they decide to ....
6 A: It's going to be hard to decide which of the job applicants to shortlist.
   B: Yes, I don't know how we are going to ....

13.4 Answer these questions about your own work or ask someone else these questions and write down the answers.

1 What kind of menial tasks does your job involve?
2 Do you think this job will allow you to realise your potential?
3 Do you ever have to work unsocial hours? If so, why? If not, why not?
4 Does there tend to be a high turnover of staff at your workplace?
5 If you do overtime, is it paid or unpaid?
6 Have you ever thrown a sickie? If so, why? If not, why not?
7 Have you ever taken or would you ever consider taking industrial action?
8 In your job is it necessary to work as a team?
9 Do you have a heavy workload?

FOLLOW UP It will probably be particularly useful for you to learn work collocations that relate to your own professional life. Look on the Internet for information in English about the job that you do or are interested in doing in the future. Make a note of any interesting collocations that you come across.

14 Thoughts and ideas

A Talking about thoughts

I **honestly think** we can win the match tonight. [NOT I ~~strongly~~ think]

I'm not sure if I want to invest in your business or not, but I'll **give it some thought**.

Bear in mind that there are often delays to flights during bad weather. [remember]

It's common knowledge that Jane is looking for a new job. [everyone knows]

My teenage son hasn't yet **grasped the importance of** revising for exams. [understood how important something is]

I **take the view** that we are all responsible for our own actions. [believe]

It's **a foregone conclusion** that Jaime will win the race. [absolutely certain]

I'm not quite sure what I'm going to do but I've got a **rough idea**. [general idea]

I don't **subscribe to the theory** that nature and nurture are of equal significance but it is now a **widespread belief**. [hold that opinion]; [generally held view]

Opinions are divided as to whether mothers of young children should go out to work or not, but **it is my firm conviction** that different things suit different families. [people hold different views]; [I am totally convinced]

ERROR WARNING

We say I am **becoming aware** of the problem, NOT I am ~~getting~~ aware.

B Judging

collocation	example	meaning
judge someone harshly	Don't **judge** him too **harshly**. He really couldn't have done things differently.	be very critical of someone
poor judgement	Deciding to set up a business now shows **poor judgement** of the economic situation.	
pass judgement on	Di's quick to **pass judgement on** other people but she's far from perfect herself.	criticise
against your better judgement	I finally agreed to go out with him, **against my better judgement**.	despite the knowledge that something is a bad idea
a lack of judgement	His approach to his children showed **a lack of judgement**.	an inability to judge a situation wisely
an error of judgement	Promoting Alec was a serious **error of judgement**.	bad decision

C Metaphors of thinking

We can talk about **thinking laterally** [approaching a problem in an imaginative and original way rather than using a traditional approach]. We can say someone has a **fertile imagination** [one that produces lots of original and interesting ideas]. We can **wrestle with a problem** [struggle to find a solution] and we can have a **nagging doubt** [an unpleasant feeling of doubt that will not go away]. We can also talk about something **fuelling speculation** [encouraging people to consider that something may be true], and sometimes people **jump to conclusions** [guess the facts about a situation without having enough information].

Exercises

14.1 Look at A. Correct the collocation errors in these sentences.

1 Opinions are separated on the issue of single-sex schools and there are sound arguments on both sides of the case.

2 I believe that the government will win another term in office but my girlfriend takes a different opinion.

3 I strongly think that you'd be making a serious mistake if you took that job.

4 I don't believe it's a foregone fact that the larger company will win the contract.

5 People are gradually getting aware of the problem of climate change.

6 You should bear in thought that your visitors will be tired after their long flight.

7 I've got a raw idea of what I want to say in my essay but I haven't planned it properly yet.

8 Increasing numbers of people today subscribe for the theory that small is beautiful.

14.2 Complete the paragraph using words from the box.

error	firm	grasped	laterally	pass	poor

Recent research shows that people who spend time meditating each day improve their mental abilities. It seems that meditation particularly enhances our ability to think in creative, unusual ways, in other words, to think 'outside the box' or think (1) .... It may, then, have been an unfortunate (2) .... of judgement on the part of the management at BNM and Co. to put a stop to the yoga classes that staff had organised for their lunch-breaks.

'It would seem that our managers have not yet (3) .... the importance of these classes,' explained yoga instructor Zandra, 'but it is not my place to (4) .... judgement on them. Their judgement may be (5) .... at the moment but it is my (6) .... conviction that as people come to understand yoga better, they will see how it could benefit the company as well as individual members of staff.'

14.3 Rewrite each sentence using the word in brackets.

1 It's unwise to draw conclusions too quickly about people's motives. (JUMP)
2 Everyone knows that Ellie has been taking money from the till. (COMMON)
3 I agreed to help him though I knew it was wrong. (AGAINST)
4 I'm afraid your decisions show you are unable to judge situations well. (LACK)
5 We have to decide when to have the party. Can you think about it? (THOUGHT)
6 I think you are being too critical of him. Remember he's only 18. (HARSHLY)
7 Surprisingly, a large number of people believe left-handed people are more intelligent. (WIDESPREAD)

14.4 Use a dictionary to find frequent collocations with these words. Your collocations can use the words literally or metaphorically.

1 a fertile   2 to fuel   3 to wrestle with   4 a nagging

14.5 Use a dictionary or an online corpus (see Unit 4) to decide whether these are common collocations or not.

1 bear in memory   2 personal conviction   3 harshly treated   4 a rough belief

15 Business reports

A Business news

Charles Park and Sons have **announced record profits** for last year despite a slight **decline in demand** for one of their key products, caused by increasingly **fierce competition**[1] in the sector. They say they are already well on the way to **meeting their targets** for the first quarter. Their new models will **go into production**[2] in the spring and this is expected to **boost**[3] their **sales** and **profits** even more.

The government today announced its intentions to **stimulate growth** in the south-west by **allocating** a large **part of its** development **budget** to industrial projects in the area. Roger Middle, who **chaired the committee** working on this scheme, said that local people welcomed the decision, which should **generate** more **business** for local firms. They appreciate that their area has many **unique selling points** for businesses and their employees, and feel that development will **pay dividends**[4] for everyone living and working in the area.

Clothing firm G and L has announced plans to build a new factory in the Midlands. Their spokesperson, Mark Mulloy, said yesterday that the proposal **made sound business sense**. 'It will be easier for us to **maintain quality** and **promote the interests** of our shareholders at the same time as **satisfying the demands** of our **target market**,' he said.

SIB Distribution held an **emergency meeting** last night to discuss the crisis caused by yesterday's rise in fuel prices. Their MD said, 'This **hike in prices**[5] will seriously **affect the bottom line**[6]. It's a considerable challenge for us as we already operate on **narrow profit margins**. However, we have **set ourselves clear objectives** and are confident we will still be able to **balance the books**[7]. We have no intention of **calling in the receivers**[8] yet!'

[1] NOT ~~high~~ competition
[2] start being made
[3] increase
[4] bring advantages

[5] (journalistic) rise in prices
[6] affect the net income
[7] make sure the amount spent is not more than the amount earned
[8] going bankrupt

B Describing trends

An important part of many business reports is the description of trends. The *Cambridge Learner Corpus* shows that there are a number of collocation errors which are frequently made when candidates write about business in advanced English exams.

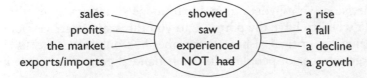

sales — showed — a rise
profits — saw — a fall
the market — experienced — a decline
exports/imports — NOT ~~had~~ — a growth

ERROR WARNING

We say a **slight decrease/increase**, NOT a ~~little~~ decrease/increase and a **substantial decrease/increase**, NOT a ~~strong~~ decrease/increase.
When comparing two things in terms of quantity, we say, for example, Exports were **five times greater than** imports, NOT Exports were five times ~~larger~~ than imports.

Exercises

15.1   Are these sentences true or false?

1 A business executive will feel worried if the company experiences a decline in demand for its products.
2 A business CEO is pleased if the company does not meet its quarterly sales targets.
3 A hike in the price of raw materials is likely to present a difficult challenge for a business that uses those materials.
4 Marketing and sales staff will promote their products' unique selling points.
5 Business managers are likely to be happy about calling in the receivers.
6 A company is likely to feel more secure if it has narrow profit margins.

15.2   Complete each sentence using a word from the opposite page.

1 It was a sad day for the company when it finally had to call in the ....
2 I'm sure you'll agree that our new mobile phone has a number of unique selling
   ....
3 We use a professional accountant to help us balance our ....
4 The bank agreed that our plans make sound business ....
5 We must ensure that the research project does not negatively affect the bottom
   ....
6 We look forward to next spring, when our exciting new line will go into ....
7 All your hard work will eventually pay ....
8 We are confident that our new business strategy will help boost both sales and
   ....

15.3   Correct the collocation errors in these sentences.

1 The company is pleased to report a strong increase in profits over the last quarter.
2 The new health and safety committee is to be tabled by a retired doctor.
3 There is increasingly high competition between airline companies.
4 The company's exports to Japan had considerable growth over the last decade.
5 The sales figures for March show a little decrease on those for February.
6 Our sales in the domestic market are certain to have a rise next year.
7 Last year sales were three times larger in Europe than in Australia.
8 We feel that this proposal does considerable business sense.
9 Although we need to reduce our costs, it's important we attain the quality that our reputation is built on.
10 Business leaders hope new government policies will stimulus growth.

15.4   Answer these questions about the collocations in this unit.

1 When might the Managing Director of a company call an emergency meeting?
2 What kind of age group is a sports car company likely to have as its target market?
3 Why would shareholders be pleased if their company announced record profits?
4 In what situations other than business do people set themselves objectives?
5 Name three things that a business would have to allocate part of its budget to.
6 How might a company try to stimulate growth in demand for its products?

 FOLLOW UP   On the website www.companieshouse.gov.uk you can find reports on several million companies. Look up a company that interests you and make a note of any interesting collocations that you find.

16 Customer services

A Shopping in the high street or online?

Most companies **carry out surveys**[1] to find out what customers or potential customers feel about their products and services. I answered one recently about **online shopping**. I personally much prefer to **go shopping** on the high street rather than to shop on the Internet. You get a much better impression of whether something is good **value for money** or truly **fit for purpose**[2] when you can touch it. And I feel if you have a problem with a purchase, it's easier to go back and **make a complaint** if you've bought something from a shop. But shopping online has its advantages, and many companies **offer** you **a discount** when you **place an order** online. And, of course, lots of online companies have plenty of **regular customers** and plenty of **satisfied customers**. I suppose the bottom line is that it's good for us as consumers to have as much **healthy competition** as possible.

[1] or **do surveys**, NOT ~~make surveys~~   [2] good at doing what it is supposed to do

ERROR WARNING

We say **do the shopping** or **go shopping**, NOT ~~do shopping~~. **Do the shopping** means the regular daily, weekly or monthly shopping that people do for food and household items. It is a household chore (compare: do the *ironing/washing*). While **go shopping** also means this, it has the additional meaning of shopping as a leisure activity (compare: go *fishing/swimming*).

B Complaining about service

I ordered this skirt on the Internet and I'm furious. On their website they promise **prompt service**. In fact they said they offered **a next-day service** but it took ten days to come. When I rang up to complain they **put me on hold** and then never got back to me! Then, when the skirt eventually arrived, the zip was broken. It's really **poor quality** – though the advert says all their clothes are **top quality**. I'm going to **kick up** such **a fuss**[1]. Of course, I'll demand **a full refund**[2], but I'd really like an apology as well. And I'll certainly **take my custom elsewhere**[3] in future.

[1] (informal) make a very forcible complaint
[2] ask for all my money back (NB NOT ~~strongly~~ demand because the verb *demand* cannot be made stronger in English – it is already strong enough)
[3] not buy from the same place again

C Company promise

If you have **grounds for complaint**[1], please contact our Head Office at the address below. We pride ourselves on **providing an excellent service** and all our products **conform to safety regulations**[2]. We **honour all commitments**[3] to customers. We **take** very **seriously** any **complaints** about poor service. So if you feel that one of our products does not **come up to standard**[4], then we will immediately offer you a replacement. We promise to **handle all complaints** promptly.

[1] a reason for complaining   [3] do what we said we would do
[2] obey all the rules or laws relating to safety   [4] reach appropriate standards

TIP

Learn more collocations relating to the topic of customer services by looking at the customer services page of a company website, for example, that of John Lewis, a British department store: www.johnlewis.com/Help/HelpHome.aspx. Make a note of any interesting collocations.

Exercises

16.1 Look at A. Correct the collocation errors in these sentences.

1 Have you ever made a complain to the management about the food in a restaurant?
2 I hate making shopping on Saturdays as the town is so crowded then.
3 If you want your shopping delivered, you can put your order with us online or by phone.
4 We made a large-scale customer survey before developing our new product range.
5 On-the-web shopping is proving increasingly popular.
6 I was surprised by the weak quality of the acting in that film we saw last night.

16.2 Choose the correct collocation.

1 This shop gives very good *worth / cost / value* for money.
2 Every business wants *satisfactory / satisfied / satisfying* customers.
3 He is an economist who believes in the advantages of *healthy / rich / fertile* competition.
4 Service doesn't have to be next-day but it should be reasonably *punctual / prompt / present*.
5 I hate it when you phone a company and get put on *hole / hang / hold* for ages.
6 Dan kicked up a terrible *fuss / foot / fever* about the service we received.
7 The hotel manager *dealt / handled / honoured* our complaint very efficiently.
8 We can't sell our old sofa because it doesn't *perform / inform / conform* to modern safety regulations.
9 I would prefer not to take my custom *somewhere / anywhere / elsewhere*.
10 The service at the hair salon did not *run / come / do* up to standard.

16.3 Complete the letters using words from the opposite page.

Dear Sir/Madam,
I am writing to complain about the service I received in your Cambridge branch.
I bought a suit there recently but it is poorly cut and does not fit well, even though it is the size I normally take. I am a (1) .... customer of yours and have never had any problems before. I returned the suit to the shop the next day, but the manager refused to give me a full (2) ....
I request that you look into this matter and (3) .... this complaint seriously. Otherwise I may be forced to take my (4) .... elsewhere.
Yours faithfully,
John Cole

Dear Mr Cole,
Thank you for your letter regarding your purchase of a suit from us. We apologise for the inconvenience caused to you.
Our company is committed to (5) ....
an excellent service and selling (6) ....
quality garments. We therefore enclose the requested refund and trust that you will continue to shop with us and will never again have (7) .... for complaint about our goods.
Yours sincerely,
Jason Campbell
Customer Services Manager

16.4 Complete the crossword.

Across
1 When choosing new offices you must ensure that they will be fit for — .
3 To get your money back you'll have to prove you have — for complaint.
4 I have no option but to demand a — refund.
5 I am afraid that your service simply fails to come up to — .
6 As a respected firm we always — all our commitments.
7 It is our policy to offer students a — on books and stationery.

Down
2 Your helmets do not conform to safety — .

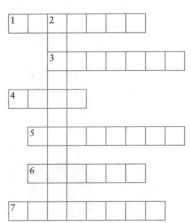

17 Student life

A Courses and qualifications

When she was a small child, Amelia's teachers identified her as having unusual intelligence and remarkable **mental agility**[1], and they put her on a special programme for **gifted children**. Amelia **won a scholarship** to **attend** a local grammar **school**. By the age of eighteen, she was a **straight A student**[2], and she **secured a place**[3] at one of the country's most prestigious **seats of learning**[4] to **read**[5] English Literature.

In the first **academic year** of the English Literature programme, the **core subjects**[6] were *The development of the novel* and *Contemporary poetry*. Amelia had a large number of **set texts**[7] to read. It was hard work but she loved it. Her professors were all **distinguished scholars** and her courses were taught by some of the world's **leading authorities** in the field. She completed her studies with considerable success and **graduated from university** last year. In the meantime, her parents have decided that it is time they made up for their lack of **formal education** and they have **signed up for** a number of evening **courses**[8]. Eventually they hope to **meet the entry requirements** for university entrance and to be able to complete a degree as **mature students**[9].

[1] ability to think quickly and clearly
[2] a student who always gets very good marks
[3] (formal) was accepted as a student; (informal: **got a place**)
[4] (very formal) educational institution with a very good reputation
[5] (formal and increasingly old-fashioned) do or study
[6] subjects which all the students on the course have to do
[7] specific books which students must study
[8] or **enrolled on … courses**
[9] students who are older than average

B Harry's school report

Mathematics	Harry's work has shown a **marked improvement** this term. However, his **attention** occasionally **wanders** in class.
English	Harry has a **natural talent** for English. He achieved **full marks**[1] in the last class test.
French	There is **room for improvement** in Harry's work in French. He seems to find it difficult to **learn** vocabulary **by heart**.
Geography	Harry has a **thirst for knowledge** and is **a quick learner**. It is a pity that sometimes his **concentration** in class **wavers**[2].
Science	Harry has **demonstrated an ability** to apply what he learns to the wider world. He **showed** considerable **initiative** in the way he approached his project on energy.
Physical Education	Although Harry has a **proven ability**[3] for tennis, he will not make any progress until he stops **playing truant**.[4] This must not continue.

[1] 100%
[2] concentration is not steady
[3] ability shown by his achievements
[4] being absent without permission

ERROR WARNING

You attend school to **acquire knowledge**, NOT ~~get~~ knowledge.

Exercises

17.1 Answer the questions using collocations from A.

1 What happens when you successfully complete a degree course?
2 What do you call students who are in their thirties or older?
3 What are, for example, Harvard, the Sorbonne and Cambridge University?
4 What kind of people teach at Harvard, the Sorbonne and Cambridge University?
5 What do you call children who are particularly intelligent or have special talents?
6 What do you call students whose marks are always excellent?

17.2 Match the beginning of each sentence with its ending.

1 We were all very impressed by the student's mental   heart.
2 My grandmother is very intelligent but she's had little formal   place.
3 I've never found it easy to learn scientific formulae by   education.
4 I'd love to study medicine there but it's very hard to get a   ability.
5 For the first year Shakespeare exam we had to read six set   requirements.
6 I am so proud of you for managing to get full   agility.
7 Your work is not too bad but there is certainly still room for   learner.
8 Your little girl has shown herself to be a very quick   marks.
9 The test has been designed to enable pupils to demonstrate their   texts.
10 I hope to study there but I may not be able to meet the entry   improvement.

17.3 Complete this teacher's letter to the parents of a problem pupil.

> Dear Mr and Mrs Wolf,
>   We are very concerned about Peter's behaviour. He has played (1) .... from school three times this month and has been seen in town in school hours. When he does come to class, his attention (2) .... and he does not seem able to concentrate on his lessons. He does not seem to understand the work and yet he never asks any questions or requests any help. The only time he (3) .... any initiative is in devising excuses for not having done his homework. Although he has a (4) .... talent for art, he is not even taking any interest in art lessons.
>   This is disappointing, as last year there was a (5) .... improvement in Peter's work and we hoped he might (6) .... a scholarship. However, unless he starts to (7) .... school regularly and to put more effort into his studies, he will certainly not even meet the (8) .... for the college course he has plans to (9) .... on next year.
>   I would be grateful if you could come into school to discuss this situation further.
>   Yours sincerely,
>   Thomas Chips
>   (Headteacher)

17.4 Answer these questions.

1 What are the core subjects for pupils at primary school in your country?
2 What would you say are the most prestigious seats of learning in your country?
3 Have you ever signed up for a course that you didn't complete?
4 If you could take a degree course now, what subject would you like to read?
5 When does the academic year begin and end in your country?
6 What do you need to do to secure a place at university in your country?

17.5 Use a dictionary to find different words to complete each collocation.

1 a thirst for ....   3 his .... wavers
2 join a ....   4 proven ....

18 Writing essays, assignments and reports

A Preparing for a research assignment

Here is an extract from a study skills leaflet given to students at a university, containing advice on how to tackle a research project. Note the collocations in bold.

- All students are expected to **submit a** 5,000-word **report**, detailing their research project and **presenting** their **findings**.
- **Select a research topic** in discussion with your tutor. You will need to formulate a **working hypothesis**[1] when you begin your study. The purpose of your research is to see if your data **supports the hypothesis**[2].
- If you are **undertaking**[3] **a study** which involves informants or volunteers, read the advice on **research ethics**[4] in the department handbook.

- A key section of your report will be a **literature review**. This is not simply a summary of your **background reading**, but an **in-depth critique**[5] of the most important books and articles, where you can show your awareness of current research.
- Make sure you **provide**[6] **a rationale** for your study, and always **back up your conclusions** with evidence; never exaggerate any claims you make.
- Wherever appropriate, you should **lay out your results** in the form of tables, charts and diagrams.

[1] a theory which can be used provisionally but may change
[2] We usually do not say *prove the hypothesis*; *prove* is too strong.
[3] (formal) carrying out; (informal: doing)
[4] a system of standards which control how research is done
[5] examination and judgement of something, done carefully and in great detail
[6] (formal) give

B Other collocations often used in essays, reports and assignments

The book offers a **vigorous**[1] **defence** of free market economics and **makes the case for** privatisation of all state-owned industries. It **confronts issues** which are of current importance in developing countries.

McGraw **puts the case for** single-sex primary education but he fails to **tackle** all of **the issues** that opponents of this approach to early schooling have raised.

This essay cannot give an **exhaustive**[2] **account** of climate change; it focuses only on the risk to sea levels. Recent **research indicates** that sea levels are rising very rapidly.

Physicists have recently begun to **formulate new theories** about the nature of the universe. The big question is how to **test** these **theories**.

Although Kristov's book **covers a lot of ground**, it does not offer a **full explanation** of the events leading to the civil war. Indeed, **the thrust**[3] **of Kristov's argument** is that such an account cannot be written, since the people with **first-hand**[4] **knowledge** of those events are no longer living.

This essay provides a **critical analysis**[5] of international trade agreements.

[1] very strong and forceful   [2] extremely detailed   [3] the main idea or opinion that is discussed
[4] experienced directly   [5] a detailed study or examination which assesses quality

 ERROR WARNING   We say **do research**, NOT ~~make~~ research. The Internet is a good place to **do research**.

Exercises

18.1 Complete each sentence using a verb from the box in the appropriate form.

cover	indicate	present	provide	put
review	tackle	test	undertake	

1 It is a huge task to .... a study involving hundreds of participants.
2 Fischler .... her findings at an international biochemistry conference last year.
3 Chapter 2 .... the literature on urban regeneration and concludes that more research is needed.
4 I have .... a rationale for the study in the introduction to this essay.
5 The research .... that owning a pet increases life expectancy by five years.
6 The next step was to .... the theory by carrying out a set of experiments.
7 The essay .... a lot of ground.
8 The book .... a number of issues which were previously ignored.
9 The lecturer .... the case for a dramatic change in economic policy.

18.2 Rewrite each sentence using a form of the words in brackets.

1 The system of standards for conducting research are described in the university's research manual. (ETHIC)
2 You need to make an examination and judgement of the arguments which is very detailed. (DEPTH, CRITIQUE)
3 You need to read books and articles which give you information about the subject. (BACKGROUND)
4 You do the analysis in order to find out whether the data indicate that your initial idea was correct. (HYPOTHESIS)
5 All the interviewees were people who had knowledge of the situation from direct experience. (FIRST)
6 It is impossible to give a complete explanation of the decline of agriculture in the 1960s. (FULL)

18.3 Complete each sentence using a word from the box in the correct form. Then number the events in the order in which they would occur in real life.

☐ Write a .... analysis of previous studies.
☐ Form a .... hypothesis.
☐ .... out your results in tables and diagrams.
☐ .... your report.
☐ 1 .... a topic.
☐ Make the .... for studying the topic in the introduction.

case
critical
lay
select
submit
work

18.4 Correct the collocation errors in these sentences.

1 The trust of Torsten's argument is that public transport can never replace the private car.
2 Economists reformed a new theory of inflation in the late 1980s.
3 It is important that we should front the issue of climate change immediately.
4 In her essay, she put forward a vigorated defence of the European Union constitution.
5 I shall not attempt to give an exhausting account of population growth in this essay.
6 The article does not back down its conclusions with enough convincing evidence.

FOLLOW UP Find an article on the Internet relating to an academic subject that is important for you. Print it off and highlight any useful collocations you notice in it.

19 Social life

A Organising your social life

Hi Nadia,

How was your weekend? My old school friend Emma came on a **flying visit**[1], which was fun. We had a **girls' night out** on Saturday with a couple of other friends. We **went out for a meal** to a local restaurant. So much for me **sticking to** my **diet**!

Emma was here for a **surprise party** for her parents on Sunday. She and her brother wanted to **spring a surprise on**[2] them for their 30th wedding anniversary – they thought 30 years together definitely **called for a celebration**[3] – so they decided to **throw a party** for them. They had it at a hotel near their house and invited all their parents' old friends. The vicar who'd married them even **put in an appearance**[4]! They asked me along too and it was lovely, a really **special occasion** with a fun atmosphere. I was just sorry I couldn't **spend** much **quality time**[5] with Emma, but she promised the next time she comes it won't be such a **whirlwind visit**[6]. Anyway, what about you? Is life its usual busy **social whirl**[7]? Do you still **go clubbing** every weekend?
Claire

[1] a visit that doesn't last long
[2] to surprise
[3] meant that a celebration was appropriate
[4] came just for a short time
[5] time where people can give their complete attention to each other
[6] brief and very busy visit
[7] non-stop set of social events

B Formal entertaining

To: Councillor D. M. Patel
County Hall, Swithick

Penniston International Youth Festival

Dear Councillor Patel,

First let me thank the County Council, on behalf of the Festival Organising Committee, for **playing host to**[1] the welcome reception for our international colleagues and for **making us** so **welcome** at County Hall last week. We were also grateful that you were able to **find time** to **pay us a visit** at our weekly planning meeting, where we were delighted to hear that you intend to **join the festivities** at the opening ceremony of the festival.

We would further like to invite you and your spouse to **attend a formal function**, to be held at the Castle Hotel, Penniston on Friday 27 July, from 7.30pm to 10.30pm, to mark the closing of the festival.

Yours sincerely,
Mark Janowski (Committee Chair)

[1] providing the facilities for

[2] social event where a family comes together, usually to celebrate something

[3] take out for dinner and drinks

[4] (rather formal) a very friendly and welcoming atmosphere

[5] place where a public event or meeting happens

ERROR WARNING We say **organise a barbecue** or **have a barbecue**, NOT ~~make~~ a barbecue.

⊔⊔⊔⊔⊓ *Castle Hotel Penniston* ⊔⊔⊔⊔

Whether you are planning a formal party, a **family gathering**[2] or simply want to **wine and dine**[3] new business contacts in a **convivial atmosphere**[4], the 16th-century Castle Hotel is **the perfect venue**[5]. Our 24 bedrooms, three restaurants and Function Room can be reserved by calling us on 1327 5547655 or by booking online at www.castlepenniston.com.

Exercises

19.1 Complete the conversation words from the opposite page.

Suki: How was Bill's (1) .... retirement party?

Dave: Great. You should have seen his face; he really had no idea about it and he was so moved. It was a really nice gesture for the company to (2) .... a party for him like that. They really wined and (3) .... us. And even the MD put in an (4) .... ! What happened to you? I was surprised not to see you there.

Suki: Oh, well I was planning to come, but then my friends (5) .... a surprise on me too that same night.

Dave: Was it a (6) .... occasion?

Suki: Yes, it was my birthday and my friends had arranged a girls' (7) .... out and invited lots of friends that I hadn't seen for ages.

Dave: Sounds great. Happy Birthday, by the way.

19.2 Choose the correct collocation.

1 My parents have always *gave / made / had* my friends feel very welcome.
2 My aunt came on a *quality / whirling / flying* visit last week.
3 It's quite difficult to *hold on / keep with / stick to* a diet when you're eating out with friends.
4 You've passed your exam! Well, that *takes / gives / calls* for a celebration!
5 We hope you will *give / find / spend* time to visit our exhibition of students' artwork.
6 It's important to try to spend plenty of *welcome / convivial / quality* time with your family.
7 My sister's life is a constant *special / active / social* whirl.
8 I recommend you *pay / spend / go* a visit to the folk museum while you're in Dekksu.
9 Athens *threw / gave / played* host to the first modern Olympic Games in 1896.

19.3 Rewrite each sentence using a collocation from the opposite page. Then say whether the sentence you have written is more or less formal.

1 We could go to a nightclub later.
2 The restaurant has a really friendly atmosphere.
3 London is holding the Olympics in 2012.
4 She has a mad social life.
5 I have to go to a formal function on Thursday.
6 We invite you to join in the fun at the opening of the Arts Festival.
7 Grapsley Park is a great place for an outdoor concert.

19.4 Which do you prefer:

1 when you're too tired to cook, ordering a takeaway or eating out?
2 plain food or rich food?
3 having a family gathering or having a barbecue with friends?
4 giving a dinner party or going out for a meal?
5 paying your friends a visit or playing host to friends at your own home?
6 a whirlwind visit from a friend, or a relative who stays for a week?

20 Talking

A ## Types of language and conversation

Some conversations are not serious. They consist of **idle chatter**, in which the speakers just **exchange pleasantries**[1] or share **juicy**[2] **gossip** about their friends and colleagues, **exchanging news** and **spreading rumours**. **Rumours are always flying around** in any society, of course. But sometimes when you **engage someone in conversation**, it may become more serious. You may **open your heart** to the person you are talking to, for example. You may even find yourself **drawn into an argument**. Some people always want to **win an argument**; for others **losing the argument** is not important as they simply enjoy a good discussion. If you are in a very noisy place, it can become impossible to **carry on a conversation** of any kind and it is also hard for parents to **hold a conversation** when there are small children in the room.

[1] (formal) make polite conversation   [2] (informal) interesting because it is shocking or personal

B ## Managing topics

Hi Jane,
As you know, I wanted to talk to my parents yesterday about my plans for dropping out of university but I didn't have much luck. First of all, I found it very hard to **broach the subject**[1]. As soon as I started explaining how badly I wanted to start earning, one of them would **change the subject**. It was as if they were deliberately trying to avoid something they sensed was going to be a problem. Eventually I managed to **bring up the subject** again and they finally started to **take me seriously**. I tried not to **overstate my case**[2] for leaving and just put things as simply as I could. But then they started to **bombard me with questions**[3]. Why did I really want to leave? What would I do? Did I realise that I would get a much better job with a degree? Dad didn't listen to my answers – he just started making **broad generalisations** about the importance of education. He went on and on for about half an hour before telling me to **drop the subject** and never refer to it again. So I'm not sure what to do next. Any advice?
Bob

[1] begin a discussion of a difficult topic   [3] ask me lots of questions
[2] give too much importance or seriousness to a point of view

C ## Adjective + noun phrases

collocation	example	meaning
bad/strong/foul language	TV dramas today use much more **bad/strong/foul language** than they did 40 years ago.	swear words, taboo language; *foul* suggests much stronger disapproval than *bad* or *strong*
four-letter words	Please try to express your feelings without using **four-letter words**.	swear words, taboo words (many of which have four letters in English)
opening gambit	'You're a teacher, aren't you?' was his **opening gambit**.	a remark made in order to start a conversation
a rash promise	Don't make any **rash promises**. Think before you agree to anything.	promises made without thinking
an empty promise	She's full of **empty promises**. You shouldn't believe a word she says.	promises made which the speaker has no intention of keeping
a tough question	Do I regret anything? That's a **tough question**.	difficult question to answer

Exercises

20.1 Look at A. Correct the collocation errors in these sentences.

1 It can be hard to carry out a serious conversation in a noisy room.
2 He finds it very difficult to open his head and talk about his feelings to anyone.
3 I don't like discussing things with people who always want to gain every argument.
4 My mother always used to tell me not to spill unkind rumours.
5 I usually find it better not to get driven into an argument with Paul.
6 We had a very enjoyable time just sitting in the park enjoying some idling chatter.
7 I managed to resist all his attempts to engage me into conversation.
8 I've never talked to him much – we've done no more than change pleasantries.

20.2 Complete each sentence using a word from the box in the appropriate form.

| bring | broach | drop | hold | lose | strong | take | tough |

1 I .... the argument because I didn't know enough about the subject.
2 I think it's time we .... the subject of our marriage with our parents.
3 No one will .... your ideas seriously unless you present them more effectively.
4 My mother can't get used to hearing well-dressed young people using .... language in public places.
5 Whenever I try to .... up the subject of moving to London, he leaves the room.
6 I've said I'm sorry – why can't you just .... the subject?
7 They're sure to ask you some .... questions at your interview but you can take time to think before you answer.
8 I felt so ill last week that I could barely .... a conversation.

20.3 Match the two parts of these collocations.

1 juicy   promise
2 broad   generalisations
3 exchange   gambit
4 take   question
5 four-letter   seriously
6 tough   word
7 rash   gossip
8 opening   news

20.4 Rewrite each sentence using the word in brackets.

1 Please stop talking about this subject immediately. (DROP)
2 Sam has a habit of promising things that he has no intention of doing. (EMPTY)
3 You must give due importance to the lab's safety regulations. (SERIOUSLY)
4 It's better not to spend too long trying to make your point. (OVERSTATE)
5 Could we please start talking about something else? (SUBJECT)
6 Did you hear the rumours that people were spreading about your boss last year? (FLYING)
7 There are rather a lot of rude words in the play. (LANGUAGE)
8 Such general statements tend to be rather meaningless. (BROAD)
9 The way he began the conversation took me by surprise. (GAMBIT)
10 The children asked me lots and lots of questions about my trip. (BOMBARD)

21 News

A Politicical headlines

A **PM CALLS APRIL ELECTION**[1]

B **MINISTER RESIGNS FROM OFFICE**

C **PARTY SECURES SLIM MAJORITY**[2]

D **ISLANDS DECLARE INDEPENDENCE**

E **GOVERNMENT'S HUMILIATING DEFEAT**

F **PARTY PRESENTS SHOW OF UNITY**[3]

G **UNPOPULAR REGIME TOPPLED**[4]

H **LEFT PROCLAIMS VICTORY**[5]

I **ARMY SEIZES POWER**

J **PRESIDENT DELIVERS KEY SPEECH**[6]

[1] officially announces that an election will take place
[2] wins a small majority
[3] publicly appears to be united
[4] (journalistic) made to fall (of regime or government)
[5] makes an official announcement of victory
[6] (formal, journalistic) makes/gives a speech

B News reports

The police have been carrying out a **nationwide search** for 22-year-old Chris Tait, who has not been seen since **trouble broke out** on Saturday night at the hotel where he was working. This evening they announced that they had found some **vital clues** but there are currently no plans to **call off the search**[1].

Following the robbery of over $10m from its main city branch, the bank has offered a **substantial reward** to anyone providing information leading to the **recovery of the money**.

Management and workers at the troubled Longside car factory have finally agreed to **enter into talks** and hopes are growing that they may soon **reach agreement**. The **dispute arose** some weeks ago when management tried to introduce new working conditions. Workers have **held demonstrations** in the city in support of Longside staff. Management described the situation as **a test of strength** and union attempts to **negotiate a settlement**[2] have so far proved unsuccessful. However, an independent arbitrator has **acted as a go-between**[3] and has succeeded in **brokering**[4] **an agreement** to talk.

TV chiefs have **bowed to**[5] public **pressure** and have **entered into an agreement** not to show scenes of gun violence on **prime-time**[6] television. They will **hold a press conference** later today where they will explain their decision to **impose** this degree of **censorship**.

[1] stop searching   [2] have formal discussions in the hope of coming to an agreement
[3] delivered messages between people who were reluctant or unable to speak to each other
[4] arranging   [5] given in to   [6] most popular time of day for watching TV

Exercises

21.1 The sentences below come from the stories beneath some of the headlines in A. Which headline does each sentence go with? Two of the headlines are not used.

1 A military coup has taken place in the island kingdom of Grammaria and the country's popular monarch now faces exile.
2 In last night's vote, the Government's new education bill was rejected.
3 Paul Cox, minister in charge of public finance, has decided that he wishes to spend more time with his family.
4 Previous rifts between rival ministers would appear to have been healed.
5 The Conservatives have succeeded in gaining 200 of the 390 seats.
6 The country will now be going to the polls somewhat earlier than anticipated.
7 Widespread and well-orchestrated rebellions have achieved their aim of overthrowing the country's dictator.
8 The country has voted that it no longer wishes to be ruled by its 19th century colonisers.

21.2 Complete this newspaper item with collocations from the opposite page. The first letters are given to help you.

> Last night the Culture Minister (1) d............................ a s........................... in which she promised
> to try to (2) b.......................... an a........................... between the Government and the film industry
> with regard to the decision to (3) i...................... stricter c........................... on films. After the
> speech, which was broadcast (4) on p........................... t........................... , the Minister
> (5) h........................... a press c........................... . She promised to appoint an independent
> negotiator to (6) a........................... as a (7) g........................... -b........................... in the hope
> that the Government and the film industry would soon (8) r........................... a........................... .

21.3 Rewrite each sentence using the word in brackets.

1 The President has finally agreed to the public's demand to hold a referendum. (BOWED)
2 Early this morning the Eco-democratic Party announced it had won the election. (VICTORY)
3 The police detective discovered the clue which led to the stolen jewels being found. (RECOVERY)
4 The police will not stop searching until the child has been found. (CALL)
5 We were on holiday when the recent political troubles started. (BROKE)
6 The police are searching the whole country for the missing boy. (CARRYING)
7 The two parties will try to come to an agreement today. (SETTLEMENT)
8 Today thousands of students demonstrated against the increase in fees. (HELD)

21.4 Explain the difference between the sentences in each pair.

1 The rally is a test of the army's strength.
  The rally is a show of the army's strength.
2 The police have found vital clues.
  The police have found significant clues.
3 The woman has offered a small reward for the return of her cat.
  The woman has offered a substantial reward for the return of her cat.
4 The politician delivered a passionate speech.
  The politician made a passionate speech.
5 The countries involved in the dispute have agreed to enter into talks.
  The countries involved in the dispute have entered into an agreement.

FOLLOW UP Use a dictionary to find extra collocations for:

to hold a ....   to broker a ....

to .... (an) agreement   a .... majority

22 Current affairs

The collocations in this unit are typically used in the news media.

A Current affairs in the press

Golfer Rick Tate has issued an **abject**[1] **apology** for his **disorderly behaviour** at the weekend. However, he **refused point-blank**[2] to **provide an explanation** for his behaviour and today further **damaging disclosures**[3] about his private life have been published in *The Daily Planet*.

The President has **issued a statement** relating to the health of her husband, who is **critically ill** in a private hospital following a massive heart attack. **Regular updates** on his condition will be provided.

The Leader of the Opposition has accused the Prime Minister of **misleading the electorate** in his **public pronouncements** on security. He has demanded that the PM **clarify his position** without delay. The PM's office has **declined to comment**.

Migrant workers **seeking permission**[6] to stay in this country may have to submit a **detailed account** of their work and personal lives to the visa authorities before they are **given leave** to stay.

[1] (formal) humble   [2] completely refused
[3] sensitive, private information which has been revealed
[4] (formal) position   [5] (formal) completely denied
[6] (formal) asking permission

The head of the National Union of Students (NUS) has **re-opened the debate** on tuition fees as **evidence emerges** of government plans to raise them still further. The NUS is committed to **taking a firm stance**[4] against tuition fees and has **flatly rejected**[5] claims that it may be about to change its position.

B Feelings and reactions in connection with current affairs

verb + noun	example	meaning
take issue with	I **take issue with** some of the points made in the speech.	(formal) disagree with
gauge reaction	The government leaked the story to the press in order to **gauge** public **reaction**.	test the response
excite speculation	The incident has **excited speculation** that the couple may be about to divorce.	(formal) caused rumours to circulate
air a grievance	Workers have **aired their grievances** to reporters about the new pay structure.	(formal) complained

adjective + noun	example	meaning
a dissenting voice	When it came to the vote, there was only one **dissenting voice**.	(formal) person who disagreed
a vociferous opponent	Our local MP is a **vociferous opponent** of having a casino in our city.	someone who opposes something loudly and publicly
passionate entreaty	Plans to extend the airport went ahead, despite **passionate entreaties** from local residents.	requests made because of strong beliefs
a throwaway comment	I don't think the politician really meant to say he was leaving the party – it was just a **throwaway comment**.	an unintentional remark which should not be taken seriously

Exercises

22.1 Correct the two collocation errors in each sentence.

1 The committee, with one disagreeing voice, voted to take a firm post on the issue.
2 It was only a throwoff comment but it has thrilled a lot of speculation.
3 As new evidence submerges of government involvement in the scandal, people are beginning to question the Prime Minister's public pronunciations on the affair.
4 The prince refused blink-point to provide a detailing account of his actions that night.
5 The Minister was accused of mislaying the electorate when he said that very few migrant workers had been handed leave to stay in the country.

22.2 Look at A. Complete each sentence using the word in brackets in the appropriate form.

1 The film star's son was arrested for .... behaviour. (ORDER)
2 The reporter asked the Minister to .... the government's position on health service reform. (CLEAR)
3 The jury felt that the accused had been unable to provide a satisfactory .... as to why he had gone to the house. (EXPLAIN)
4 The council will issue a .... at the close of their meeting today. (STATE)
5 She .... rejected the allegation that she had a financial motive. (FLAT)
6 Anyone seeking .... for permanent residence here is subject to a set of standard checks. (PERMIT)
7 There have recently been a number of damaging .... in the press about the politician's personal financial affairs. (DISCLOSE)
8 After years of silence on the issue in the press, teachers are now hopeful that the debate on school discipline will be .... (OPEN)

22.3 Complete the second sentence using a collocation from the opposite page. Both sentences should have the same meaning.

1 The singer has strongly and publicly opposed the war.
   The singer has been a .... of the war.
2 We carried out market research to see whether the public would like our new car.
   We carried out market research to .... to our new car.
3 The rock star made an emotional request for the earthquake victims, which produced a huge response.
   The rock star's .... for help for the earthquake victims produced a huge response.
4 The team will post accounts of their progress on their website every few days.
   The team will post .... on their progress on their website.
5 The newsletter allows staff to complain openly about conditions.
   The newsletter gives staff the chance to .... publicly.
6 I opposed the committee's stance on this matter.
   I .... with the committee's stance on this matter.
7 The actor would not say anything about the accusations that had been made.
   The actor .... on the accusations that had been made.
8 The doctors announced that the film star was very ill indeed.
   The doctors announced that the film star was ....
9 The politician made a public statement humbly regretting his derogatory comments about the town.
   The politician issued an .... for his derogatory comments about the town.

23 Festivals and celebrations

A Talking about festivals

Ballynoe Fiddle Festival (18 July)

This fun **festival falls on** the third Saturday of July, and the village becomes the centre of wild music for the whole day. The **festival celebrates** the birthday of Pat Davey, a famous local musician. This year's special guests include Anne O'Keeffe (fiddle) and Ger Downes (guitar), who will **uphold**[1] **the annual tradition** of playing at the house where Darvey was born.

[1] also *keep up*
[2] (journalistic/literary) very old
[3] also **festival marks**
[4] usually refers to the time around Christmas and New Year

Golden Apple Week (3–9 Sep)

Every year, the villagers of Hartsby **hold an unusual festival** – the Week of the Golden Apple. Hartsby, at the centre of the apple-growing region, celebrates this **tradition**, which **dates back to** the Middle Ages, at the beginning of every September. The festival is held to celebrate the apple harvest. Come and **join in the festivities** and eat as many apples as you want! Tickets £5 (children £2)

Fire and Light Festival (18 Dec)

It may be winter, dark and cold, but the village of Taft will be in **festive mood** on December 18th. **Wearing traditional dress**, the women of the village **perform dances** around a huge fire in the main square, while the men keep up **the age-old**[2] **tradition** of wearing large, brightly-coloured hats and carrying lanterns. The **event marks**[3] the beginning of the **festive season**[4].

B Traditional festivities

Different religions often have **movable feasts**[1] which depend on the phases of the moon.
There is a **rich tradition** of music and dance in central Sweden.
Jazz and blues are part of the **cultural heritage** of the southern United States.
Every year the town **puts on a** firework **display** as part of the festival.
We have a **proud tradition** of raising funds for charity through our annual town festival.
This month some of our students are **observing the festival of** Ramadan.
In a **break with tradition** this year's festival will feature modern dances alongside traditional ones.

[1] can refer to any arrangement, plan or appointment where the date is flexible

C A wedding celebration

Look at this speech by the best man (usually the bridegroom's best or oldest male friend) at a wedding. He mixes informal and formal collocations, which can have a humorous effect.

"Ladies and Gentlemen, according to **long-standing**[1] **tradition**, I now have to make a speech, but it'll be very short, so here goes. I never thought Jim would ever **get hitched**[2], but he's finally decided to **tie the knot**[3]. Yesterday he was suffering from **pre-wedding nerves**, but today he looked calm and happy as he and Sally were **joined in matrimony**[4]. So now, I'd like to **propose a toast**[5] to the bride and groom. Please **raise your glasses**. To Sally and Jim! May they have many years of **wedded bliss**[6]!"

[1] which has existed for along time   [2/3] (informal) get married   [4] (formal: used as part of the marriage ceremony) married   [5] also **make a toast**   [6] (usually used slightly humorously) happiness through being married

ERROR WARNING
Dress is an uncountable noun when it refers to a style of clothing (e.g. **traditional dress**, **formal dress**). Don't say *traditional dresses*; this would mean dresses for women only.

Exercises

23.1 Match the beginning of each sentence with its ending.

1 This year's National Day festival	a traditional dance from the region.
2 In this region we have a rich	the tradition, despite opposition.
3 A group of children performed	festival in spring.
4 This year's festival represents a break	celebrates 50 years of independence.
5 The tradition of carol singing dates	of giving food to older villagers every new year.
6 The people are determined to uphold	with tradition, as it will be held in May.
7 The town holds its annual	tradition of poetry, music and dance.
8 Our village has a proud tradition	back hundreds of years.

23.2 Correct the collocation errors in these sentences.

1 All the men wore traditional dresses consisting of green jackets and white trousers.
2 The festival makes the beginning of the Celtic summer.
3 The festival is part of the region's cultural inherit.
4 Hundreds of people, locals and tourists, join on the festivities.
5 The annual 'Day of the Horse' drops on 30 March this year.
6 Everyone in the village was in feast mood as the annual celebrations began.
7 The average age at which couples tie the strings is rising.
8 This region has a ripe tradition of folk singing and dancing.
9 Getting joined to matrimony is a significant reason for celebration.
10 The area is famous for observing a number of age-standing traditions.

23.3 Read these remarks by different people. Then answer the questions.

Alicia: Grandparents Day is a movable feast, depending on when Easter falls.
Brona: Every year we put on a display of traditional arts and crafts.
Monica: Nowadays, only older people observe the Festival of the Dead.
Erik: The festive season usually gets underway towards the middle of December.
Evan: The harp is part of the cultural heritage of Wales.

1 Who is talking about the beginning of a period of celebration?
2 Who is talking about something that represents the identity of a group of people?
3 Who is talking about something that happens on a different day each year?
4 Who is talking about something that not everyone celebrates?
5 Who is talking about people organising an exhibition of some sort?

23.4 Answer these questions about weddings.

1 Does *get hitched* mean get (a) engaged (b) married (c) divorced?
2 What kind of happiness do married couples hope for?
3 What do the bride and bridegroom 'tie' when they get married?
4 What is the difference between making toast and making a toast?
5 What phrase means the nervousness people feel before they get married?
6 What formal expression is used in the marriage ceremony meaning to marry?
7 Why do people raise their glasses?
8 Are the two expressions referred to in questions 1 and 3 formal or informal?

 FOLLOW UP Look up a festival that is special in your country on the Internet. What information in English can you find about it? Make a note of any interesting collocations in the text. A good starting-point for your search might be: www.festivals.com.

24 Advertisements and fashion

A The language of advertisements

Relax in the **sheer luxury** of a Florella Foam Bath.

The Luxe is a very special hotel. With us you experience **gracious living** in truly **grand style**.

EcoCream has **anti-ageing properties**. It has been **clinically proven** to **banish wrinkles**[1]. One application of this **luxury cream** will make **fine lines** and other signs of ageing disappear, leaving you with a **flawless complexion**.

Enjoy the **unrivalled service** at our **exclusive restaurant** in London's West End.

You won't **pile on the pounds**[2] if you eat one of our **tasty snacks** whenever you're **feeling peckish**[3]. Each one is a mere 40 calories.

For **long-lasting colour** and to treat **sun-damaged hair** use *Tressy products*.

Daisy Oil will bring out the **natural highlights** in your hair.

[1] get rid of lines
[2] put on weight
[3] (informal) feeling hungry

B Interview with a fashion model

Reporter: Would you say that fashion has always been important to you?

Beth: Well, ever since I was a child, I've loved reading **glossy magazines**[1], looking at the photos and finding out **what's in fashion**.

Reporter: And as you grew up, did you buy **designer label** clothes?

Beth: Oh, no! I couldn't afford them, and I was actually quite happy with **high-street fashion**[2]. But I loved looking at fashion shows on TV, especially when Paris or Milan designers **launched their new collections**.

Reporter: And now you are the one showing us the **new season's look**[3] and **setting the trend**[4]!

Beth: That's right. I still can't quite believe it.

Reporter: So what should we be wearing this year?

Beth: Well, there is a **stunning range** of new leisurewear about to **hit the high street**[5]. It's based on the new adventure-influenced trend we saw coming out of Paris and I think it's going to be a **hugely popular** look. And it's going to be comfortable to wear too.

Reporter: That's good. So, have you ever let yourself become a **fashion victim**[6]?

Beth: Well, I must admit I've worn some **excruciatingly uncomfortable** shoes in the past, so I'm happy to report that flat shoes are definitely **back in fashion**!

[1] magazines printed on high quality paper with lots of photos and adverts
[2] clothes bought in ordinary shops rather than from special fashion designers
[3] the new fashion style
[4] starting the fashion
[5] become available in chainstores
[6] a person who always wears fashionable clothes even if they make them look ridiculous or don't suit them

Exercises

24.1 Look at A. Add a word to each sentence to make the language typical of advertisements.

1 These vitamins have been proven to protect the body from winter viruses.
2 Our snacks cost only 24p.
3 Enjoy a weekend of luxury at the Highlands Health Hotel.
4 We manage a number of restaurants in Paris and New York.
5 Our new shampoo will subtly bring out the highlights in your hair.
6 Our lipsticks come in a range of colours.
7 We guarantee you will be impressed by the service provided by all our hotels.
8 Our new concealer will make the lines around your eyes disappear.

24.2 Match the beginning of each sentence with its ending.

1 I don't believe those ads that claim their creams have anti-ageing   peckish.
2 While working in Austria I ate so many lovely cakes that I piled on the   hair.
3 Why not have a bowl of soup or a banana if you're feeling a bit   wrinkles.
4 We guarantee that you will see instant results with our luxury hand   magazines.
5 You should use this shampoo to revive your sun-damaged   style.
6 Sometimes I wish it were really possible to banish   cream.
7 The hotel gives all its guests the chance to experience gracious   restaurants.
8 We were invited to a banquet, where they entertained us in grand   properties.
9 At the airport she bought herself a couple of glossy   pounds.
10 This part of town is famous for its classy hotels and exclusive   living.

24.3 Complete this article from a fashion magazine using collocations from B. The first letters are given to help you.

A stunning (1) r....................... of new summer clothes is about to (2) h....................... a high street near you. Vibrant colours are (3) b....................... in fashion, and there were also many more practical designs in the collections (4) l....................... last week at the Paris fashion show than we have seen for some time. The Paris designs instantly (5) s....................... the trends which have quickly been taken up and adapted for the mass market. Such adaptations for the (6) h....................... street fashion stores may not carry designer (7) l....................... but they allow us all to wear the new (8) s....................... look. We are confident that this will be a hugely (9) p....................... look as it is designed with comfort as well as elegance in mind. So there's no need to be a fashion (10) v....................... this summer!

24.4 Find three collocations for each word. One is in this unit. Use a dictionary or online corpus (see Unit 4) to find two more.

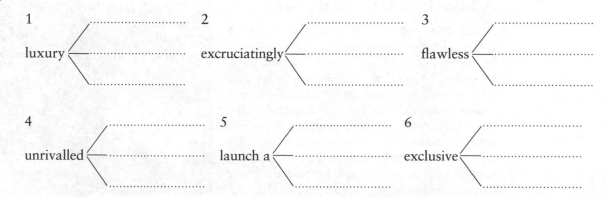

25 Traffic and driving

A Traffic problems

Traffic has been **severely disrupted**[1] on the M82 motorway, owing to an accident. Currently all **traffic** is being **diverted**[2] through the village of Oxtoe. Motorists are advised to avoid the area as **heavy traffic** is expected on many side roads for the rest of the day.

Traffic is very **dense**[3] on all routes into the city at the moment because of this evening's football cup final. **Lengthy delays** are expected around the National Stadium area. The heavy **traffic** is not expected to **die down**[4] till around 10pm. So walk or cycle to the match if you want to avoid getting **stuck in traffic**.

If you're thinking of using the N27 this morning, don't! **Traffic** is currently **tailing back**[5] over ten kilometres, following an accident near junction 14. Police say **traffic** is **building up** on all approach roads and is not expected to **ease off**[6] during the next three hours.

[1] prevented from continuing as usual
[2] made to take a different route
[3] very close together
[4] gradually become less
[5] forming a long queue
[6] gradually become less (similar to *die down*)

B Learning to drive

Hi Nina,
I'm learning to drive at last! All the jobs I want require a **valid**[1] **driving licence**, so I've no choice. I'm hoping to **take my driving test** in about four months' time, but the last lesson didn't go too well. I'm finding it really hard to **change gear**. **Getting into reverse** is particularly hard and I can sense my instructor flinching whenever I **grind the gears**[2]. Perhaps I should have opted to learn on an **automatic car**!
Paul

Hi Paul,
Much better to learn on a **manual car** – then you can drive anything after your test. Driving tests are awful. I remember mine when I came to the UK and needed a **current** UK **licence**. The examiner told me to **bear left**[3] at a junction and I went right! I'd never driven a **right-hand-drive** car before.
I had to remember to **keep to the left** instead of to the right. It was a nightmare.
Nina

[1] currently in use or acceptable   [2] change gear roughly and noisily   [3] change direction slightly towards the left

C A new kind of transport

A bike that travels sideways

It has been **hailed as** the first **major development** in bicycle design for 150 years. The Sideways Bike has a steerable wheel with **a set of handlebars** at either end. The cyclist sits sideways and operates a wheel with each hand. However, some people don't like the fact that the rider doesn't face the **oncoming traffic**. Its **key advantage** is that it's more manoeuvrable than a conventional bike. It's very like snowboarding because you're **moving sideways**. That affords you tremendous grace, though it will never win you the Tour de France!

Exercises

25.1 **Choose the correct collocation.**

1 After the accident the traffic *failed / tailed / held* back for more than five miles.
2 The traffic didn't die *back / up / down* until long after the rock concert.
3 Traffic is being *disrupted / dispensed / diverted* onto the B2534 because of an accident on the M73 motorway.
4 The traffic starts *rising up / building up / massing up* in the city centre around 4pm.
5 When the lorry broke down, traffic was severely *disrupted / diverted / disturbed* for several hours.
6 When you come into the town, *hold / maintain / keep* to the left, then *bear / drive / hold* left at the first roundabout.

25.2 **Replace the underlined part of each sentence using a collocation from the opposite page with the opposite meaning.**

1 There was <u>light traffic</u> on the motorway at the time of the accident. (give two answers)
2 The <u>traffic built up</u> after the match was over. (give two answers)
3 I have <u>an outdated driving licence</u>. (give two answers)
4 <u>Brief delays</u> are expected on all routes because of the start of the holiday weekend.
5 <u>Bear right</u> at the next junction.
6 I much prefer to drive <u>an automatic car</u>.
7 I don't know how he manages to <u>change gear smoothly</u> like that.
8 His invention was <u>said to be a minor development</u> in aeronautics.

25.3 **Complete each sentence using a word from the opposite page.**

1 I always find it difficult in this car to get into .... when I need, for example, to back into a parking space.
2 The handlebars on my bike got twisted in the accident – I'm going to have to get a new ....
3 Being able to get through rush hour traffic quickly is the key .... of travelling by bike.
4 Electric cars were hailed as a major .... in automotive engineering.
5 In an automatic car you don't need to .... gear manually.
6 The policeman pointed out that my licence was no longer .... – it expired last week.
7 I .... my driving test three times before I eventually passed it.
8 The traffic is always particularly .... on the main road coming into town in the rush hour.

25.4 **Rewrite the underlined part of each sentence using the word in brackets in the appropriate form.**

1 I was in <u>a car with the steering-wheel on the right</u>. (HAND)
2 Crabs are one of the few creatures that <u>do not move in a forwards direction</u>. (SIDE)
3 I took <u>the examination to become a qualified driver</u> in 1999. (TEST)
4 The jet engine <u>was soon understood to be a major development</u> in aircraft design. (HAIL)
5 <u>The best thing about</u> manual cars is that there is less that can go wrong with them. (KEY)
6 <u>People were being delayed</u> at the airport <u>for hours</u> because of the fog. (LENGTHY)
7 <u>There were major traffic problems</u> on the ring road this morning. (SEVERE)
8 I <u>got held up by a traffic jam</u> on my way to the airport. (STUCK)
9 Be careful and always be aware of <u>the traffic that is coming towards you</u>. (COME)

26 Travel and adventure

A An exciting trip

Read Catherine's account of her trip to South America.

I'd always had **a thirst for adventure** and often **get itchy feet** so I could hardly **contain my excitement** when I set off for South America for a year. After a 12-hour flight to São Paulo, Brazil, I had another long flight to Manaus in the Amazon. Then I went by bus to a smaller town. It was a very **arduous**[1] **journey**. I should have **broken the journey**[2] somewhere but I did it all in one go. Next time, I'll **have a stopover**[3] in São Paolo, have a bit of a rest and **do the sights** there before travelling on.

After two fantastic weeks in the Amazon I got a flight on a **low-cost airline** to Rio de Janeiro. I then tried to get a flight to Peru but they were all full, so they **put me on standby**[4]. Luckily I got a seat on the flight I wanted.

In Peru I **went trekking** in the Andes with a group. The guide took us **off the beaten track** and I felt like an **intrepid**[5] **explorer** from another century in some **unexplored wilderness**. There was a real **sense of adventure**. One day we actually got **hopelessly lost**. It was getting dark and we were afraid they'd have to **send out a search party** to look for us. But then we met some locals who were very friendly and helped us get back on to our path. It was a great trip.

[1] difficult, tiring, needing a lot of effort   [2] stopped for a short time   [3] have a brief (usually) overnight stay in a place when on a long journey to somewhere else, usually by air   [4] made me wait to see if a seat became available   [5] brave, with no fear of dangerous situations

B Articles about travel adventures

Note the collocations in these brief magazine items about travel adventures.

Some longed-for **sunny spells** have **boosted** the **spirits**[1] of three British women hoping to set a polar trekking record. The women have **faced severe weather conditions** since setting off to walk to the North Pole 18 days ago. However, the team's base camp manager said she had spoken to them yesterday by satellite phone and they had been relieved to report the weather was sunny and **their spirits were high**[2].

London to Tangier by train: Whilst this journey may not compare in terms of **sheer epic grandeur** to some of the great American train journeys, it does **have a special charm** all of its own. It may not be cheap but if you **keep your eyes peeled**[3], you can find some surprisingly good deals. If **your budget doesn't quite stretch to**[4] a sleeping compartment, you can always just curl up in your seat for the night. Let the rhythmical motion and the dull rumbles of the train **lull you to sleep**. The first **leg of the journey** gives you very little indication of what lies ahead ...

[1] made feel more cheerful   [2] they were in a positive mood   [3] (informal) keep your eyes open
[4] you can't afford

> **TIP**
>
> There are many English language websites relating to the theme of travel and adventure. Try, for example, a magazine site such as www.nationalgeographic.com or an adventure travel company such as www.keadventure.com.

Exercises

26.1 Complete these descriptions of TV documentaries using a word from the box.

arduous	beaten	intrepid	sense	sights	trekking	unexplored

1 John Howes presents essential holiday tips for those heading off the .... track, while Anneke Zousa does the .... of New York in record time.

2 In this fascinating film, Grieshaus gives us a picture of the largely .... wilderness of the Kara Kum Desert.

3 Like a(n) .... explorer of the nineteenth century, James Westly travelled with only two companions.

4 In 1957, Anna Trensholm went .... through the mountains of North-Eastern Turkey and filmed every step of her way. This unique footage reveals the harshness of her .... journey.

5 This film conveys a genuine .... of adventure, as we travel with its makers through the dense jungles of Guyana.

26.2 Choose the correct collocations.

I have always had itchy (1) *hands / feet / fingers* and last summer I had the amazing opportunity to travel to the – for me at least – (2) *unexplored / unplanned / unprepared* territory of the Gobi Desert. My budget wouldn't (3) *spread / stretch / afford* to travelling on a normal flight but I couldn't find a (4) *low-cost / low-key / low-cut* airline to fly me there. In the end, I got a (5) *stand-up / stand-off / standby* ticket and it was not too expensive. Once there I joined a group and we made a journey on horseback into the desert. You wouldn't believe the sheer (6) *very / mere / epic* grandeur of the region. If you keep your eyes (7) *peeled / scaled / washed* you can see all sorts of amazing plants and creatures. We were lucky with the weather. We were told that the previous group had had to (8) *meet / face / address* severe weather (9) *circumstances / coincidences / conditions*. Our main problem was that one day we got (10) *hopelessly / fearlessly / carelessly* lost and they had to send out a search (11) *group / party / set* to find us. We felt so stupid. Anyway, the Gobi Desert may not be everyone's choice of holiday destination but I can assure you that it (12) *does / gets / has* a very special charm of its own.

26.3 Rewrite each sentence using the word in brackets.

1 At the beginning the journey was straightforward. (LEG)
2 I couldn't afford to travel first class. (STRETCH)
3 After we arrived at our base camp we felt more cheerful. (BOOSTED)
4 There will be periods of sunshine in most areas today. (SPELLS)
5 We broke our journey to Australia in Singapore. (STOPOVER)
6 Jack has always longed to have adventures. (THIRST)
7 Grandmother is very cheerful today. (SPIRITS)
8 The movement of the ship helped me to fall asleep. (LULLED)

26.4 Use a dictionary or online corpus (see Unit 4) to find two more collocations for these words.

1 arduous   2 wilderness   3 uncharted

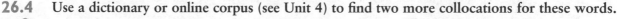

27 Sport

A Emails about a sports camp

Hi Greg,

How are things with you? I'm having a great time here at this sports camp in New Zealand. I'm taking the opportunity to **do**[1] several **extreme sports** like white-water rafting and rock climbing. At the weekend we went to the mountains and I've **acquired** quite **a taste for**[2] snowboarding. I didn't like it much at first – I found it really hard to **keep my balance**. But my instructor said she was sure I'd **get the hang of it**[3] in a couple of hours. I thought there was **precious little chance**[4] of that happening but I decided to **take up the challenge** and, sure enough, I mastered it. I thought I was **pretty fit**[5] but I'm really having to **push myself to the limits**[6] to be able to cope. I'm so shattered at night that it takes me about two seconds to fall into a deep sleep. Anyway, despite the tiredness, I'm **having a whale of a time**[7]. Hope you are too.

Philippe

[1] NOT ~~make~~
[2] begun to enjoy
[3] (informal) become able to do something
[4] (informal) very little chance
[5] (informal) fairly fit
[6] make a considerable effort
[7] (informal) having a fantastic time

It sounds like you are having a fantastic time! I'd **jump at the chance**[8] to try out some of those sports. The only sport I'm doing at the moment is running for the bus. But I am sharing your exhaustion. We're so busy at work that I can't **summon up the energy** to do anything in the evenings to **keep in shape**[9].

Greg

[8] (informal) really like to do something [9] stay in good physical condition

B Sports news

The mood amongst the crowd **reached fever pitch**[1] at yesterday's match between India and Pakistan. In the last few minutes of the game Khan **played a blinder**[2] and secured a **convincing victory** for Pakistan.

In the cricket match between Australia and South Africa the **score** currently **stands at** 65 for 3 wickets. We'll bring you the **latest scores** on the hour, every hour.

[1] became very excited/agitated   [2] (informal) performed brilliantly, usually in sport

C Match reports

The teams **took the field**[1] to the applause of 5,000 spectators. Despite **putting up** a determined **performance**, the England team seemed unable to **break through the** formidable Australian **defence**. After some impressive tackles, Australia was **awarded a penalty** just before half time. The **penalty was missed**, much to the delight of ...

Yesterday's match was full of excitement with three players being **given yellow cards** and some controversial **free kicks**. The game was lost when the Blues **scored an own goal**[2] in the last two minutes. The crowd **went wild**[3].

[1] went on the pitch   [2] scored a goal in error against their own team   [3] became crazy with excitement (can also be used for other emotions, such as rage)

TIP

Listen to commentaries in English relating to a sport that interests you and find a website dedicated to that sport. Note down any collocations about that sport that you notice being frequently used. You may find this website useful: www.bbc.co.uk/fivelive/sport.

Exercises

27.1 **Look at A. Choose the correct collocation.**

1 I'm finding it hard to *summon up / acquire / reach* the energy to do anything much in the evenings these days.
2 Have you ever tried any *formidable / fever / extreme* sports?
3 I didn't realise how difficult the marathon would be when I originally *took / had / got* up the challenge.
4 I don't think I could ever *acquire / educate / achieve* a taste for bungee jumping.
5 I'd *rise / jump / take* at the chance of a trip to Venice if I were offered one!
6 It won't take you long to get the *balance / taste / hang* of cross-country skiing as you're such an experienced downhill skier.

27.2 **Complete each sentence using a word from the page opposite.**

1 Don't .... yourself to the limits now. Conserve some strength for later on.
2 I'm having a .... of a time learning how to surf, though I find it almost impossible to .... my balance.
3 There's precious little .... of your getting her to go for a long walk today.
4 I've just heard the .... scores. Italy's winning and excitement's reaching fever ....
5 The score in the rugby match currently .... at 27 to 5 and France looks set to win a convincing ....
6 You must try harder to keep in .... over the winter. You could walk to work instead of going by bus, for example.
7 John Shane was given a yellow .... for performing an illegal tackle on an opponent.
8 The captain took the free .... and it reached Jobbs, who instantly scored.
9 Fortunately for Wales, Scotland .... every penalty that they were .... during the match.
10 When the headteacher offered a prize to the pupils who built the best raft over the holidays, children from every class decided to take up the ....

27.3 **Rewrite each sentence using the word in brackets.**

1 I'd love to meet Johnny Depp, wouldn't you? (JUMP)
2 The spectators stood and clapped as the teams went on to the pitch. (TOOK)
3 You should only attempt this climb if you have a reasonable level of fitness. (PRETTY)
4 The crowd was extremely excited at the end of the match. (WILD)
5 We very much enjoyed our time in Australia. (WHALE)
6 I decided to be brave and start my own business. (CHALLENGE)
7 The little boy soon learnt how to ride his bike without stablisers. (HANG)
8 The team captain felt dreadful when he kicked the ball into his own team's goal. (OWN)

27.4 **Complete each sentence using the word in brackets in the appropriate form.**

1 I get the .... football scores sent through to my mobile. (LATE)
2 The home team won a .... victory. (CONVINCE)
3 Our team put up an excellent .... (PERFORM)
4 It took some time before our team succeeded in breaking through the Reds' .... and scoring our first goal. (DEFEND)
5 The team captain helped to win the game by playing a .... (BLIND)

28 Plans and decisions

A Decisions and solutions

Hans Brokaw, head of a company making garden furniture, is announcing to his senior staff **plans** he is **making** to move the business exclusively to the Internet.

As you know, for some time now we've been **toying**[1] **with the idea** of transferring all our business to Internet-only sales as a **long-term solution** to the problem of finding good retail outlets. You'll remember that at the last team meeting Rob **unveiled**[2] **a plan** to move the line to the web in three phases over nine months. And Philippa did a great job **drumming up support**[3] for the move among the sales and marketing people. Since then, as you also know, we've had a **slight change of plan**, and, **acting on a suggestion**[4] from the logistics team, we've now decided that the move should happen over 12 months. In order to **implement**[5] such **a plan**, we need to **draw up a schedule** and **stick to**[6] that **schedule**.

So I'd like to make a **tentative suggestion**[7]. Before we **launch the scheme**, I think we should invite the web designers to come here and take us through the process from their side. That will give us the opportunity to **exercise greater control** over things. I don't think we should just **leave** everything **to their discretion**[8]. I'm just aware of how important it's going to be to **cover every eventuality**[9] before we commit 100% to the Internet.

We propose to end our relationship with the garden centres where we currently sell. We've reached this decision **after careful consideration**. We do believe that realistically it's the only **option open to us. The deciding factor** was losing our biggest customer – the Greenway garden centre chain. After that, we really had no choice.

[1] considering, but not in a focused way   [2] showed / made known for the first time
[3] increasing support for something   [4] doing something as a result of a suggestion
[5] put into operation   [6] keep to   [7] a suggestion that you are not sure will be accepted
[8] leave everything to their judgement   [9] consider all possible situations and difficulties

B Making plans

Note the collocations in this speech at the start of an annual youth summit.

Good morning, friends, and welcome to our summit, the first of what we plan as an annual event! I have been waiting for this day with **eager anticipation**[1] for a long time. We **came up with the idea** five years ago and **preparations have been underway**[2] ever since. There was a certain amount of **necessary groundwork**[3] to do, of course, before our sponsors were able to **reach the decision** to support us. But then we were able to turn our attention to how best to **put** our ideas **into practice**.

[1] feeling of great excitement about something that is going to happen   [2] happening
[3] work done in preparation

C Rejecting plans

Someone may **declare outright opposition** or **outright hostility** to a plan. [say they are completely opposed/hostile] A plan can be **rejected out of hand**. [totally rejected] Those who do not like a plan or piece of work may offer **constructive criticism**. [criticism which is useful and intended to help or improve]

ERROR WARNING | Note that we **come to** or **arrive at** a conclusion, NOT ~~make~~ a conclusion.

Exercises

28.1 **Match the two parts of these collocations.**

1 unveil   every eventuality
2 stick to   a lot of support
3 make   something a reality
4 leave it   a schedule
5 drum up   a plan
6 cover   to someone's discretion

28.2 **Complete each conversation to make B agree with what A says.**

1 A: I think we should do what Hilary is proposing.
   B: Yes, I think we should definitely act .... her suggestion.
2 A: We need to make a timetable for what needs to be done.
   B: Yes, we need to draw .... a schedule.
3 A: We need a lot of discussion before we can put the scheme into operation.
   B: Yes, we need a couple of meetings before we can implement the ....
4 A: We need to be able to have more influence over what's happening.
   B: I agree. We must .... greater control over things.
5 A: It's not an answer to the problem that will solve it permanently.
   B: I agree. It's not a .... solution.
6 A: We don't really have that choice.
   B: I agree. That .... is not open to us.

28.3 **Complete each sentence using a word from the box.**

| change | consideration | factor | groundwork | launch | outright | suggestion |

1 After careful .... , we decided not to sell the business.
2 We'll do the necessary .... and then .... the scheme in May.
3 I was very shocked to encounter such .... hostility to my plan.
4 Money is always the deciding .... in business decisions.
5 It was only a tentative .... , not a final decision.
6 There's been a slight .... of plan, I'm afraid.

28.4 **Correct the collocation errors in these sentences.**

1 Final preparations for the music festival are now undergone.
2 I was very upset when they rejected my suggestions out of foot.
3 The company came on with the idea of encouraging customers to recycle packaging.
4 I don't think you will find it easy to get your ideas into practice.
5 He declared his offright opposition to the plan.
6 Constructed criticism is always welcome, but negative criticism is not.

28.5 **Complete the word puzzle.**

Across
1 It's difficult to put the idea into — .
Down
1 There's been a change of — .
2 We need to — a decision today.
3 He always leaves me to — the plans for our holidays.
4 We should — on this suggestion at once.
5 I tend to — with an idea before making a decision.
6 The kids are full of — anticipation.

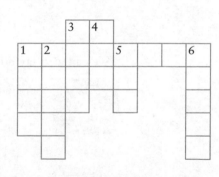

29 Film and book reviews

Note the collocations in these reviews of the same film from different publications.

Quality newspapers

Larissa is an excellent film. It tells the story of what happens when a young woman decides to try to find out what really happened to her grandmother, who disappeared in Russia in the 1930s under mysterious circumstances. As the **suspense builds up**, Larissa sets off **an amazing chain of events**. It's an incredibly gripping film and its direction shows **startling originality**.

It was certainly a **bold experiment**[1] to cast Jenni Adams as a woman twice her age, but Jenni is a very **accomplished actor** and a **consummate professional**[2], and she carried it off brilliantly. And the rest of the **star-studded cast** gave a **dazzling display** of their talents too. The film, which documents an extraordinary **series of events**, was **spectacularly successful** in the US – the New York Times gave it **glowing reviews**[3], and not without good reason.

[1] a brave and risky thing to do   [2] (formal) complete professional   [3] very positive reviews

Popular (tabloid) newspaper

Whoever decided to **cast** Jenni Adams **in the role of** the disappearing grandma in *Larissa* must have been out of their mind. An **unmitigated disaster**[4], **strongly influenced**[5] by the very worst kind of Hollywood sentimentality. The only good thing was the theme music. Perhaps they'll **release the CD** of it – that would be something. The cinema next door was showing *Screech of the Vampire* – now that I would **highly recommend**[6] ... if you **can bear the suspense**[7]!

[4] total disaster   [5] or **heavily influenced,** but NOT ~~highly~~ influenced
[6] **thoroughly recommend** is also possible   [7] can stand the excitement

Entertainment magazine

I usually **think highly** of Joel Hanson's films but this one, based on a novel by Slevan Gorsky, is a **dismal failure**. In spite of the **all-star cast**, the film just didn't **hold my attention** the way the book did. I was a college student when I read it, but it made a **lasting impression**[8] on me. It **fired my imagination** more than any other book has ever done, and **awakened my interest** in Russia in the 1930s so much that my poor old bookshelves are groaning with books on Russian history! The film, however, simply failed to **create**[9] **the atmosphere** of Leningrad in the 1930s which the book achieved so successfully.

[8] We can also say **an indelible impression**, meaning a permanent one   [9] also **evoke an atmosphere**

ERROR WARNING

Someone can have a **considerable reputation** or a **well-deserved** reputation, but NOT a ~~high~~ reputation.

Exercises

29.1 Complete the review using words from the opposite page. The first letter is given to help you.

The recently released film, *1,000 Nights*, does not have a (1) s.............................. cast
but it will not fail to make a (2) l.............................. impression with its startling
(3) o.............................. and its dazzling (4) d.............................. of new talent.
Jon Hayden is cast in the (5) r.............................. of Tim Alexon, a man
of principles trying to make his way in the world of big business. It is
Hayden's first appearance on the big screen, but he shows himself as an
exceptionally (6) a.............................. actor playing the little man caught
up in an intriguing and at times terrifying (7) s.............................. of
events. The use of unknown actors was a bold (8) e..............................
but it turned out to be (9) s.............................. successful. *1,000 Nights*
will (10) f.............................. the imagination of even the most cynical
of viewers.

29.2 Cross out the option which *cannot* be used in each sentence.

1 Alla Repina has a *high / considerable / well-deserved* reputation as a character actor.
2 The *all-star / star-studded / starring* cast is set to make the film a box-office success.
3 My cousin *highly / spectacularly / thoroughly* recommended the play.
4 The plot is based on an extraordinary *series / burst / chain* of events that happened in New York in the early 1800s.
5 The stage sets were obviously *strongly / highly / heavily* influenced by the work of the surrealist artist, Salvador Dali.
6 The film made a(n) *consummate / lasting / indelible* impression on me.
7 The author *evoked / created / wrote* a magical atmosphere.

29.3 Complete each sentence using a word from the opposite page.

1 I admire that producer because he is such a consummate ....
2 We all began to feel increasingly nervous as the suspense built ....
3 All that writer's books have received glowing ....
4 The central character's actions set off an amazing chain of ....
5 To my mind the play is an unmitigated ....
6 Making a film lasting six hours was quite a bold ....
7 I'm afraid the novel didn't really succeed in holding my ....
8 I couldn't watch the film at the most exciting point – I just couldn't bear the
....

29.4 Name the following:

1 a CD that has been recently released.
2 a film director whom you think highly of.
3 a film that has recently been spectacularly successful.
4 a book that has awakened your interest in a different place or period of history.

29.5 Two of the collocations on the opposite page are strongly negative ways of saying that something did not succeed. Which are they?

Go to www.imdb.com (The Internet Movie Database) and read some of the items and reviews there. Make a note of any useful collocations not in this unit.

30 Regulations and authority

A Health and safety regulations

Dear colleague,

As you are probably aware, the Government has recently **passed** new **laws** relating to health and safety in the workplace. These new **regulations** have been **introduced**[1] to **standardise procedure** in workplaces across the country and ensure that employers **adhere to standards**.

The enclosed guide details the steps you need to take in order to **comply with** these new **laws**. All employers **have an obligation** to **carry out a risk assessment**[2]. Failure to do so will leave us **in breach of the law**[3]. The purpose of the risk assessment is to **minimise danger** to employees and also to make it easier for employers to **satisfy the requirements** of the regulations.

All department heads **have an obligation** to read the information in the guide carefully. Please do so, and if you have any further questions, I will be happy to answer them.

Bill Lloyd
Health and Safety Officer

[1] also *brought in*   [2] an exercise to identify and assess risks   [3] (formal) breaking the law

ERROR WARNING
We say We could not **arrive at an agreement** or We could not **reach an agreement**, NOT We could not ~~get to~~ or We could not ~~find~~ an agreement.

B Planning permission

If you wish to build, say, an extension to your house, it is **absolutely essential**[1] to **seek permission**[2] to do so. If your **plan is approved**, then you will be **granted permission**[3] to build. But it is becoming more difficult to **obtain permission**[4] as the government has **introduced new legislation** which has **tightened controls**[5]. It can take quite some time after **putting in an application** for **permission to be given**. This is because the planning officers have to ensure that your plans do not **infringe the regulations**[6] relating to building in your area.

Be wary of treating the planning officers as **faceless bureaucrats**[7]; they are **in a position of** considerable **authority**, though some of them are more vigorous about **exercising authority**[8] than others. Some will be prepared to **cut through the red tape**[9] for you, whereas others might seem to be doing everything they can to block your plans, especially if they think you are trying to **flout the rules**[10].

[1] NOT ~~very~~ essential
[2] (formal) ask for permission
[3] (formal) given permission
[4] (formal) receive permission
[5] made the rules tougher
[6] (formal) break the rules
[7] used as an insult to officials, suggesting that they lack character
[8] (formal) using that authority
[9] deal quickly and effectively with bureaucratic procedures
[10] (formal) intentionally break the rules

TIP
Language relating to the law and to regulations often has its own very special, often formal, collocations. These are more likely to be used in written than spoken English so avoid using them in informal speech.

Exercises

30.1 Complete these collocations from A using a word from the box.

1 .... requirements
2 .... an obligation
3 .... at an agreement
4 .... out a risk assessment

5 .... a new law
6 .... in regulations
7 .... to standards
8 .... authority

adhere	arrive
bring	carry
exercise	have
pass	satisfy

30.2 Rewrite the underlined part of each sentence to make it more formal.

1 You will be punished if you continue to <u>ignore</u> the rules.
2 All our sister organisations <u>stick</u> to the standards listed in the Code of Practice.
3 We <u>asked for</u> permission to build on a field next to our house and after some time we were <u>given</u> that permission.
4 It is important that all citizens should <u>do what the law says they should do</u>.
5 If your business doesn't <u>meet</u> the legal requirements, you may find yourself prosecuted for <u>breaking</u> company law.

30.3 Complete this letter of complaint using words from the opposite page.

> Dear Sir/Madam,
>
> I am writing to complain about the behaviour of our town council. When its members were elected to (1) .... of authority, they promised to (2) .... the ridiculous amount of red tape that is choking modern society. Yet all they have done is (3) .... still more pointless new legislation, thus (4) .... controls over the ordinary family. They have turned out to be no better than their predecessors, (5) .... bureaucrats, all of them. Their latest decision – to (6) .... a plan to build a multi-million new council office block – is an absolute disgrace!
>
> Yours faithfully,
>
> W. Hinger

30.4 Complete the word puzzle.

Across

1 The builders had friends in high places and got away with flouting the —— for several years.
2 It is hard to find staff who —— all our requirements.
3 Extreme sports are risky, but we do all we can to minimise the —— to participants.
4 I chose not to —— my authority and impose a punishment as it was a special holiday.
5 It is absolutely —— that we do not put staff at risk.
6 By building a house without permission the builder found himself in —— of the law.
7 It took time but eventually we —— permission to demolish our garage.

Down

1 Before the shop opens for business you must carry out a —— .

30.5 Find one other possible collocation for each of the verbs in the box in 30.1. Use a dictionary to help you.

31 The environment

A Damaging the environment

Read this extract from a report on getting rid of waste.

> **Disposal of household waste** is a daunting task for local authorities. Towns and cities cannot just **dump**[1] such **waste** and hope it will go away. Household waste contains many materials and substances which are extremely **harmful to the environment**, and authorities need long-term solutions. Efforts to **recycle waste** are only a partial solution. Meanwhile, the problem of **toxic**[2] **waste** remains. One expert recently warned that the risks to **public health** are so great that we may have less than a decade to avoid an **environmental catastrophe** on a global scale.

[1] dispose of in an irresponsible manner [2] poisonous

B Climate change and its consequences

Here is an interview with Gary Prime, the American rock star known for his support of environmental campaigns, who is visiting London.

Interviewer: Would you agree that climate change is the most urgent issue facing us today?

Prime: Definitely. You only have to look at the changing **weather patterns** in many parts of the world. It's **absolutely vital** that we **change our ways** before it's too late. Parts of Europe which used to be cooler now experience intense, **searing heat**[1], and **temperatures soar** above the average every summer. Other areas suffer **widespread flooding** on a regular basis. We can't continue in this way without there being **dire**[2] **consequences**.

Interviewer: So what can people do in the face of this **irreversible climate change**?

Prime: Yes, there is. We can all **reduce our carbon footprint**[3] by flying less, and reduce our **food miles**[4] by buying local produce. Some airlines have schemes now for **offsetting carbon emissions**[5].

Interviewer: Flying's only one part of it, though. Most of the problems come from **vehicle emissions** and power stations.

Prime: True, but there are things we can do about that too. Buy a **hybrid car**[6], develop **alternative energy sources** for homes, **solar heating** for instance, and build more **offshore**[7] **wind farms**. Oil supplies will **run dry**[8] within 50 years. **Renewable energy** can make a real difference. And politicians shouldn't be afraid of **introducing green taxes**[9] and incentives to encourage **eco-friendly design** in architecture. With sufficient will, we can **find a solution**.

Interviewer: Gary Prime, thank you for giving up your time for this interview.

Prime: No problem, I've got just enough time to catch my flight to Los Angeles.

[1] extreme heat [2] extremely serious [3] amount of carbon dioxide created by an activity/person/business [4] distance food has to travel between where it is grown or made and where it is consumed [5] paying for an equivalent amount of carbon dioxide to be saved elsewhere [6] a car which can alternate between different energy sources (e.g. petrol and battery) [7] at sea, away from the coast [8] finish [9] taxes which relate to the protection of the environment

ERROR WARNING
- We say **absolutely** *vital*, NOT *very vital*.
  It's **absolutely vital** that everyone plays their part in combating climate change.
- We say **find a solution**, NOT *give a solution*.
  We need to **find a solution** to the problem of energy supplies.

Exercises

31.1 Read these remarks by different speakers, and then answer the questions.

> Sylvia: We found that poisonous chemicals had been thrown into the river.
> Tomas: We have to protect everyone from illnesses caused by environmental problems.
> Marcos: We can collect glass and plastic from homes which can then be re-used.
> Gerard: We are heading for a major disaster in terms of the pollution of the oceans.
> Ulla: We must stop using this chemical. It can destroy plant and animal life.

1 Who mentions public health?
2 Who is complaining about people dumping toxic waste?
3 Who is talking about avoiding the use of something which is harmful to the environment?
4 Who is explaining about recycling household waste?
5 Who is sounding a warning about an environmental catastrophe?

31.2 Complete each sentence using a word from the opposite page.

1 We looked out to sea and spotted some .... wind farms.
2 Oil supplies are likely to .... dry within the next 200 years.
3 It's absolutely .... that we all do something to reduce global warming.
4 As a green organisation we only use architects who specialise in .... design.
5 Continued use of fossil fuels will have .... consequences in the long term.
6 The airline has a scheme where you can .... your carbon emissions.

31.3 Rewrite the underlined part of each sentence using a collocation from the opposite page based on the word in brackets.

1 <u>How far our food travels before we consume it</u> should be a concern for everyone. (MILE)
2 <u>Energy which comes from inexhaustible sources</u>, such as wind, is our greatest hope for the future. (RENEW)
3 The region has experienced <u>flooding over large areas</u> in recent years. (WIDE)
4 We have caused <u>the world's climate to alter in a way that cannot be changed back</u>. (CHANGE)
5 We must <u>do something to eliminate</u> the problem of toxic waste. (SOLVE)
6 We should all try to reduce <u>the amount of carbon we emit</u>. (FOOT)
7 <u>Wind farms located out at sea</u> can provide a partial solution to the problem. (SHORE)
8 The Minister chairs a committee aiming to improve <u>the way we get rid of rubbish from our homes</u>. (DISPOSE)

31.4 Correct the collocation errors in these sentences.

1 Temperatures expanded during the summer months and reached a record high.
2 We must change our way before it is too late.
3 They now have a sun heating system in their house; it's very economical.
4 The desert experiences soaring heat during the day but is cold at night.
5 The weather designs have changed in recent years: winters are milder, summers are hotter.
6 He has one of those mixed cars which alternates between petrol and battery power.
7 The government must present green taxes so people who damage the environment pay more.
8 Vehicle transmissions are the main source of pollution in big cities.
9 We need to find alternative energy origins for private homes.

 Go to the United Nations Environment Programme website at www.unep.org, and make a note of useful collocations you find there connected with the environment.

32 Town and country life

A   City life

Read this advertisement for new houses in the city, and note the collocations.

Secure your new home now in the exciting city of Lorchester. In Lorchester's **bustling**[1] **centre** you can enjoy high-quality **urban living**, with **reliable public transport** and shops and restaurants whose **long opening hours** will suit your busy lifestyle.

Phone us now on 00345 877223 to visit our extensive range of show houses and apartments, or take a virtual tour at www.incitilife.com.

[1] full of busy activity

B   Country life versus city life

Jerome has just moved from his home village into a big town. He emails Rosie about it.

Hi Rosie,
Well, I did it. I moved into town. I must say I don't miss the **rustic charm**[1] of life in **the back of beyond**[2]! For some people Little Snoring is a **rural idyll**, but for me it was always just a **quiet backwater**[3] **in the middle of nowhere** where nothing ever happened and where I was **bored rigid**[4]. I've only been in town a week, but I love everything about it – the **crowded streets**, the **hectic pace**[5] **of life**, the fact that you can get a cappuccino or **hail a taxi** at two in the morning.
So when are you coming to visit?
Jerome

[1] appeal that is simple and picturesque   [2] an extremely isolated place   [3] a quiet, isolated village
[4] (informal) extremely bored   [5] very busy and fast pace

C   City Council plans

GOOD NEWS FOR INNER CITY LIFE

City Councillors last night approved extensive plans for **urban regeneration**.

Key features of the plan include the restoration of **derelict buildings**[1] and a **tree-planting scheme**.

The hope is that the **inner city** will soon resemble the **leafy suburbs** as an attractive and **desirable place to live**.

Planners believe that an increase in the number of **residential dwellings**[2] in the town centre will ease the problem of **congested roads** and night-time crime: with commercial and recreational facilities **within walking distance** and **open all hours**, it is hoped that many people will choose to leave their cars at home, and that it will be safer to walk on the street at night.

[1] buildings that are not cared for and are in a very bad condition   [2] (formal, official) homes

Exercises

32.1 Complete each sentence with *the city* and *the country* in the correct space.

1 There is a less hectic pace of life in .... than in ....
2 It's much easier to hail a taxi in .... than in ....
3 You are less likely to find reliable public transport in .... than in ....
4 You are more likely to find rustic charm in .... than in ....
5 You are more likely to find congested roads in .... than in ....

32.2 Explain the difference in meaning between the sentences in each pair.

1 The roads are very congested.   The streets are very crowded.
2 We live in the inner city.   They live in the leafy suburbs.
3 He lives in a quiet backwater.   She lives in a bustling city centre.
4 I enjoy urban living.   I love my rural idyll.

32.3 Put the collocations in the box into pairs that are similar in meaning.

city life	long opening hours	rustic charm	in the back of beyond	open all hours
urban living	in the middle of nowhere	rural idyll		

32.4 Rewrite the underlined part of each sentence using a collocation from the opposite page.

1 The village is regarded as a <u>quiet place where nothing happens</u>, but the people who live there love it.
2 She lives in a simple cottage <u>miles away from any other inhabited places</u>.
3 The government plans to provide funds to subsidise <u>the modernisation and improvement of our cities</u>.
4 The city announced <u>a plan to plant more trees</u> in 2007.
5 The south side of the city is <u>an area where many people would like to have a home</u>.
6 The city council has declared that part of the town may only be used for <u>people's homes</u>.

32.5 Find collocations on the opposite page with the opposite meaning to these phrases.

1 smart, modern buildings   ....
2 quiet roads (2 answers)   ....
3 a quiet city centre   ....
4 urban decay   ....
5 the urban nightmare   ....
6 restricted opening times   ....
  (2 answers)

32.6 Use a dictionary to find three collocations for these words.

1 countryside   2 landscape   3 village

32.7 Answer these questions.

1 Do any types of TV programmes or films bore you rigid? If so, what types?
2 Would you consider living in a remote country village in your country to be living in a rural idyll?
3 Do you have a reliable public transport system in the place where you live?
4 Are there any derelict buildings where you live?
5 What sort of facilities are there within walking distance of the house or flat where you live?

33 Personal finance

A Managing your finances

Read this leaflet on personal financial management given out by a university to its students. Note the collocations.

> £££££ **Keeping afloat[1] – how to manage your finances** £££££
>
> While you're doing your degree, your main **source of income** may be a student loan or, if you're lucky, a grant or scholarship. But you may well still need to **supplement[2] your income** by getting some kind of part-time work. Here are some tips for avoiding financial problems:
>
> ▶ **Open a current account** at the campus bank – they have a team there which specialises in helping students with their financial matters.
>
> ▶ If you **get into debt**, try to **clear[3] your debts** as soon as possible.
>
> ▶ If things are difficult, you may have to economise by, say, **cutting down on luxuries**. This is far better than **running up huge debts[4]**.
>
> ▶ If you have a credit-card debt, try to **make a payment** every month, however small. Never exceed your **agreed credit limit**.
>
> ▶ It's a bad idea to **borrow heavily** to repay your debts. Always seek advice from your bank about how to clear **outstanding[5] debts** and **pay back loans**.
>
> ▶ Never **run up an overdraft[6]** if you can avoid it. If you do need one, remember that most banks will offer students an **interest-free overdraft**.

[1] having enough money to pay what you owe (can also be **staying afloat**) [2] add something to something to make it larger or better [3] pay in full [4] continuing to spend and therefore owing a large amount of money [5] not yet paid [6] amount of money that a customer with a bank account is temporarily allowed to owe to the bank

B Financial crimes and disputes

These newspaper clips are all concerned with financial crimes and problems.

Credit-card fraud[1] has reached an all-time high. One in ten people are the victims of **identity theft[2]** and the crime is on the increase.

Mr Ambrose **spent a fortune** staying at expensive hotels. He managed to **run up[3] a bill** of £7,000 at one hotel. He used his employer's funds and **falsified[4] records**. He made **fraudulent claims** for travel expenses.

People are being encouraged to **put down a deposit[5]** on new homes, thanks to low interest rates. But if borrowers **default on repayments[6]**, banks are obliged to **call in loans[7]**.

The company is now under new management. Its backers have **written off debts[8]** of £100,000 on the promise of new **cost-cutting measures** designed to solve the company's financial problems.

[1] crime of misusing another person's credit card without their permission [2] stealing someone's personal details, usually in order to access their bank accounts or credit cards [3] accumulate [4] changed something, e.g. a document, in order to deceive people [5] pay a sum of money in advance as part of a total payment [6] fail to pay a debt [7] demand that a person pay back the money the bank has lent to them [8] accepted that an amount of money has been lost or that a debt will not be paid

Exercises

33.1 Match words from each box to form collocations from the opposite page and use them to complete the sentences below.

| borrow | make | spend | stay | supplement | | afloat | a fortune | heavily | my income | a payment |

1 I .... of €500 every month to my credit-card account.
2 When I was a student I got a job in a fast-food outlet to ....
3 I used to .... on books when I was at university.
4 I had no grant or scholarship, so I had to .... to finance my studies.
5 Small firms find it difficult to .... when costs and interest rates are high.

33.2 Copy and complete the collocation bubbles using words from the box. Some words collocate only with *debt*, some only with *overdraft* and some with both. Use a dictionary to help you find one more collocation for each bubble.

to arrange a(n)	a bad	to be in
to clear a(n)	deep in	facility	to get a(n)
to get into	a hefty	the national
to pay off a(n)	-ridden	to run up a(n)
an unauthorised		

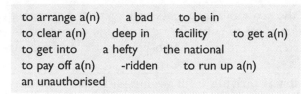
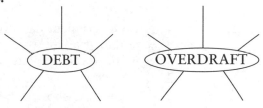

33.3 Correct the collocation errors in these sentences.

1 The firm has huge debts and has had to borrow $10 million. The new Chief Executive has introduced cost-cutting methods.
2 When I left university I had no upstanding debts, unlike most of my friends, who owed thousands of pounds.
3 The manager falsified company recordings and stole money from her employer.
4 I had no resource of income, so I had to get a job, and quickly.
5 We placed down a deposit on a new car last week.
6 She faulted on her loan repayment and had to sell her business.
7 Many people don't trust online banking because they are afraid of identification theft.
8 If we don't cut up on luxuries, we're going to find ourselves in serious debt.
9 There are special offers for students who enter a current account at the university bank.
10 You will pay a lot of interest if you go over your discussed credit limit.

33.4 Answer the questions about collocations from the opposite page.

1 What object is a person or company being compared to when we use the collocation *keep* or *stay afloat* metaphorically?
2 What are you eventually expected to do with a loan?
3 If a bank *calls in* a loan, do they (a) give it (b) write it off (c) demand full payment?
4 If someone defaults on a payment, do they (a) not make it (b) make it in full (c) partially make it?
5 What is the crime called when someone makes illegal use of another person's credit card?

33.5 Complete each sentence using the word in brackets in the appropriate form.

1 The accused was found guilty of .... company records. (FALSE)
2 The insurance company takes all .... claims very seriously. (FRAUD)
3 I try to make a .... into my savings account every month. (PAY)
4 Identity .... is becoming an increasingly common crime. (THIEF)
5 I was glad that the bank was able to offer me an .... overdraft. (INTEREST)

34 The economy

Budget speech

As we can all testify, this country's economy is strong and getting stronger.

Our measures to **curb inflation**[1] have proved highly successful. The **rampant inflation**[2] of the previous government is a thing of the past. Inflation currently stands at 2 per cent. The strength of the **current economic climate** suggests that **interest rates** are unlikely to be raised again this year. This should help us to build up a culture of **investing for the long-term**.

This Government has **steered the economy** through seven years of **uninterrupted economic growth**; a trend which is set to continue with our major success in **stimulating growth**. And in the latest quarter, the economy has been growing at an annual rate of 2.5 per cent.

All indicators show that **industry is thriving**[3]. But we are particularly proud of the **steady growth** experienced by small businesses. We have made it our aim to **safeguard their interests**[4] and the healthy economy we have created has enabled them to **increase output**. The **plummeting profits**[5] caused by the previous government's misguided policies are now safely behind them.

Our goal is to establish world-class public services through investment and reform in order to ensure that taxpayers receive real **value for money**. **Public spending** goes to provide strong and dependable public services. These are vital to **extend opportunity**, tackle **social exclusion**[6] and improve people's life chances.

The **taxes** that we **levy**[7] allow us to **allocate resources** to achieve that goal. And we have **met with** considerable **success**[8]. In particular, we must now **build on the success**[9] of the climate-change **levy we introduced** last year.

Another of our goals is to win the battle against the **black economy**. If **left unchecked**[10], the black economy – I think here particularly of the loss to our economy of **undeclared earnings**[11] and other tax evasion practices – will **push up costs**[12] and lead to **rising unemployment**. This government is committed to its eradication.

[1] control inflation [continuous increase in prices]
[2] very dramatic, uncontrolled, inflation
[3] doing very well
[4] protect their interests
[5] rapidly falling profits
[6] the problems of the underprivileged, of those who have less fortunate places in society than others
[7] impose or introduce
[8] been very successful
[9] develop previous success
[10] not stopped
[11] income that people fail to report to the tax authorities
[12] make costs rise

Exercises

34.1 Match the beginning of each sentence with its ending.

1 The government is finding it very difficult to curb	exclusion.
2 The country is suffering because of the current economic	interests.
3 Although heavy industry is in decline, service industries are	inflation.
4 The CEO is anxious to safeguard his company's	climate.
5 New machinery has enabled the factory to increase its	resources.
6 The tax authorities plan to tackle the issue of undeclared	output.
7 The budget plan explains how we intend to allocate our various	thriving.
8 We must tackle and solve the problems caused by social	earnings.

34.2 Which of these phrases would a Finance Minister be likely to use about the economy under his/her own guidance and which about the economy under a previous rival government?

build on success   extend opportunity   leave inflation unchecked   levy heavy taxes

meet with success   poor value for money   rampant inflation

rising unemployment   safely steer the economy   steady growth

thriving black economy   thriving industry   uninterrupted growth

34.3 Find the opposite of the underlined words in these collocations on the opposite page.

1 to invest for the <u>short</u> term
2 to <u>restrict</u> opportunity
3 <u>declared</u> earnings
4 <u>falling</u> unemployment
5 <u>stunting</u> growth
6 <u>soaring</u> profits
7 <u>private</u> spending
8 to <u>reduce</u> costs
9 to <u>lower</u> interest rates
10 to <u>abolish</u> a levy

34.4 Complete each sentence using words from 34.3 (either those underlined above or their opposites) in the appropriate form.

1 The government has more control over .... than over .... spending.
2 Tax inspectors make spot checks to ensure we do not have any .... earnings.
3 If you have a steady and secure income, then it may be sensible to invest for the .... rather than the .... term.
4 .... unemployment is a sign of a healthy economy.
5 If the government wants to slow down the economy by .... interest rates, then a company's costs will be .... and so their profits may ....
6 A progressive government will want to .... opportunity and to .... growth.
7 A political party might think it was a good idea to slow growth down but it would be very unlikely to say that it wanted to .... growth.
8 The government has decided to .... a levy on commercial waste collection in order to encourage recycling.

 Go to www.economist.com/index.html. Enter your own country in the Search box and select an article that interests you. Make a note of any more useful collocations relating to the topic of the economy.

35 Social issues

A Facing and solving social problems

Read these short reviews of books about social problems, and note the collocations in bold.

> *To Dream a Better Life* by Ken Lomond
> How can we best **address the issues** surrounding large-scale economic migration? Can economic migration be seen as a **force for good**[1], rather than always seen as a problem that must be tackled? This book offers a **novel**[2] **solution**.

> *Disaster and After* by Sandra Haley
> Should rich nations **provide relief** when disasters occur in poorer countries, or is this too little, too late? Haley's book calls for a **fresh drive**[3] to address the issue, and **makes a plea**[4] for governments to **break the cycle**[5] of dependency.

> *A Fragile Calm* by Alexander Fleig
> When **law and order break down**, when **riots erupt**[6] and **public disorder**[7] threatens **the social fabric**[8], politicians tend to take **draconian**[9] **measures** which rarely work. Fleig's book looks at alternatives and offers lessons from history.

> *Cities in Crisis* by Mark Golanz
> Problems of **run-down**[10] **areas** in big cities are the subject of this book. **Antisocial behaviour**, **underage drinking**, **dysfunctional**[11] **families**, all come under intense scrutiny in this wide-ranging study.

[1] a positive influence [2] new and original [3] new effort [4] an urgent or emotional request
[5] bring a stop to a negative pattern of behaviour [6] burst out suddenly
[7] expression of dissatisfaction by crowds of people, especially about a political matter
[8] social structure [9] extremely severe [10] in a very bad condition [11] not behaving normally

B Neighbourhoods and housing

In these extracts from meetings where local problems are being discussed, the second speaker echoes the ideas of the first speaker by using the collocations in bold.

A: The problems faced by poorer households are very complex indeed.
B: Yes, there are many issues affecting **low-income families**, and they are indeed complex.

A: When someone becomes homeless, our immediate task is to find a roof for them.
B: Yes, our job is to **provide shelter** as quickly as possible.

A: Fifteen per cent of families are living in houses without running water. Many are in houses which are so bad no one should be living in them.
B: That's right. Too many people are living with **poor sanitary conditions** and it's unacceptable that there are houses which are **unfit for human habitation**.

A: The problem is that houses are too expensive for most ordinary families.
B: Yes, the government should do something to provide **affordable housing**.

A: The people who encourage others to commit violent acts should be dealt with firmly.
B: That's right. Anyone **inciting violence** deserves harsh punishment.

A: The thing is, people should be more vigilant about crime in their local communities.
B: Yes, it would be good if more **neighbourhood watch schemes** could be **introduced**.

C Other collocations connected with social issues

He was arrested for possessing an **illegal substance**. [formal: an illegal drug]
Families who **claim benefits** often feel ashamed. [financial support from the state]
Green organisations are increasingly important as a **force for change** in the world today.

Exercises

35.1 Complete each sentence using a verb from the box in the appropriate form. You do not need to use all the verbs in the box.

address	answer	break	break down	break up
finish	give	incite	make	provide	supply

1 How can we .... the issue of alcohol abuse?
2 Aid agencies .... emergency relief, but is this always the best thing?
3 In 1997, law and order .... completely and there was chaos.
4 Social workers try hard to .... the cycle of abuse in families where violence occurs.
5 Community leaders .... a plea for understanding and tolerance of cultural differences.
6 People who .... violence should be severely punished.

35.2 Complete each sentence using a collocation from the opposite page.

1 The house has no roof, and there are rats in it. It is unfit ....
2 The lack of a mains water supply means that they have very poor ....
3 At night you often see 14- and 15-year-olds consuming alcohol. The city has a big problem with ....
4 That part of the city has many homes where people behave very badly with regard to others around them. There is a big problem with ....
5 Hundreds of people protested in the streets, and sometimes things got violent. For several days there was major ....
6 Neighbourhood committees can have a positive influence in the community, and indeed most people believe they are a force ....

35.3 Match the beginning of each sentence with its ending.

1 Poor people often have to claim   the issues of global poverty and disease.
2 The city council introduced a   shelter and food to the earthquake victims.
3 The government took some draconian   benefits in order to survive financially.
4 All governments need to address   erupted in all the major cities.
5 The authorities had to provide   neighbourhood watch scheme.
6 As the discontent grew, riots   measures to prevent public disorder.

35.4 Correct the collocation errors in these sentences.

1 The violence threatened the sociable fabric.
2 The Minister said it was time for a fresh driving to cut crime.
3 Customs officials found some illegitimate substances in the passenger's luggage.
4 The run-out areas of the city are often dangerous at night.
5 We hope our new organisation will be a force for political changing.
6 He proposed a novelist solution to address the issue of social inequality.
7 Multifunctional families are a difficult problem for social workers.
8 The union representative did a plea for the workers to stand firm.
9 There were scenes of publicity disorder on the streets last night.
10 It is very difficult for young people to find affordable building.

FOR SALE
£349,077,275 ONLY

36 Science and technology

A Technology in business

Scientists and technologists are **pushing back the frontiers**[1] of knowledge every day. Scientists **publish** their **findings**[2] and those findings are developed into commercial applications. We have become very skilled at **harnessing**[3] **technology** in all sorts of creative ways. New **cutting-edge design**[4] is transforming our daily lives and our businesses. But even with technology we are already familiar with, things do not always **run smoothly**[5]. There can be difficulties **installing equipment** and hardware can suffer from **wear and tear**[6]. More serious are viruses, which can cause **systems** to **crash** and lead to the loss of important data. A **power cut** may cause machinery to lose power and **production may be halted** until **power is restored**. If **computers** have to be **shut down**[7] for even a short time, it can cause a variety of problems, all of them costly.

[1] extending the limits [2] results [3] making use of [4] the most innovative design
[5] work without problems [6] damage caused by ordinary use [7] switched off completely

ERROR WARNING

Findings is almost always used in the plural. Scientists **publish** their **findings**, NOT ~~finding~~. *Research* is uncountable; it is not used in the plural. They **published** some **interesting research**, NOT ~~researches~~.

B Innovations

We asked our readers to remind us of the little technical innovations that have quietly entered – and improved? – our lives over the last 20 years. Here are some of their replies.

- I never carry much 'real money' and I hardly ever even write a cheque. I just put a piece of plastic in a slot, **enter my PIN** and take out the cash!
- You're more likely to have to **swipe a card** than use a traditional key these days.
- Remember when you had to rush out of work to get to the bank in your lunch hour? I never need to go into a bank today. **Online banking** is fantastic.
- My music collection used to take up a whole wall of my room. Now I've got far more **music stored** on my little MP3 player.
- How did people manage without mobile phones? And I love all the extra bits. I love being able to **download** new **ringtones**!
- **Wireless hotspots**[1] are fantastic – I can easily get online using my own laptop.
- I travel a lot and it's great to be able to **remote access** my **email**.

- Remember when you had to get off the sofa to **switch channels** on your black and white TV? Now you turn your huge **flat-screen TV** on and off **by remote control**!
- **High-definition TV** – the picture is fantastic compared with before.
- I **use SATNAV**[2] in the car all the time – much easier than looking at a paper map.

I SAID TURN LEFT, NOT RIGHT

[1] public places where people can access the Internet via a wireless signal
[2] short for satellite navigation

TIP Collect collocations that relate to the specific areas of science and technology that interest you. Go to www.newscientist.com and click on a link that appeals to you.

Exercises

36.1 Look at A. Correct the collocation errors in these sentences. In some sentences there is more than one error.

1 If you switch off your computer without shutting it properly, you may lose data.
2 I didn't expect everything to run gently in my new job but I didn't imagine it would be quite so difficult as it was.
3 Alex had some technical problems initiating his new computer equipment.
4 The company is famous for its cutting-side design.
5 If they'd serviced their machines regularly, they wouldn't have had to halt producing.
6 Vic dreams of making a discovery that would help to push out the frontiers of science.
7 Scientists usually publicise their findings in academic journals.
8 There was a power break this morning. The power went off at ten and it wasn't restorated till midday.
9 Urs loves pure research but his brother is more interested in the application of research to practical projects and in harassing new technology for commercial ends.
10 They carried out researches over a ten-year period and finally published their finding this month.

36.2 What are the people in the pictures doing? Answer using a collocation from B.

1

He's ....

3

She's ....

2

She's ....

4

He's ....

36.3 Answer these questions using collocations from the opposite page.

1 What three technological developments have made watching television a better experience?
2 What is an MP3 player used for?
3 What might happen if the computer systems in a company suddenly became overloaded, or there was a serious problem with the software or hardware?
4 Is it always necessary for people to visit the bank personally to do their business?
5 What might you try to find at an airport if you, say, wanted to check your email from your own laptop?
6 You want to watch TV but a boring programme has come on. What do you do?
7 You are tired of the sound your phone makes when a call comes in. You want something different. What can you do?
8 What eventually happens to electrical items that you use a lot?

36.4 Use a dictionary to help you answer the questions.

1 What collocations with *screen* can be used to mean (a) TV and (b) the cinema?
2 What can *online* collocate with as well as *shopping* and *banking*?
3 What can *remote* collocate with as well as *access* and *control*?

37 Health and medicine

A Maintaining good health

Do you want to **enjoy good health**? Or perhaps you want to **reduce your stress levels**? **Build up your strength** by **doing plenty of exercise**[1]. It's better to start with **gentle exercise** unless you already **do** a lot of **sport**[2]. It's equally important to **watch what you eat**. There's no need to **go on a diet**: just eating the right food will help you to **build up resistance** to disease.

[1] NOT ~~making~~ exercise   [2] NOT ~~make~~ sport

B Treatment

When Alexa was diagnosed with a **serious medical condition**, she was worried that she might have to **have an operation**[1]. However, her doctor first prescribed a **course of medication**. Fortunately, she **responded well to treatment**, and **made a full recovery**.

[1] NOT ~~make~~ an operation

PATIENT INFORMATION LEAFLET
- Do not **exceed the recommended dose**.
- If you think you have **taken an overdose**[2], consult a doctor immediately.
- If you suffer any of the **side effects**[3] mentioned in this leaflet, or any other **adverse**[4] **reactions**, consult your doctor or pharmacist.

[2] taken too much of a drug
[3] unwanted secondary effects of a drug
[4] negative

C Illness

collocation	example	meaning
a streaming cold	I've had **a streaming cold** for days now.	a heavy cold
shake off a cold	I wish I could **shake off this cold** – I've had it for nearly two weeks.	get rid of a cold
be in poor health	My gran's **been in poor health** for years.	not be very well
an infectious disease	There are a number of **infectious diseases** which mainly affect children.	diseases caught from someone with that disease
a rare illness/disease	The baby was born with **a rare illness**.	an illness that seldom occurs
critically ill	She's still **critically ill** in hospital.	extremely/dangerously ill
fight for one's life	The accident has left three people **fighting for their lives**.	in danger of dying
fall into / come out of a coma	The boxer **fell into a coma** after receiving a blow to the head and didn't **come out of the coma** for five days.	become unconscious; regain consciousness
a massive heart attack	He suffered **a massive heart attack**.	a very serious heart attack
untimely/premature death	We were all saddened by the young woman's **untimely/premature death**.	death at too early an age

> **TIP** If you need to know more about the language of health and medicine, have a look at: www.nhsdirect.nhs.uk – a site aimed at the non-specialist.
> For more specialist language, try www.doctorupdate.net, which is aimed at medical professionals.

Exercises

37.1 Look at A. Combine the words in the box to form eight collocations.

your	build	watch	do	do	enjoy	exercise	sport	good
exercise	what	gentle	on	health	levels	of	your	you
plenty	reduce	resistance	eat	stress	diet	up	go	a

37.2 Complete the collocation forks.

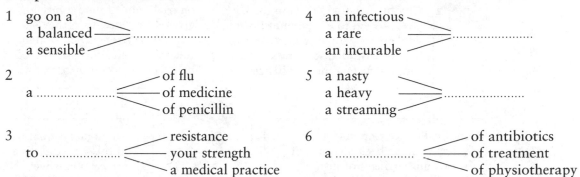

1 go on a
   a balanced ....
   a sensible

2 a .... of flu
           of medicine
           of penicillin

3 to .... resistance
           your strength
           a medical practice

4 an infectious
   a rare ....
   an incurable

5 a nasty
   a heavy ....
   a streaming

6 a .... of antibiotics
           of treatment
           of physiotherapy

37.3 Match each question with its answer.

1 Is the man still in a coma?	a He had to have an operation.
2 What did Pat's grandfather die of?	b A massive heart attack.
3 How did Tim's uncle respond to treatment?	c A rare but not incurable disease.
4 Why did Sam have to stay in hospital?	d His friend is critically ill.
5 Your little boy has a runny nose, hasn't he?	e Yes, he's had a streaming cold since Sunday.
6 What sort of medical condition has he got?	f A course of medication.
7 What cured Meg's brother?	g By doing some gentle exercise.
8 Why does Tony look so worried?	h He initially had some adverse reactions.
9 How does Joe plan to build up his strength?	i He's still fighting for his life.
10 Is the patient recovering yet?	j He came out of it this morning.

37.4 Complete each short dialogue using a collocation from the opposite page.

1   Anna: Did the medication the doctor prescribed help you?
     Ben: Yes, but it has had some rather unpleasant ....
2   Clara: Mozart died when he was just 35.
     Dean: Yes, he had a very ....
3   Ellie: Have you still got that cold?
     Fran: Yes, I just can't ....
4   Grant: Your aunt doesn't look very well.
    Harry: Yes, I'm afraid she is in rather ....
5   Inga: Why do they only sell these tablets in small packets?
     Joan: To try to prevent people ....
6   Karl: Make sure you don't take more than the doctor told you to.
    Lotte: Don't worry. I would never ....
7   Masha: What did the doctor say about your grandfather's painful leg?
     Nina: She has referred him to a surgeon. He has to ....
8   Orla: Do you have to change your diet if you're diabetic?
      Pat: Well, you have to ....
9 Quasim: What's the prognosis for your uncle now he's had a kidney transplant?
     Rita: He's still feeling rather weak but he's expected to ....

38 Criminal justice

A Expressing views about crime and punishment

Look at these extracts from calls to a radio phone-in programme called 'Your Call to Jeremy', which on this occasion is about crime and punishment.

Hello, Jeremy. I want to know why financial criminals in the City always seem to **escape punishment**, while poor people always seem to receive **custodial sentences**[1] even for **committing minor offences**.

My view is that if someone is **put on trial** and is **found guilty** and **given a sentence**, then they should have to **serve out**[2] **their sentence**. Releasing someone early for **good behaviour** is a complete nonsense.

Jeremy, I'd like to point out that there have been a couple of serious **miscarriages of justice**[3] recently and people don't seem to realise how damaging this is. No one should **face trial** on the basis of **unreliable evidence** or **trumped-up charges**[4].

We're facing **soaring**[5] **crime rates** in this city and it's about time the criminals were **brought to justice**. And I'm sick of hearing about **extenuating circumstances**[6] – that someone had a deprived childhood, or they're not fit to **stand trial**. Rubbish!

[1] a sentence to be served in a prison or similar institution   [2] serve the full amount of time
[3] situation where innocent people are found guilty   [4] invented and false accusations
[5] rising very fast   [6] circumstances that lessen the blame, also **mitigating circumstances**

B Courts and trials

These newspaper clips contain typical collocations about courts and trials.

A key witness **gave evidence** today in the Misthorpe murder trial. The witness claimed to have seen the accused leaving Ms Bartram's house. **The trial was adjourned**[1] until March 7th. The accused, 27-year-old Liam Grout, was **remanded in custody**[2].

In a **unanimous verdict**[3] today in Raylton District Court, Clare Irene Wilson, 37, was **found not guilty** of murder. The judge said the prosecution had failed to prove **beyond reasonable doubt** that Ms Wilson was guilty.

Mr Hanry had **denied all knowledge** of the alleged fraudulent business deal. His lawyers attempted to show that Derek Yardley was an **unreliable witness**. Despite suggestions that the judge might **dismiss the case**[4], he found in favour of Mr Hanry and **awarded damages**[5] to him.

Mary Jones was released this morning after her lawyers successfully **contested the verdict**[6] which sentenced her to prison for three years. The judge, Mr James Egdon, **overturned the verdict** in the Court of Appeal. Mary Jones herself did not **appear in court** but later said that she felt **justice had been served**.

[1] was suspended till a later time or date
[2] send to prison until the trial begins or continues
[3] verdict which all the decision makers agree to
[4] decide that the case is not worth considering

[5] ordered the organisation or person who has been responsible for causing injury or loss to pay money to the victim as compensation
[6] disagreed with the verdict and tried to change it

Exercises

38.1 Rewrite the underlined part of each of these extracts from conversations to make them sound more like extracts from newspaper reports.

1 <u>An increasing number of crimes per head of the population</u> have been recorded in the last twelve months.
2 Why should young criminals <u>get away without being punished</u> for crimes just because of their age?
3 The lawyers <u>disagreed with the court's decision</u>.
4 The judge <u>threw out</u> the case because he felt the evidence was <u>not strong enough</u>.
5 John Jones <u>said he didn't know anything about</u> the robbery.
6 The judge <u>said that</u> the trial <u>would now take place</u> next month.

38.2 Choose the correct collocation.

1 Someone might get out of prison early for *soaring / extenuating / good* behaviour.
2 If you get a custodial sentence, you *go to prison / only serve the sentence if you commit another crime / have to do some community service*.
3 If you are remanded in custody, you are *allowed to go home / obliged to pay some money / kept in prison*.
4 If you serve out a sentence, you are *released from prison early / kept in prison for the full amount of time / kept in prison for life*.
5 If charges are trumped-up, they are *accurate / invented / exaggerated*.

38.3 Correct the mistakes with prepositions in the collocations.

1 He was put in trial for murder.
2 He was later remanded on custody.
3 The witness appeared on court for the first time today.
4 The murderer was soon brought into justice.
5 The case against Mr Sharp was proved over reasonable doubt.

38.4 Complete each sentence using a word from the opposite page.

1 Unfortunately, there have been a number of .... of justice recently.
2 The lawyer claimed that there were some .... circumstances.
3 This is the sixth time the accused has .... in court.
4 The jury was quick to reach a .... verdict, finding the accused guilty.
5 The accused .... all knowledge of the crime, but no one believed her.
6 Charles Weiss was .... damages for the injury he had suffered.
7 The newspaper said .... had been served by the conviction of Joe Lee.
8 The trial has been .... until next week.
9 He has been in court on several previous occasions but only for committing .... offences.

38.5 For each word in box A find two collocating words in B. Then write sentences using each of the ten collocations.

A	find	give	trial
	unreliable		verdict

B	contest	face	evidence	evidence	guilty
	not guilty	overturn	sentence	stand	witness

Look up the following legal words in the British National Corpus, searchable online at
www.natcorp.ox.ac.uk: verdict witness custody
Note down any other interesting collocations that you find.

War and peace

A   Ten days of war

> **Bitter enemies**, the Sornak Republic and Vorinland are once more **engaged in hostilities**. Our timeline charts the latest fighting.
>
> Jan 1   The Sornak Republic accuses Vorinland of **stockpiling weapons**[1]. Vorinland accuses the Sornak Republic of **creating instability**[2] in the area. Both sides **deploy troops**[3] to the region.
>
> Jan 4   Vorinland attacks a Sornak Republican border town. The Sornak Republic claims it was an **unprovoked attack** and **violence erupts** along the border. The **violence escalates**[4] with a **spate of attacks**[5] on both sides of the border. Both countries claim that innocent victims have been **caught in the crossfire**[6].
>
> Jan 6   The Sornak Republic **goes on the offensive** and makes a **pre-emptive strike**[7] on the capital of Vorinland. Bombs are dropped in the city centre and it is claimed that they hit their intended targets, but that some **collateral damage**[8] was inevitable.
>
> Jan 8   Vorinland **launches a counter-attack** on the Sornak Republic by making '**surgical strikes**[9]' on a number of industrial cities. They also **seize power** in Tensington, the Sornak Republic border town and major rail centre.
>
> Jan 10   Both sides **suffer** a large number of **casualties** but neither is willing to **call for a ceasefire**[10].

[1] building up large quantities of weapons
[2] making the area unsafe
[3] send soldiers
[4] violence increases dramatically
[5] a large number of attacks
[6] shot by accident as they were in the wrong place at the wrong time
[7] an attack made to prevent the enemy from attacking you
[8] unintentional killing of civilians and destruction of non-military targets – term used by those who cause it to make it sound less serious
[9] short and narrowly targeted military attacks
[10] an agreement to stop fighting

B   Ending fighting

collocation	example	meaning
uneasy truce	The **uneasy truce** came to an end when the rebels attacked the capital.	a truce that could easily be broken
fragile peace	There is a **fragile peace** in the area with hopes it will soon strengthen.	a peace that could easily be destroyed
ceasefire comes into effect	The **ceasefire will come into effect** at midnight.	agreement to stop fighting starts from this time
restore peace	The aim of the talks is to **restore peace** in the area.	stop the fighting
bring stability	At last the treaty has **brought stability** to the region.	made the region feel safe
disband an army	It will be hard to persuade the warlords to **disband their army**.	send the soldiers home, as the army is no longer in existence
lift a blockade	They have agreed to **lift the blockade** on our ports.	stop preventing goods from entering
withdraw troops	The country agreed to **withdraw their troops** from the area.	take their soldiers out

Exercises

39.1 Look at A. Complete the collocations used in these newspaper headlines.

1
BORDER AREA HIT BY
.... OF ATTACKS

2
.... ERUPTS AFTER
ELECTIONS

3
PRE-EMPTIVE ....
LAUNCHED LAST NIGHT

4
JOURNALISTS ....
IN THE CROSSFIRE

5
ARMY SEIZES ....
IN NIGHT-TIME COUP

6
CIVIL SOCIETY CALLS FOR A
....

39.2 Read the article and answer the questions using full sentences.

UN attempts to restore peace to this troubled region
may finally be meeting with some success. A
ceasefire has been agreed and will come into effect
from midnight tomorrow. It is hoped this will bring
an end to a decade of escalating violence between
these two historically bitter enemies.

1 What is the UN's aim?
2 What success have they had?
3 When will it start?
4 For how long have they been
   engaged in hostilities?
5 Has the situation been getting better?
6 What is the relationship generally
   like between the two sides?

39.3 Complete each sentence using a collocation from the box.

collateral damage	create instability	fragile peace	go on the offensive
launch a counter-attack	lift the blockade	suffer casualties	surgical strikes

1 The enemy have agreed to .... on our ports.
2 The General said that we have carried out some .... on the enemy.
3 There are hopes that the .... will develop into something more lasting.
4 It was their decision to .... first ...
5 ... and so we had no choice but to ....
6 It is believed that the aim of the invading army is to .... in the region.
7 He mentioned .... but didn't say exactly how many civilians died.
8 Our army is certain to .... , given the strength of the opposition.

39.4 Correct the collocation errors in these sentences. In some sentences there is more than one error.

1 The two countries have been engaged in hostile for a long time.
2 The ceasefire makes into effect today and all hope it will bring stable to the area again.
3 The government has promised to retreat its troops next year.
4 There is an uncomfortable truce between the two sides at the moment.
5 When peace is replaced, we shall be able to deform the army.
6 The newspaper reported that the enemy had felt a defeat despite the fact that they had
   employed large numbers of troops to the area.
7 They accused us of piling weapons and of preparing to launch a provoked attack.
8 Some argue that the nuclear deterrent has prevented violence from excavating.

FOLLOW UP

Choose a conflict currently in the news and find reports of it in different English-language
newspapers. At this website www.thebigproject.co.uk/news you can find links to large numbers of
these. Note down collocations that you notice being used in several different reports.

40 Friendship

A Friendship over a lifetime

Read this introduction to an article about friendship from a popular science magazine.

Do you have a lot of **close friends**? Are they **lifelong friends**? **Childhood friends**? Have you ever met someone and instantly felt that you've made **a friend for life**?

People with a large **circle of friends** may well have discovered the secret of a long and happy life, according to recent scientific research which suggests that having good friends may actually help us live longer.

For many, the most important friendship is a **long-term relationship**[1] with a partner or a spouse. However, the research shows that **platonic relationships**[2] are equally valuable. Whether your **social network** is made up of **firm friends** or **casual acquaintances**, socialising could impact positively on your life expectancy.

[1] usually referring to a romantic relationship   [2] relationships which are not romantic or sexual

B Making, keeping and losing friends

Note the collocations in these magazine horoscopes.

Capricorn   22 Dec–19 Jan
Relations are **cordial**[1] at work, but they could be better. It will take hard work to **remain on friendly terms** with everyone, but it will be worth the effort.

Aquarius   20 Jan–19 Feb
A **complete stranger** comes into your life and friendship quickly develops. However, a **close confidant**[2] is uneasy and advises you to **put some distance** between yourself and the newcomer. It's advice you don't want to hear.

Pisces   20 Feb–20 March
It takes a long time to **win someone's trust**, so when somebody **abuses that trust** it hurts. It's going to take a lot of effort to **make the relationship work**. Is it worth it? Yes.

Aries   21 Mar–19 Apr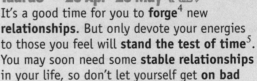
Someone **takes** something you say **the wrong way**. A good **relationship breaks down**, but don't worry, a **heart-to-heart chat** will soon help to **heal the rift**[3].

Taurus   20 Apr–20 May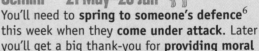
It's a good time for you to **forge**[4] new **relationships**. But only devote your energies to those you feel will **stand the test of time**[5]. You may soon need some **stable relationships** in your life, so don't let yourself get **on bad terms** with those around you.

Gemini   21 May–20 Jun
You'll need to **spring to someone's defence**[6] this week when they **come under attack**. Later you'll get a big thank-you for **providing moral support**[7] when it was most needed.

[1] friendly, but formal and polite   [2] person you trust and share your feelings and secrets with
[3] end a serious disagreement between friends   [4] form or create   [5] last   [6] act very quickly to defend them   [7] showing that you approve of someone and what they are doing

ERROR WARNING

Remember, the collocation is **make friends**, NOT ~~get~~ friends or ~~find~~ friends.
At first it was difficult to **make friends** at my new school, but then I met Richard.

Exercises

40.1 Choose the correct collocation.

1 I was contacted by a *childish / childhood / childlike* friend I hadn't seen for years.
2 I am sure that my friendship with Louisa will *pass / sit / stand* the test of time.
3 *Foraging / Forcing / Forging* good relationships helps us live longer.
4 Mason was a *long-life / lifelong / lifelike* friend of my father's.
5 She has quite a wide *circle / circulation / cycle* of friends.
6 It's hard to form *life-term / long-time / long-term* relationships when you're in a job that involves a lot of travelling.

40.2 Complete each sentence using an adjective from the box.

bad	casual	close	complete	cordial	firm	friendly	moral	social	stable

1 I don't know her well – we're just .... acquaintances.
2 We have been on .... terms ever since Jack refused to return the money I lent him.
3 For many people the Internet plays an important role in developing new .... networks.
4 Jack Whitley was a .... confidant of the Prime Minister in the 1980s.
5 Their relationship hasn't been very .... They've broken up and got back together again several times.
6 She told her entire life story to a .... stranger on a train.
7 Bethan and I have been .... friends for many years.
8 Thanks for all the .... support you gave me when I needed it.
9 Despite their political differences the two leaders have always enjoyed .... relations.
10 Leslie and I have remained on .... terms despite our professional disagreements.

40.3 Rewrite each sentence using a synonym of the underlined words to create collocations from the opposite page.

1 From the moment they met they knew they would be friends for <u>ever</u>.
2 She always <u>leapt</u> to Angela's defence if anyone criticised her.
3 He very quickly <u>gained</u> his employer's trust and was given a very important job.
4 She <u>gave me</u> a lot of moral support when I had problems at work.
5 I arranged a meeting to try and <u>resolve</u> the rift between Hilary and Jake.
6 I'm sorry that you <u>interpreted</u> what I said the wrong way.
7 Their relationship <u>collapsed</u> when she discovered he was seeing someone else.
8 We've been <u>very good</u> friends ever since our first day at primary school.

40.4 Correct the collocation errors in these sentences.

1 We should have a head-to-foot chat to resolve our differences.
2 She got under attack from some colleagues at work who didn't like her.
3 If you disuse someone's trust you deserve to lose their friendship.
4 We tried hard to have the relationship work but failed.
5 I think you need to make some distance between yourself and Eduardo.

FOLLOW UP Horoscopes are a good source of vocabulary on relationships. Read English ones now and then in a newspaper or online at, say, www.horoscopes.co.uk, and make notes of any useful collocations you find.

41 Youth and age

A Childhood

Ever since he was a **newborn baby**, Horace's adoring parents were convinced he was **a child prodigy**[1] and **pandered to his every whim**[2], so that he soon grew into a **spoilt brat**[3]. As a young teenager, he hung around with the rest of the town's **disaffected youth**[4], and was on the verge of becoming a **juvenile delinquent**[5]. But then a music teacher realised he had a talent for singing and helped him to **see the error of his ways**[6]. He spent the rest of his teenage years singing for a group which made a considerable contribution to popular youth culture.

[1] young genius
[2] did every little thing that he wanted even when it was not appropriate
[3] (informal, disapproving) an unpleasant child, one who behaves badly and whose parents allow to behave as he/she wishes
[4] young people who do not accept society's values
[5] a criminal who is still legally a minor
[6] understand his mistakes

B Middle age

Amy and Stewart got married young. They **had a baby**[1] and then another almost at once and quickly **fell into the pattern** of family life. They concentrated so much on providing a **stable environment** for their children that they neglected their relationship and soon began to **take** each other **for granted**[2]. The children **left home** and went off to university and Stewart began to **go through a midlife crisis**[3]. He said he was bored with his daily routine and he wanted to go off and travel the world while he was still young enough. Amy thought he was just **going through a phase**[4] but she felt she had no choice but to **respect his wishes**. She said nothing to stop him as he bought a red sports car and set off on a road trip through Europe.

[1] NOT ~~got~~ a baby
[2] not value each other
[3] period of dissatisfaction in the middle of one's life
[4] going through a period of strange or difficult behaviour

C Old age

Louise and John are in their seventies now. They say they don't **feel their age**[1] except for 'the **occasional twinge**[2]'. They both admit to the occasional '**senior moment**[3]' and John can sometimes be a bit of a **grumpy old man**[4]. They don't have to **support their family** any more, so they **live quite a comfortable life**[5]. When they were younger, they were quite poor but those days are only a **hazy memory** now. At home they are surrounded by things of great **sentimental value** to them and it has **become their habit** to spend the evenings poring over their photo albums. These are full of pictures that **rekindle memories**[6] of days gone by. Louise and John are happiest when their grandchildren come to stay. They give them their **undivided attention**. In fact, they **don't let them out of their sight**. Sometimes the grandchildren complain about this but Louise always explains, 'We just want to make sure you don't **come to any harm**.'

[1] feel as old as they are
[2] a slight ache from time to time
[3] moment of forgetfulness
[4] (informal, uncomplimentary) an old man who is always complaining about things
[5] note how *live* often collocates with *a life*
[6] bring back memories

Exercises

41.1 Combine the words in the box to form five collocations presented on the opposite page.

> baby   brat   child   delinquent   disaffected
> juvenile   newborn   prodigy   spoilt   youth

A number of other collocations using words from the box are possible apart from those presented in A. What are they?

41.2 Complete these short dialogues using collocations from 41.1.

1 A: Antonio can play all Mozart's violin concertos and he's only nine.
    B: Yes, I've heard he's a ....
2 A: Meena has just had a son. I want to get him a present.
    B: Well, they've got lovely things for .... in the shop next to the
       hospital.
3 A: Why did the police decide to build that new unit for young offenders?
    B: It was suggested by a businessman who'd once been a .... himself.
4 A: Tim's older boys are nice but the youngest screams if he doesn't get his own way.
    B: Yes, he's a .... His parents give him whatever he wants.
5 A: I've read a lot recently about young people who feel alienated from society.
    B: Yes, there seems to have been a spate of headlines about ....

41.3 Correct the collocation errors in these sentences.

1 It is all too easy to make your close friends and your family for granted.
2 Liz's got four children and she's just bought herself a sports car. Do you think she's going against some kind of midlife crisis?
3 My sister got a baby boy last month.
4 You'll spoil your daughter if you keep on wandering to her every whim.
5 My parents are vegetarians, so I admire their wishes and don't eat meat in their house.
6 Sorry. I must be having an elderly moment. I just can't remember your name!
7 Jacqui insists she has seen the mistake of her ways.
8 Don't worry about your daughter leaving home. She won't go to any harm.
9 Make sure you don't let the child out of your view.

41.4 Explain the difference between:

1 leaving home and leaving the house.
2 a hazy memory and a distinct memory.
3 a grumpy old man and a dear old man.
4 an occasional twinge and a sudden twinge.
5 become a habit and develop a habit.
6 fall into a pattern and fit into a pattern.

41.5 Cross out the word in each set which does *not* form a normal collocation.

1 *live / lead / go / have* a comfortable life
2 a *firm / familiar / pleasant / stable* environment
3 *feel / look / talk / show* your age
4 go through a *crisis / stage / divorce / problem*
5 *undivided / perfect / careful / close* attention
6 *share / wake up / rekindle / stir up* memories
7 have *adventures / a baby / visitors / an increase*
8 *sentimental / sensitive / practical / outstanding* value

42 Celebrities and heroes

A Contents of a celebrity magazine

page	CONTENTS
23	AN **EXCLUSIVE INTERVIEW** WITH PAOLA SIMONE. Paola **lets us in on the secrets** of her **fairytale wedding** and the **lavish lifestyle**[1] she now leads.
27	JOEY WINTER **GOES INTO REHAB**[2]. **Sources close to** Joey **reveal the truth** about the rock star's drug problem.
30	ACTRESS PHILADELPHIA MARRIOTT tells the truth about her **prenuptial agreement**[3] and her **messy divorce**[4] from footballer Tyrone Finton.
34	A ROYAL **KISS AND TELL**[5]. Traina Grabb, ex-girlfriend of Prince Henrik of Glosvatt is ready to **sell her story** to **the highest bidder**[6]. Who will buy it?
41	COURT SCANDAL. Tennis ace Bach Handar in the second of two **in-depth interviews**. Handar **reveals** some of the **secrets** about match fixing that kept him **in the full glare of publicity** for much of last year.

[1] rich and extravagant way of life
[2] (short for *rehabilitation*), getting treatment in a clinic for an addiction
[3] legal agreement made before marriage dealing with the distribution of money and property in the event of a divorce
[4] (informal) divorce which involved many arguments and legal problems
[5] (informal, journalistic) a story sold to the press about one's love life
[6] person who is prepared to pay most in an auction

B Speech at an awards ceremony

We are here today to **celebrate the achievements** of Monty Sharpe, a remarkable film director. Monty's first full length feature film, *Lincoln's Boyhood,* about the life of Abraham Lincoln, was **highly praised** by the critics and **received nominations** for a number of prestigious awards.

Monty's film-making goes back a long way. He made several short films at university which received rave reviews in the student press. After university he soon **realised his ambition** of working in cinema when he got his first job at Sheepton Studios.

Monty soon began directing and enjoyed a **meteoric rise**[1] to fame. Critics have **heaped praise on** all his work, highlighting his unique approach to film. It is my great honour today to be **presenting this award** to him. The Director's Bowl is the **highest accolade**[2] which can be offered to anyone in his profession. We offer Monty this award not only because of his own achievements but also because his work has had a **significant impact**[3] on all of our leading young directors and will do so for many years to come. Let me share with you some of the **glowing tributes**[4] which we have received from other directors...

[1] rapid rise
[2] top symbol of praise and approval
[3] NOT ~~strong~~ impact
[4] (journalistic) extremely positive comments

ERROR WARNING

Be careful with the word *success*. We say The song **enjoyed** or **had great success** all over the world, NOT ~~made~~ great success. You can, however, **make a success of** something. For example: She **made a success** of her new job and was promoted after a short time.

Exercises

42.1   **Look at A. Are these sentences true or false?**

1 'Sources close to the Prime Minister' means 'members of the Prime Minister's family'.
2 A lavish lifestyle is one that occasionally breaks the law.
3 When someone goes into rehab, they want to learn a new skill.
4 The highest bidder is the most important person asking for something.
5 A fairytale wedding is likely to cost a lot of money.
6 If someone lets you in on a secret, they tell you something not generally known.
7 A kiss and tell story is one where a couple talk to the press about their relationship.
8 A prenuptial agreement is an agreement made just after a couple marry.
9 The 'full glare of publicity' is a metaphor based on the idea of a bright light shining on someone or something.
10 An exclusive interview suggests that the interview does not include much information about the interviewee's private life.

42.2   **Complete each sentence using a word from the opposite page.**

1 Shelly Winter enjoyed a meteoric .... to fame in Hollywood in the 1990s.
2 Carlos never realised his .... of becoming a top footballer and played for his local team for 20 years.
3 The critics have .... praise on De Suta's latest film and it has been nominated for an Oscar.
4 In 2001, his latest novel received a .... for an award but it did not win the prize.
5 The film was .... praised by some critics but it received some negative reviews too.
6 Imelda Fry gave an interview to *Celeb* magazine but she didn't .... many secrets.
7 The film .... great success on both sides of the Atlantic.
8 He .... a success of his career in music and travelled the world.

42.3   **Match each question with its answer.**

1 What kind of divorce did they have?	An exclusive one.
2 What kind of interview did you get?	The highest.
3 What kind of impact did he have?	A fairytale one.
4 What are we here to celebrate?	Glowing ones.
5 What does she want to sell?	A prenuptial one.
6 What have you got to present?	A very significant one.
7 What sort of agreement did they sign?	Her achievements.
8 What sort of accolade did she get?	An award.
9 What kind of wedding did they have?	Her story.
10 What kinds of tributes were paid to him?	A messy one.

42.4   **Which collocations from this unit are the opposites of these expressions?**

1 a superficial interview   3 a minor impact
2 a gradual rise to fame   4 a simple lifestyle

 FOLLOW UP   Read an article from a current issue of a celebrity magazine. You will find one at www.hellomagazine.com. How many collocations from this unit can you find? Highlight any interesting new collocations that you find in it.

43 Criticising people

A Lecturers and students

Students these days are not what they used to be. Half of them are **bone idle**[1] and the others **have an attitude problem**[2]. They seem to let anyone in to university these days – I have one very **slippery customer**[3] in one of my classes. He's more interested in **mindless violence** than books and is ready to **pick a fight**[4] at any opportunity.

[1] (informal) extremely lazy   [2] a negative, uncooperative attitude
[3] (informal) someone who cannot be trusted   [4] provoke a fight

Lecturers these days say that students **have no respect for** authority but they seem to **hold** us **in contempt**[5]. I always seem to **take the flak**[6] if there's a problem in class, as they have decided that I am a **disruptive influence**[7] who **poisons the atmosphere** for other students. But, as I see it, if a class is a disaster, **the blame rests**[8] fairly and squarely with the lecturer. They shouldn't be allowed to **shirk their responsibilities**[9] to us students.

[5] despise   [6] be held responsible   [7] someone who encourages others to behave in a negative way
[8] it is the fault of   [9] pay no attention to their responsibilities

B Critical exclamations

These collocations are quite forceful, but can also be used humorously. A rising intonation combined with a smile will soften them.

'I am appalled that you would **stoop to that level**!' [do something as bad as that]
'That was a really **dirty trick to play**!' [nasty/dishonest thing to do]
'I think Ron is **a nasty piece of work**!' [an unpleasant, untrustworthy person]
'Your behaviour was **totally out of order**!' [very inappropriate]
'It was **a downright disgrace** to behave like that!' [absolutely disgraceful]
'I **wouldn't trust** Eva **an inch**!' [wouldn't trust at all]

C Other collocations relating to criticising people

example	meaning
I'll never tell you a secret again. You have totally **betrayed my trust**.	disappointed me because I trusted you
He did really well, given that he is only a child. It's not fair to **belittle his achievements**.	make what someone has done seem unimportant
You're letting his good looks **cloud your judgement**.	affect your judgement negatively
Your essay was not bad, but I have a few **minor niggles**.	small complaints
How did you manage to overlook such a **glaring error**?	obvious mistake
He said he was leaving me because he was sick of my **constant nagging**.	complaining or criticising all the time

ERROR WARNING Note that we say **deep dissatisfaction**, NOT ~~strong~~ dissatisfaction, for example, I am writing to express my **deep dissatisfaction** about...

Exercises

43.1 Look at A. Find a collocation that matches each of these definitions.

1 an untrustworthy person
2 senselessly violent behaviour
3 not take one's duties seriously
4 provoke a fight

5 be blamed
6 spoil the mood
7 despise
8 a negative impact (on other people)

43.2 Find a collocation on the opposite page that could be used about these people.

1 A colleague, Sue, doesn't seem to you to do any work at all.
Sue's ....

2 Another colleague, George, seems to be making the atmosphere at work less pleasant than it used to be.
George is .... at work.

3 You suspect your neighbour, Glyn, is involved in some illegal activity.
I wouldn't ....

4 You always thought your sister, Josie, was rather silly but now she has done something particularly bad. (give two answers)
Josie's behaviour was ....

5 You are not completely satisfied with the translation work done by your student because there are a few errors.
I have some ....
with your translation.

6 You think your new neighbour looks like a very unpleasant person.
My new neighbour looks
....

43.3 Complete these collocations using a verb from the box.

belittle	betray	cloud	have	have
hold	pick	play	rests	stoop

1 .... someone's trust
2 .... in contempt
3 .... an attitude problem
4 .... a fight
5 the blame ....

6 .... someone's achievements
7 .... someone's judgement
8 .... a dirty trick
9 would never .... to that level
10 .... no respect for

43.4 Complete each sentence using the word in brackets in the appropriate form.

1 The papers are increasingly full of stories of .... violence. (MIND)
2 Your work is full of .... errors. (GLARE)
3 I'm afraid your son is a .... influence in my lessons. (DISRUPT)
4 Such dreadful behaviour is a downright .... (GRACE)
5 It's very unkind to belittle his .... in that way. (ACHIEVE)
6 His parents' constant .... made him keen to leave home. (NAG)

44 References

Note the useful collocations to use in reference letters in the texts below.

A A reference for a student

I am happy to **act as a referee** for Ilona Hradetska, who has applied to do a course in archaeology at your university. Ilona has a **keen interest**[1] in archaeology and although she **lacks experience**, she makes up for this in her enthusiasm for the archaeology of the classical world. She has an **encyclopaedic knowledge**[2] of Ancient Greece and Rome. However, she has already managed to **accumulate** some practical **experience**[3] as she worked on a dig for two weeks in Greece last April, and she is looking forward to **honing**[4] **her** practical **skills** at the same dig over the summer holiday. Her dream of **pursuing her interests** in archaeology is **of paramount importance**[5] to her and I am sure she has the ability to **meet the challenges**[6] of the course.

[1] very strong interest
[2] very extensive knowledge
[3] (formal) gain experience
[4] making perfect
[5] (formal) extremely important
[6] deal with the difficult aspects

B A job reference

It is my pleasure to **provide a reference for** Phil Lee, who has applied for the post of Marketing Manager in your company. I can **wholeheartedly recommend** Mr Lee for this position as I **have every confidence in** his ability to **perform the tasks**[1] indicated in your job description. He has remarkable **financial acumen**[2] and excellent **interpersonal skills**. He is a good team player and while working here has **revealed a** remarkable **talent**[3] for **handling** difficult **situations**. It goes without saying that you can **trust him implicitly**[4]. I am confident that if you were to offer him the position he would quickly become an invaluable member of your team.

[1] **perform tasks** is a more formal way of saying **carry out tasks**
[2] talent in financial matters
[3] (formal) **showed a talent**
[4] trust him totally

C Common errors

There are a number of errors which are frequently made when students are required to write a reference as an exam task.

error	correction
He has high computer skills.	He has **good/advanced computer skills**.
He has a high education.	He is **highly educated**. He has **a good level of education**.
A secretary with high qualifications is required.	A **well-qualified** secretary is required. A secretary **with good qualifications** is required.
He has a high knowledge of English.	He has **a good / an advanced knowledge** of English.
He has a large knowledge of all subjects.	He has **an extensive / a comprehensive knowledge** of all subjects.
He has big/great experience of teaching.	He has **considerable experience** of teaching.
He managed to get a good relationship with his boss.	He managed to **establish/develop a good relationship** with his boss.
Mr Day is a very appreciated member of staff.	Mr Day is a **highly valued** member of staff.

Exercises

44.1 Complete each sentence using a collocation from A. The first letters are given to help you.

1 Jason takes a k.............................. i.............................. in all his school subjects, but particularly in the sciences.
2 Suzie is looking forward to h.............................. her computer s.............................. on a course next month.
3 We set the job applicants a particularly difficult task in order to discover who would best be able to m.............................. the c.............................. .
4 You can rest assured that your happiness will always be of p.............................. i.............................. to me.
5 My brother chose that university because it was the best place for him to p.............................. his i.............................. in marine biology.
6 Over the years I have managed to a.............................. plenty of e.............................. of working with young people.

44.2 Rewrite each sentence using the word in brackets to make it more formal.

1 Paul knows a lot about African history. (ENCYCLOPAEDIC)
2 Karen is very good at dealing with people. (SKILLS)
3 Eric did a lot of work on farms when he was in Canada. (ACCUMULATED)
4 Toyah has an excellent teaching qualification but she hasn't done much work in the classroom yet. (LACKS)
5 I have total trust in Dr Robinson. (IMPLICITLY)
6 This job will offer you the perfect opportunity to become more skilled at working with a computer. (HONE)
7 I am totally confident you will be able to complete the course. (CONFIDENCE)
8 It was Duncan's talent for making money that led to his promotion. (ACUMEN)

44.3 Correct the reference letter below by replacing the underlined words with more appropriate collocations.

> I am happy to do as a referee for James McBride, who has applied for a teaching post at your language school. I <u>take</u> every confidence in Mr McBride's abilities as a teacher. He spent last summer working at the school where I am Principal and he was a <u>very appreciated</u> member of our staff. He was very successful in <u>getting</u> a good relationship with both students and staff. He <u>has a high education</u> with a particularly <u>large</u> knowledge of English literature. He combines <u>high</u> teaching qualifications with <u>big</u> experience of teaching students at all levels of English. He also has <u>high</u> computer skills, which should certainly prove useful in a technologically advanced school such as yours.

44.4 Choose the correct collocation.

1 Jenny *revealed / provided* some surprising talents during our expedition.
2 I'd *wholeheartedly / implicitly* recommend Mr Lee for promotion.
3 Mehmet has every ability to *meet / run* the challenges of the position.
4 I am delighted to *provide / act* a reference for Meena Mistry.
5 The position would require you to *perform / hone* a wide range of tasks.
6 Your contributions to the project are *highly / wholeheartedly* valued.

44.5 Use a dictionary to find other words to complete these word forks.

financial
.......................➤acumen
....

valued
highly◀━.......................
....

a task
perform ◀━ ....
....

45 Appearance and personality

A Describing how people look and behave

Note the collocations in these interviews where famous people discuss their own or other people's **personality traits** (or **personal characteristics**).

Film star Jerry Bowen

Interviewer: You seem to have had such a special relationship with Kara Hanson over many years. What is it about working with her?

Bowen: Kara's wonderful. She just seems to have **boundless energy**[1] and she's always been able to **boost** people's **confidence**[2], especially new young actors. She has a wonderful, **bubbly**[3] **personality** and she's got a **dazzling smile**. She **bears a striking resemblance to**[4] Ingrid Bergman, one of the great cinema beauties. She **has** some wonderful personal **qualities** that are so rare in stars nowadays.

[1] lots of energy   [2] make more confident   [3] lively   [4] looks very like

Ex-rock star Eddie Stewart

Interviewer: You always had a troubled relationship with your drummer, Kaz Porter, in the days of your band, The Loop. Kaz died in 1987. How do you remember him now?

Stewart: Well, Kaz was not an easy person to work with. He had a very **thinly disguised**[5] dislike of the music industry and the people in it. Politeness wasn't **his strong point**! He had a real **stubborn streak**[6] that made him unpopular with managers and agents. But, you know, behind that **gruff**[7] **exterior** he had a **sharp wit**[8].

Interviewer: You say gruff, some would say **downright rude**. Would that be too harsh? He always seemed full of **pent-up anger**[9] towards the world in general.

Stewart: Well, 'rude' is a bit unfair. Yeah, he had a **forthright**[10] **manner**, and he was capable of **open hostility** if he thought we were being manipulated.

Interviewer: Yes, he did **display** some rather scary **characteristics**.

[5] barely hidden   [6] a stubborn side to his character   [7] rude and unfriendly
[8] was very amusing in a clever way   [9] anger which he didn't express   [10] direct

Retired golfer Andy Barstow

Interviewer: Andy, you're retired, you're a senior citizen, but everyone would agree you certainly don't **look your age**[11]. What's your secret?

Barstow: Well thanks. I'm sure some people would say I don't **act my age**[12] either!

Interviewer: Oh, that's not necessarily a bad thing! You do always seem to be **bursting with energy**!

Barstow: That's what golf does for you!

[11] look as old as you are   [12] behave in a manner expected of your age

B Other useful collocations for behaviour and appearance

She had a **blank expression** on her face. [showing no understanding or emotion]
He always gave everyone a **warm, friendly smile**.
Tracy's new colleagues gave her a rather **cool reception**. [unfriendly welcome]
You have been guilty of **unacceptable behaviour**.
I'm surprised you find Jack unfriendly. He's always been **perfectly friendly** to me.
Angela has a rather **abrasive manner**. [rude and unfriendly manner]

Exercises

45.1 Match words from each box to form collocations from the opposite page. Then match them to the definitions below.

blank	personality
gruff	streak
striking	reception
cool	exterior
stubborn	resemblance
bubbly	expression

1 two things or people which look very similar
2 a very lively person
3 a person's face which shows no emotion
4 when someone is being inflexible
5 an apparently rude and unfriendly personality
6 a rather unfriendly welcome

Amanda often had a blank expression on her face.

45.2 Which of these things that people say would usually be compliments?

1 He/She certainly looks his/her age.
2 He/She's downright rude.
3 He/She's bursting with energy.
4 He/She has a bubbly personality.
5 He/She has a very abrasive manner.
6 He/She has a warm smile.
7 He/She's full of pent-up anger.
8 He/She has boundless energy.

45.3 Complete this conversation using collocations from the box in the appropriate form so that Nell always agrees with Zoë.

bear a striking resemblance to	boost your confidence	burst with energy
forthright manner	has a lot of admirable qualities	strong points

1 Zoë: Tom looks a bit like Brad Pitt, doesn't he?
  Nell: Yes, he does. He .... him.
2 Zoë: And he's very good at making you feel more confident, isn't he?
  Nell: Yes, he's great at ....
3 Zoë: Though of course he does say what he thinks directly to you.
  Nell: Yes, he sometimes has a rather .... but I like that.
4 Zoë: Me too. In fact, I think that it might be one of his best characteristics.
  Nell: Yes, you could say it is one of his .... , I suppose.
5 Zoë: Well, he has a lot of good points.
  Nell: Yes, I'd certainly agree that he ....
6 Zoë: He's very energetic, for example.
  Nell: Yes, I love the way he's always .... It's very attractive.

45.4 Complete each sentence using the word in brackets in the appropriate form.

1 Teresa is always .... friendly towards me. (PERFECT)
2 Can you see how Holly is looking at him with open .... ? (HOSTILE)
3 I refuse to put up with such .... behaviour. (ACCEPT)
4 He displays a lot more attractive .... than his brother does. (CHARACTER)
5 The woman looked at the official with .... disguised contempt. (THIN)
6 The star was upset that his home town gave him such a cool .... (RECEIVE)

46 Time and space

A Talking about space

Hi Liz,

How frustrating house-hunting is! We've just looked at a city-centre flat near Oliver's new job. The estate agent's ad said it was 'spacious'. Ha, ha! How anyone could live in such a **confined space**, I don't know. It was tiny. I know you have to expect **cramped conditions** in the city centre but this was ridiculous. We're **short of space** already where we are now, what with the new baby and everything. Kids **take up a lot of space**, don't they?

Love,

Emma

Dear Emma,

Sorry to hear of your problems. Yes, kids do seem to **take up a lot of room**. But listen, a friend of ours is selling her house in town and moving to Australia. It's not huge, but there's **ample**[1] **room** for a family with two children. There's even a garden, and though it's not a **vast expanse**, it's very pleasant. There's a shed on it at the moment, which is a bit of **a waste of space**[2] but that could be removed to **leave room** for a play-area. There's no garage, but it's on a quiet street and there are always plenty of **vacant parking spaces**. Let me know if you're interested and I'll have a word with her.

Best,

Liz

[1] more than enough   [2] bad use of space when there is limited amount of it

Note that you can say **ample space/room; leave space/room; short of space/room** and **take up a lot of space/room**. However, you can only talk about something being a **waste of space** (NOT a waste of ~~room~~).

B Talking about time

In these magazine clips, notice the useful collocations for talking about time.

Pop bands come and go **over the course of time**[1], but few bands have **made** such **a lasting contribution** as The Beatles. They will **go down in history**[2] as possibly the greatest pop musicians of all time. Their music represents the **golden era**[3] of British pop in the 1960s, and every one of their songs **brings back memories** of that unforgettable time. Their music is all **preserved for posterity**[4] on a new set of re-mastered CDs.

[1] as time passes   [2] be remembered   [3] can also be **golden age**; period of time when a particular art, business, etc. was very successful   [4] (formal) kept for people in the future

Buildings from a **bygone era**[5] are the main attraction at Castmere Folk Village. Homes, shops, even a cinema, have been **restored to their former glory**[6] in a massive project that has now reached completion.

[5] (literary) a time in the distant past   [6] *glory* here means 'beauty'

For many people, the 1960s are nothing more than a **dim and distant**[7] **memory**, but in the **decades** that have **elapsed**, those of us born in the 60s begin to realise how that decade, which is still well **within living memory** for much of the population, has **shaped our destiny**. Our parents worked with pen and paper, or machines, or with their hands. They couldn't have known how computers would change everything in **the not-so-distant future**[8]. All indications are that many more changes will help to **shape** our children's **lives** in **the foreseeable future**[9].

[7] remembered slightly, but not very well   [8] not the immediate future but relatively near
[9] as far into the future as you can imagine or plan for

TIP Where alternatives exist for a collocation, make a note in your vocabulary book and list the alternatives together, for example, **take up (a lot of) space/room**, **a golden age/era**.

Exercises

46.1 Match the beginning of each sentence with its ending.

1 Living in such a confined   room for a bigger kitchen and utility room.
2 The piano took up a lot of   space, so we're going to convert it into a study.
3 This office is better than the cramped   space is difficult with three kids.
4 We're moving because we're short of   room, so we sold it.
5 We demolished an old outhouse to leave   conditions I used to work in.
6 The attic is a waste of   space where we're living at the moment.

46.2 Complete the second sentence using a collocation from the opposite page so that it has the same meaning as the first sentence.

1 Einstein's ideas significantly contributed to our understanding of the universe.
  Einstein's ideas made .... our understanding of the universe.
2 The hotel car park didn't have any room, so we parked in the street.
  There were no .... at the hotel, so we parked in the street.
3 Few people now have any clear memories of the Second World War.
  The Second World War is now a ....
4 We won't have problems with our furniture as it's a big house.
  It's a big house, so there will be .... for all our furniture.
5 She crossed the enormous Senoui desert on horseback.
  She crossed .... of the Senoui desert on horseback.

46.3 Rewrite the underlined part of each sentence using a collocation from the opposite page based on the words in brackets.

1 <u>It's ten years</u> since the agreement was signed. (ELAPSE)
2 I can't see any great changes happening in the <u>future as far as we can imagine</u>. (FORESEE)
3 Machines from <u>an era which has long passed</u> are the theme of the exhibition at the city museum. (GO BY)
4 The event will <u>be remembered in history</u> as the nation's worst tragedy. (DOWN)
5 Everything changes <u>as time passes</u>. (COURSE)
6 In the <u>fairly near future</u> we can expect to be able to travel to other planets. (DISTANT)

46.4 Complete the crossword.

Across
1 The palace was restored to its former — .
3 The events have — our lives.
5 That song brings — memories.
6 Many things shape the — of a nation.
7 It all happened within — memory.

Down
1 It was the — era of Italian football.
2 My schooldays are now just a dim and — memory.
3 This table takes up a lot of — .
4 The castle has been preserved for — .
5 The cottage is a remnant of a — era.

47 Sound

The collocations marked * are rather literary and not frequent in everyday conversation.

A The human voice

Here are some brief extracts from novels, where people's voices and speech are being described.

- Lennox noticed **a trace of**[1] a foreign **accent** in the man's voice. It was a **booming**[2] voice, one he had heard before, many years ago.
- Lucy's **voice faltered**[3]* as she told her sad story.
- Wilson **gave** a loud **laugh*** as he watched Robert trying to fire the gun. Then, in a **gruff**[4] voice, he said, 'You're useless! Bring it here!' Robert **muttered** something **under his breath** as he obeyed.
- Mildred **met with a stony**[5] **silence** as she entered the room. It was as if everyone had **lost their voice**. Nobody **uttered a word**[6] as she walked across to the table.
- The woman spoke with a **broad**[7] Scottish **accent**. She had a rather **husky**[8] voice, which James found attractive, but she **slurred her words**[9] a little, as if she were too tired to talk.
- **Muffled**[10] **voices** could be heard coming from the next room, then **a strangled cry**[11]*, as though someone was in pain.
- Polly's suggestion met with **hoots of laughter**[12]*. She **raised her voice** angrily and shouted, 'Okay, do it your way then!'

[1] very slight [2] very loud [3] lost strength and hesitated [4] low, unfriendly and harsh
[5] cold and unfriendly [6] note, this collocation is normally in the negative or has a negative
subject [7] strong (of accents) [8] low and rough, often thought to be attractive
[9] spoke unclearly, running the sounds together [10] quiet and unclear
[11] weak, high, interrupted sound made by an extremely frightened or anxious person
[12] sounds of loud laughter

B Sounds and silence

Here are four winning entries from a student poetry competition. The theme of the competition was 'Sound and silence'.

1st prize: Sasha Brokenburg

A **clap**[1] **of thunder**
then a **deathly hush**[2]*.
In a **soft whisper**
the wind tells the moon
how beautiful she is.

2nd prize: Abdul Zahra

Silence descends on Carthmore Lake.
My heart is still.
Only the **distant echo** of a sad cry
can be heard.

3rd prize: Nuria Palomar

In the street below, the **incessant**[3] **noise**
of trams and vans
of trucks and cars.
But my soul **makes** no **sound**.
Here in this darkened room
silence reigns[4].

4th prize: Liu Chan

A **dull thud**[5] awakens me.
The **sound travels** from
the valley where it was made
to this place here,
where no one dares **let out a cry**.

[1] sudden loud noise made by thunder [2] extreme silence, in a way that is unpleasant
[3] which never stops [4] dominates [5] unclear sound made when something heavy falls

Exercises

47.1 Read the sentences. Then answer the questions.

Despite his gruff voice, Fabrice's boss is actually quite an approachable person.
Zara gave a strangled cry when she realised the child was injured.
Kevin spoke in a booming voice, as if he were an army sergeant.
Ilona raised her voice and angrily addressed the young man at the door.
As she entered, she could hear Joe's husky voice addressing someone.

	name
1 Who spoke in an extremely loud voice?	
2 Who spoke in a low, rough, but perhaps attractive way?	
3 Who spoke in a low, unfriendly voice?	
4 Who started to speak louder than before?	
5 Who made a high, interrupted sound of fear or anxiety?	

47.2 Complete each sentence using a word from the box in the appropriate form.

descend	falter	give	let	lose	make	slur	travel	utter

1 The woman .... a shrill laugh when she heard the story.
2 Try not to .... a sound as we pass the baby's bedroom.
3 We didn't .... a single word as Harry told his sad tale.
4 The sound .... through the thin walls of my apartment; I hear everything.
5 The patient .... out a cry of pain as the doctor took his hand.
6 Silence .... in the hall as Mr Traynor walked to the platform to speak.
7 The man's voice .... as he answered the detective's questions.
8 What's the matter with you? Have you .... your voice? Say something!
9 Travis .... his words somewhat. I thought he might have been drinking.

47.3 Correct the collocation errors in these sentences.

1 I could hear a slight track of an Irish accent in her voice.
2 Paolo was met with a rocky silence as everyone tried to absorb the bad news.
3 The old woman let off a cry of anger when she heard the result of the trial.
4 She has a wide American accent, even though she was not born there.
5 I could hear thuds of laughter coming from the next room.
6 The voices were muttered, so I could not make out what anyone was saying.
7 Silence ruled in the classroom as the pupils were all hard at work.
8 Speak up. I hate it when you mutter something under your voice.

47.4 Replace the underlined words with their opposites to form collocations from the opposite page.

1 The <u>nearby</u> echo of gunfire could be heard across the valley.
2 The <u>intermittent</u> noise of the planes kept me awake all night.
3 In a <u>loud</u> whisper she said, 'You look wonderful tonight.'
4 I heard a <u>sharp</u> thud as the men dropped the heavy box on the floor above me.
5 There was a <u>joyful</u> hush in the room as General Wilkins broke the news.
6 Suddenly there was a <u>murmur</u> of thunder and it started to rain heavily.

48 Making things easier

A Choosing your approach

COMPLETING A TASK – HOW TO DO IT

When you need to work out the easiest way to do something, you have to **explore different ways** of approaching the task. Sometimes there will be many **feasible[1] alternatives** to consider and sometimes there will only be one or two **viable[2] options**. You need to **enlist the help** of people to give you advice before you decide on which **method to adopt**.

The best advice is to take a **step-by-step approach**: **break the task down** into stages, so that you are dealing with small **manageable chunks**. This way you will soon find that something you thought was hard is in fact **simplicity itself[3]**. But be careful, don't always take what looks like **the easy option**. Think first. At the end, you can feel proud that you didn't just **take the easy way out[4]**.

[1] possible
[2] workable
[3] extremely simple
[4] do what is easiest but not what is best – which may mean avoiding doing anything at all

B Ways of remembering

Notice the collocations in this text introducing techniques for improving your memory.

A trained memory is an **immense asset[1]**, particularly in public life. Mnemonics are systems for **dealing with the complexities** of learning and remembering, and people who use them can recall things with an **amazing degree of accuracy**.

The Ancient Greeks **perfected[2]** a number of mnemonic **techniques**, some of which are still used today, for example, using the first letter of each item to form a word that will help you remember the whole list of items. For instance, you might remember the female first name, ADA, to help you recall the phrase *amazing degree of accuracy*. Or you might think of the word BAG, which will give you three colours that collocate with *hair* (*blond, auburn, ginger*).

A **simple rule** of all memory training systems is the idea of 'Initial Awareness'. This works in a **straightforward[3] way**. The **basic principle** is that the system helps you **concentrate the mind** on whatever you are trying to remember for just long enough to force Initial Awareness.

This may **sound like hard work** at first, but in fact all memory training systems are perfectly simple. Once you have **taken the time** to learn them, you will be able to **instantly recall** any new **items of information** you want to, with **remarkable ease**.

[1] something of great value
[2] the verb is pronounced /pɜː'fekt/
[3] easy to understand or simple

Do you know any mnemonic techniques to help you learn vocabulary? If possible, share them with other students.

Exercises

48.1 **Answer these questions about the text in A.**

1 Which alternatives is it best to focus on when considering ways of doing something?
2 What sort of options are those that could work well?
3 Which option is not always the best one to take?
4 What sort of approach can one take to make a big task more manageable?

48.2 **Match words from each box to form collocations from the opposite page.**

adopt	concentrate	enlist	immense
instantly	perfect	perfectly	remarkable
simple	take		

asset	ease	help	a method	the mind
recall	rule	simple	a technique	the time

48.3 **Complete B's responses using collocations from the opposite page.**

1 A: I notice your tennis serve is much better these days.
   B: Yes, I think I've finally .... the technique, though it took months of practice.

2 A: Was the new computer easy to set up?
   B: Yes, it was .... itself.

3 A: How did you get on in the charity race?
   B: Well, I actually managed it with remarkable .... , given how unfit I was!

4 A: I didn't envy you having to sort out 200 CDs for the school music library!
   B: Well, it sounded like .... at first, but it wasn't in fact that difficult.

5 A: How well does the pedometer your son made at college actually work?
   B: With an amazing .... , in fact.

6 A: I have to sort out all these old papers and I just don't know where to start!
   B: Why don't you .... the task down into smaller chunks and deal with them gradually?

7 A: Do you enjoy working with collocations?
   B: Well, it's worth .... time to learn them as they make your language sound so much more natural.

8 A: How was your computer course?
   B: Good. I find it much easier to deal with the .... of programming now.

48.4 **Choose the correct collocation.**

1 I always use mnemonics to help me recall important .... of information.
   A spots   B objects   C items   D stuff

2 We .... all the different ways of getting home before eventually deciding to fly.
   A exploded   B exploited   C explicated   D explored

3 The system works in a .... way.
   A straightforward   B strong   C straight   D forthright

4 It's a good idea to divide a task up into .... chunks.
   A portable   B manageable   C edible   D thinkable

5 All memory systems work on the same basic ....
   A promotion   B prime   C principal   D principle

FOLLOW UP Look at this mnemonics site: www.fun-with-words.com/mnemonics.html. Make a note of useful ones.

49 Difficulty

A Adjective + noun collocations

- Life seems to have been a **constant struggle** for her ever since she left home.
- When the electricity went off everyone was rushing about in a **state of confusion.**
- Losing the job she loved so much was a **severe blow** for Anna. She **took it** very **badly.**
- Our plane was cancelled because of **adverse weather conditions.**
- Unfortunately, after the **widespread flooding** came **widespread looting** of the properties that had been abandoned. Meanwhile, many families remained in **grave danger** as the flood waters showed little sign of abating.
- If you continue to smoke there is a **high risk** of your developing a number of serious diseases.
- Jasmine's birthday party was a **complete disaster.** She decided to invite all of her own and her sisters' ex-boyfriends – with **catastrophic results.**

B Verb + noun collocations

collocation	example
face a problem	My grandmother **faced** many **problems** in her life.
address a problem	How do you think we should **address** the traffic **problems** in our city?
tackle a problem	More must be done to **tackle** the AIDS **problem.**
pose a threat	Nuclear weapons **pose a threat** to the whole world.
carry a risk	Most things that we do in life **carry** some degree of **risk.**
minimise a risk	Not smoking **minimises the risk** of getting a whole range of illnesses.
relish a challenge	Rob **relishes the challenge** of a new project.
hinder progress	Our party believes that this country's complex tax laws mainly serve to **hinder progress.**
spot an error	Terry **spotted an error** in the email he was about to send.
encounter difficulties	Any new business is bound to **encounter** some initial **difficulties.**
overcome hurdles	As she was born blind she has had to **overcome** many extra **hurdles** in her life.
fight for survival	Poor people in this drought-ridden country **fight for survival.**
respond to an emergency	The international community **responded** rapidly **to the emergency.**
disaster strikes	**Disaster struck** the province last June, when torrential rains caused mudslides in many areas.

ERROR WARNING

Remember that we **make mistakes**, NOT ~~do~~ mistakes, we usually **have problems** or **experience problems**, just as we usually also **have/experience difficulties**, NOT ~~get problems/difficulties~~. We attempt to **find a solution**, NOT ~~give~~ a solution. **Problems arise** or **occur**, NOT ~~happen~~ and **difficulties arise**, NOT ~~appear~~.

Exercises

49.1 Find a collocation in A that has the opposite meaning of these collocations ...

1 favourable weather conditions
2 a magnificent success
3 an easy ride

4 isolated flooding
5 slight danger

... and the same meaning as these collocations.

6 total confusion
7 disastrous results
8 serious risk

9 a terrible shock
10 a total disaster

49.2 Complete each sentence using a verb from the box in the appropriate form.

carry	face	fight	hinder	pose	respond	spot	strike	tackle

1 The government is doing all it can to .... the drug problem in our cities.
2 We had only just set off on our holiday when disaster ....
3 Can you .... the six deliberate errors in this story?
4 The international community does not always .... as promptly as would be desirable to an emergency.
5 Any new enterprise .... some risk of failure but that should not deter you.
6 I am afraid that Sandy's problems at home may be .... his progress at school.
7 If we .... the problems together we should find it easier to tackle them.
8 By the end of the expedition the climbers were .... for their very survival.
9 A man like that in a position of power .... a serious threat to world security.

49.3 Match each question (1–6) with its response (a–f).

1 Is Roy enjoying the challenge of his new post?
2 What can I do to minimise the risk of falling ill?
3 What made them decide to postpone the match?
4 What happened after the earthquake?
5 How can we address the climate change problem?
6 What was the hardest hurdle to overcome in your job?

a By reducing our carbon footprint.
b Widespread looting.
c Eat healthily.
d He's relishing it.
e Gender stereotyping, probably.
f Adverse weather conditions.

49.4 Correct the collocation errors in these sentences.

1 We are getting a number of problems with our new car.
2 Some problems happened when we tried to follow your instructions.
3 Somehow our society must give a solution to the problem of child poverty.
4 A difficulty has appeared with regard to a member of our project team.
5 Even advanced students sometimes do mistakes with this type of collocation.
6 I've always found a lot of difficulties with English spelling.

49.5 Use a dictionary or online corpus to find two other collocations for each of these words.

1 encounter   2 tackle   3 pose

50 Quantity and size

A Countable and uncountable expressions of quantity

The expressions in the table all mean quite a large number or amount.

collocation	example	comment
a good/fair few	**A good few** students are likely to get a first-class degree.	informal, used with countable nouns
a good/fair number	We spent **a good number of** weeks planning the project.	informal, used with countable nouns
a substantial/significant number	**A significant number of** people pledged their support.	formal, used with countable nouns
a substantial/significant quantity	We took **a significant quantity of** provisions with us.	formal, used with countable or uncountable nouns
a substantial/significant amount	He'll get **a substantial amount of** money when his father dies.	formal, used with uncountable nouns

B Other expressions about size and quantity

We couldn't believe **the sheer quantity** of food on the table. [the surprisingly large amount]
There's only a **finite number** of days until the exam.
[limited number]
The room is a **good size**. [quite large]
A teacher needs to possess **unbounded enthusiasm** as
well as **infinite patience** and an **endless supply** of
good jokes.
They charge **astronomical fees** for the course. [very high]
We had a **bumper crop** of tomatoes last year and I gave
masses away to our neighbours. [informal; very large crop]
Unemployment reached **epic proportions** and this led to
social instability.
The rock star died from a **massive overdose** of barbiturates.

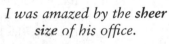

*I was amazed by the sheer
size of his office.*

An **overwhelming majority** of the population are in favour of reform.
I visited a lot of different relatives yesterday and drank an **inordinate amount** of tea.
Try to use a **wide range** of vocabulary in your essay.
There is a **wide variety/choice** of things to do here in the evenings.
The new maths teacher is **an unknown quantity**. I hope she'll get on well with the students.
[a person or thing whose characteristics are not yet clear]

C Common errors

There are a number of errors often made by learners when talking about quantity or size.

correct word(s)	collocates with ...	wrong word(s)
small	minority, amount, number, quantity, percentage	little
large	quantity, amount, number, majority	great, big, high
large, high	percentage	great
great	importance, significance	high, big

Exercises

50.1 Rewrite each sentence using the word in brackets.

1 We had a large number of apples from our trees last year. (BUMPER)
2 A lot of their income comes from the apartments they rent out. (SUBSTANTIAL)
3 I feel confident that quite a few people will vote for Mac. (NUMBER)
4 Jill's room at college is quite big. (GOOD)
5 We don't have an unlimited number of tickets, so we're offering them on a first-come-first-served basis. (FINITE)
6 I was terrifed when I saw how big the dog was. (SHEER)
7 I still don't know what my new colleague is like. (QUANTITY)
8 There were rather a lot of careless mistakes in your homework. (FAIR)

50.2 Complete each sentence using a word from the opposite page.

1 The Green Party won the election with an overwhelming ....
2 He did not realise how strong the tablets were and died of a massive ....
3 Some lawyers are known to charge astronomical ....
4 The government didn't take action until inflation had reached epic ....
5 I have a profound admiration for your sister's infinite ....
6 We didn't have many plums last year but this year we enjoyed a bumper ....
7 Paul doesn't really like coffee but I drink a substantial ....
8 There never used to be any nightclubs here but now there are a good ....

50.3 Match the two parts of these collocations from the opposite page.

1 unbounded	quantity
2 bumper	amount
3 astronomical	enthusiasm
4 infinite	patience
5 fair	fees
6 endless	few
7 inordinate	supply
8 sheer	crop

50.4 Put a tick in the box if the collocation is possible.

	minority	majority	amount	number	percentage	quantity	importance	significance
small								
little								
large								
great								
big								
high								
wide								

50.5 Use a dictionary or online corpus to find two other collocations for each of these words.

1 infinite   2 epic   3 overwhelming   4 endless   5 massive

51 Change

A Collocations with *change* as a noun

There have been **dramatic changes** in the climate of the Arctic region in the last decade. [very sudden or noticeable changes]

The government is proposing **fundamental changes** to the laws on marriage and divorce. [basic changes, and more important than anything else]

There was a **radical change** in party policy in 2003. [great or extreme change]

The new manager made **sweeping changes** to the way the company was run. [change affecting many people/things]

Let's go swimming this morning instead of jogging – it **would make a change**. [be pleasantly different to one's usual routine]

Read the teacher's comments on your essays, then **make** any necessary **changes**.

The **changes** in the system **will be implemented** soon. [will be put into operation/practice]

The **change** in the electoral system **came about** because of widespread public protest.

Many **changes** had **taken place** in my home town – and not always for the better.

B Collocations with *change* as a verb, adjective or adverb

Things can **change dramatically, fundamentally** or **radically** but NOT ~~sweepingly~~.

Pronunciation **changes imperceptibly** over the years. [changes so slowly that you hardly notice it]

In the ten years since our last meeting, Irene had **changed beyond recognition**. [changed so much one couldn't recognise her]

If we call someone **a changed man/woman** we mean that he or she has changed for the better.

Life in the village **remained unchanged** for centuries. [formal: **stayed the same**]

Some people are much better than others at **adapting to changing circumstances**.

C Other ways of talking about change

example	comment
The hotel had **undergone a transformation** since our last stay.	also **undergo a revival**
The exchange rate has been **fluctuating wildly** over the last few days.	= going up and down in an unpredictable way (also used with *temperature(s)* and *share prices*)
We have had a **modest increase** in students enrolling on our courses.	also a **modest improvement, modest gain, modest recovery**, where modest = slight or small
There has been a **sudden shift** in public opinion in favour of the ban on smoking.	also a **dramatic shift**
Amy's work **shows** considerable **improvement**.	one opposite might be: There is **room for improvement** in her work.
Our children's **lives were turned upside-down** when we moved.	= **changed dramatically**, usually for the worse
Elderly people sometimes find it difficult to **move with the times**.	= keep up with changes and adapt to them

ERROR WARNING
Profits **show an increase/decrease** and **show an upward / a downward trend**, NOT ~~have~~ an increase etc.
Figures **increase dramatically** or **significantly**, NOT increase ~~strongly~~.

Exercises

51.1 **Answer these questions about the collocations on the opposite page.**

1 What is the opposite of:
   a) to change imperceptibly   b) to cancel planned changes
2 Which of these words suggest major changes and which minor changes?
   a) dramatic   b) slight   c) fundamental   d) superficial   e) radical
3 Which is the more formal alternative in each pair:
   a) The town remains unchanged.   The town is the same.
   b) Over the years the school has changed a lot.
      Over the years many changes have taken place in the school.
4 If someone says Emma is a changed woman, do they approve of the change in Emma?
5 Is it easier for a young person or an elderly person to adapt to changing circumstances?
6 If someone says 'It made a nice change going out for a meal last night', what changed
   – the fact that they went out, or the restaurant they went to?

51.2 **Complete each sentence using a word from the box in the appropriate form.**

dramatic	make	implement	increase	recognise
show	times	turn	undergo	wild

1 The figures .... a dramatic increase in the number of women in paid
   employment in the 1940s.
2 My grandmother loves her laptop and her mobile phone – she has no problem moving
   with the ....
3 I can't face moving house again – I don't want to have my life ....
   upside-down another time.
4 The pop music of the 1980s seems to be .... a bit of a revival.
5 The weather's been odd this month – temperatures have fluctuated ....
6 We have experienced a modest .... in profits this year.
7 I .... some changes to the document but forgot to save them!
8 I think you'll find that the school has changed beyond ....
9 The new leader promised that things would change .... and for the better.
10 When are they planning to .... the changes to the school curriculum?

51.3 **Rewrite each sentence using the word in brackets.**

1 Your coursework assignment is still not quite as good as it should be. (ROOM)
2 Public attitudes towards the issue of capital punishment suddenly changed. (SHIFT)
3 There were several changes in our management structure last year. (PLACE)
4 The school programme has changed a lot since I was a pupil here. (SWEEPING)
5 Some quite significant changes took place last year. (CAME)
6 Penny has been much nicer since she got the job she wanted. (CHANGED)
7 My life changed dramatically when I lost my job. (TURNED)
8 It'd be nice to do something different and stay in
   a hotel rather than go camping this summer. (CHANGE)

 FOLLOW UP Go to www.bbc.co.uk and search for 'climate change'. Click on one of the items, read it and make a note of any collocations relating to change that you find in it.

52 Stopping and starting

A Stopping

example	comment
The accident **brought** traffic **to a halt** for several hours.	often used about transport (trains, etc.)
The union **called a halt to** the strike after 21 days.	= prevent something from continuing (e.g. military action, protests, etc.)
The chair **brought** the meeting **to a close** at 5pm.	often used about discussions.
The new teacher soon **put a stop to** bad behaviour in the class.	used about unpopular activities or habits (e.g. crime, antisocial activities)
They **terminated his contract** since he failed to meet his sales targets.	formal; also **terminate a pregnancy**
The government may **abandon their policy** on ID cards.	also **abandon an attempt** to do sth
Police **called off the search** as darkness fell.	= cancelled; also **call off a match** or other sports event
The police have **closed off** the **street** while repairs are being carried out there.	= block the entrance to stop people entering a street
Wait until there is a **lull in the conversation**, then we can leave.	= a pause; also **lull in the fighting** (in a military conflict)

B Starting

As **dawn broke** we set off up the mountain. [as the sun first appeared]
Jasmine suddenly **broke into song**. [started singing]
William **broke into a run** when he saw the bus leaving. [started running]
The rain set in for the day. [it started and seemed likely to continue]
The smoke **set off the fire alarm**.
Customs have **instigated measures** to deal with illegal immigration. [formal: introduced]
The chairperson made some **opening remarks**, others then **entered into the discussion**.

C News headlines

VIOLENCE **SPARKS FEARS**[1] OF FURTHER UNREST

MINISTER **ALLAYS FEARS**[6] **OF** TAX INCREASE

PEACE PROCESS **TALKS COLLAPSE**[2]

ARMY **QUELLS UNREST**[7] ON BORDER

STADIUM FINALLY NEARS COMPLETION[3]

NEW REPUBLIC **BREAKS DIPLOMATIC RELATIONS WITH NEIGHBOURS**

STAR **DISPELS RUMOURS**[4] OF DIVORCE

SINGER **CLEARS UP CONFUSION**[5] ABOUT LYRICS

[1] makes people worry about
[2] come to an unsuccessful conclusion
[3] is almost finished
[4] makes a statement to end the rumours
[5] ends confusion
[6] stops people worrying about
[7] stops disturbances

Exercises

52.1 Look at A. Which word fits in both sentences in each pair?

1 The Minister may be forced to .... his policy on constitutional reform.
The climbers had to .... their attempt to reach the summit because of bad weather.

2 During a .... in the fighting, aid workers were able to get food to people in need.
Have something ready to say in case there is a .... in the conversation.

3 I think we should .... the meeting to a close now.
Did the demonstration .... the traffic to a halt?

4 It's time the union .... a halt to the industrial action.
The college .... off the match because of the bad weather.

52.2 Match the beginning of each sentence (1–8) with its ending (a–h).

1 I'm afraid it was me burning the toast that set
2 As soon as she saw her mother the little girl broke
3 Because of the President's visit, they've closed
4 I didn't manage to fall asleep until dawn
5 I hope they won't decide to terminate
6 The missing child was found, so the police called
7 The school is planning to instigate some
8 We were halfway up the mountain when the rain

a the contract.
b off the smoke alarm.
c anti-bullying measures.
d off the area.
e set in.
f into a run.
g off their search.
h was breaking.

52.3 Match each topic of a newspaper article to the most likely headline in C.

1 There was a disagreement about who wrote a particular song.
2 A problem between two neighbouring countries is solved by military means.
3 A country recalls its ambassador from another country.
4 Two countries at war fail to reach agreement.
5 People are beginning to worry that there will be more disturbances.
6 A celebrity denies that her marriage is over.
7 Some sports facilities will soon be ready for use.
8 The government promises that rumours are untrue.

52.4 Choose the correct collocation.

1 First I'd like to make a few *beginning / opening / starting* remarks.
2 I'm not going to *enter / bring / come* into any further discussion of the issue.
3 I hope I can manage to *collapse / staunch / allay* your fears.
4 I wish we could put a *close / stop / halt* to the redevelopment plans.
5 I love it when she *sparks / clears / breaks* into song as she prepares our meal.
6 We must do something to *close off / dispel / break off* the rumours about us.
7 The guards soon managed to *quell / collapse / allay* the unrest at the prison.
8 At long last the building is nearing *finish / termination / completion*.

53 Cause and effect

A Collocations with *cause* and *effect*

We have yet to **establish the cause** of this latest outbreak of foot and mouth disease.
Mass unemployment is believed to be the **root cause**[1] of the riots.
The research team thinks that a virus is the **primary cause**[2] of this type of cancer.
The President said it would take time for the reforms to produce the **desired effect**.
It is likely to be some weeks before we **feel the full effect** of the rise in interest rates.
This morning's delays to flights have **had a knock-on effect**[3] on departures all day.
The children involved in the hijack are not expected to suffer any long-term **ill effects**[4].

[1]	origin	[3]	indirect result (NOT ~~make~~ an effect)
[2]	main cause	[4]	negative results (Note that *ill* here means *bad* rather than *sick*)

B Other words meaning *cause*

example	meaning
The advertising campaign didn't **produce the results** we hoped for.	lead to the results
The Finance Minister's decision to raise income tax **provoked an outcry**.	caused a lot of public anger
If teachers show favouritism, it **breeds resentment**.	makes others feel angry and unhappy
Mary didn't believe the rumours about her boss but they **planted doubts** in her mind.	made her feel uncertain
The film star's photo **prompted speculation** that she may be pregnant.	caused people to suspect
Email has more or less **rendered** the fax machine **obsolete**.	caused to be no longer used
If you want to make an insurance claim, you can **set the wheels in motion** by filling in this form.	make something start to happen
This wind will **wreak havoc** with my flowers!	cause a lot of damage to
Our new neighbours are so noisy, it's enough to **drive** anyone **crazy**!	informal, make angry and upset
The strike could **spell disaster** for the country.	cause serious problems

C Talking about reasons and consequences

Mr Ball: Why did Jack behave so badly in class? There must have been some **compelling reason**[1] surely. He must have known there'd be **dire consequences**[2].
Miss Cane: I don't know. I think his parents' financial problems might be a **contributing factor** but he refused to **give me a reason**. Anyway, I sent him to the headteacher and I'm sure she'll **demand an explanation**.
Mr Ball: Yes, she'll certainly make him **face the consequences** of his actions!

[1] very powerful reason   [2] very serious consequences

Exercises

53.1   Match the beginning of each sentence with its ending.

1 I think that computers will eventually render	havoc in low-lying areas.
2 The preliminary meeting set the wheels	an outcry from the staff.
3 Her mother calling her sister 'the pretty one' bred	speculation that he is unwell.
4 I always suspected the new tax law would spell	a positive result.
5 I'm sure that your hard work will produce	us crazy.
6 The boss's decision to cut wages provoked	disaster for the economy.
7 The way he behaved last night planted	a lot of resentment.
8 The Minister's absence has prompted	of the new project in motion.
9 The uncertainty of the situation is driving	books obsolete.
10 The floods last week wrought	doubts in my mind about his honesty.

53.2   Complete each sentence using a word from the opposite page. The first letters are given for you.

1 Henry's mother d................................... an explanation for his extraordinary behaviour.
2 Fortunately the consequences were not as d.................................. as we had anticipated.
3 Now I dread having to f................................... the consequences of my over-hasty decision to hand in my notice.
4 Do you have any c................................... reason for wanting to invite Zoë to come too?
5 When I asked the doctor why I felt so exhausted, he said that stress might be a c................................... factor.
6 Can you give me any sensible r................................... why we should do something so risky?
7 Unfortunately, the sleeping pills she's taking are not having the d................................... effect.
8 The hurricane has w................................... havoc along the Florida coast.
9 I suspect that the journalist deliberately wanted to p................................... doubts in his readers' minds about the effectiveness of the recent security measures.

53.3   Order the words to form sentences.

1 the / next / nearly / crazy. / dust / site / building / The / me / is / from / driving / door
2 them / will / time / establish / of / It / a / the / the / take / cause / long / accident. / to
3 motion / If / now, / your / week. / things / we / next / visa / ready / should / set / in / be
4 out / customer / produced / results. / The / survey / company / surprising / carried / which / the / some

53.4   Answer these questions.

1 What is the desired effect of any medication?
2 Is a knock-on effect usually welcomed or not?
3 Which other collocation in A has a similar meaning to *primary cause*?
4 If a dentist gives you a local anaesthetic injection, how long does it usually take before you feel the full effect of the injection?
5 Do you think society has suffered any ill effects as the result of the invention of television?
6 Can you name an invention that has been rendered obsolete by new technology?

 FOLLOW UP   Use a search engine or corpus to find sentences using (a) cause and (b) effect. Note down five sentences for each word, illustrating typical collocations.

54 Describing groups and amounts

A Groups of animals

When we describe a group of animals, the word we use depends on the animals we are talking about. So, we talk about **a pack of dogs, hounds** or **wolves** but **a herd of cattle** and **elephants** (and other large herbivorous mammals). We say **a swarm of bees/locusts** (and other flying insects) but we say **a flock of birds** and also **a flock of sheep**.

Other more unusual examples include **a pride of lions, a shoal of fish** or **sardines** (or other specific small fish), **a school** or **pod of dolphins** or **whales, a tribe of monkeys** or **baboons**.

B Feelings and behaviour

Here are some collocations using 'amount' words relating to feelings and behaviour. Note that the futher collocations listed in the third column do not all relate to feelings or behaviour.

example	comment	further collocations
There was **a flurry of activity** as the children fetched their paints.	*Flurry* suggests a sudden, short period of interest or activity.	**a flurry of interest/excitement/ speculation/snow**
I didn't detect **even a flicker of emotion** in his cold eyes.	*Flicker* suggests a brief expression of emotion.	**a flicker of hope/interest**
The company's figures are beginning to offer **a glimmer of hope** for the future.	*Glimmer* suggests a faint indication of something.	**a glimmer of interest/light/ understanding**
There was **a touch of sadness** in her voice as she told us her news.	*Touch* suggests a small amount of something.	**a touch of humour/irony** **a touch of class** = sophistication
I've experienced the **whole gamut of emotions** from joy to sorrow.	*Gamut* means the entire range of something.	collocates very strongly with *emotions*, though it can also be used about colours or musical notes
Inviting José to join our project team was a **stroke of genius**.	A *stroke of* means a bit of.	**a stroke of luck;** he never does **a stroke of work** (always used with the negative)

C Food

Set menu

Soup
freshly made soup of the day, with **a hunk[1] of bread**
Garlic chicken
(10 **cloves[2] of garlic** in every helping!) served on
a bed of rice or with baked potato and **a knob of butter[3]**
Apple pie
served with a generous **dollop of cream[4]**
To finish, try our speciality coffee with **a drop of brandy**,
a dash[5] of cream and **a sprinkling[6] of cinnamon** on top.

[1] thick slice (of cheese, bread or meat)
[2] one piece taken from a head of garlic
[3] small lump of butter
[4] large spoonful of jam or cream
[5] small amount of liquid
[6] small amount of herb or spice

Exercises

54.1 Look at A. Which creature in each group has a different group word?

1 birds, bees, flies	4 whales, dolphins, fish
2 zebras, cattle, wasps	5 elephants, baboons, monkeys
3 sardines, sheep, birds	6 wolves, lions, dogs

54.2 Complete the answers to the questions using a word from the opposite page.

1 A: What have the stock exchanges been like this morning?
   B: Well, there was a .... of activity first thing but it's quietened down now.
2 A: Would you like your coffee black or white?
   B: Can I have just a .... of milk, please?
3 A: *(on the phone)* What's the weather like with you?
   B: Cold! There was even a .... of snow here this morning.
4 A: Do you think it was a good idea to write our new advert in verse?
   B: It was brilliant, a .... of genius! Everyone's talking about it.
5 A: Do I need to do anything more to finish off the sauce?
   B: Add a .... of brandy and a .... of herbs and it'll be perfect.
6 A: What do the critics say about the film?
   B: The Times critic says it takes viewers through a whole .... of emotions.
7 A: Shall we have our picnic here?
   B: No, look at that .... of ants. Let's go a bit further.
8 A: Do you think the pupils enjoyed the lecture?
   B: Well, I saw an occasional .... of interest but it didn't last.
9 A: Do you think she knows what's going on?
   B: I thought there was a .... of understanding in her eyes but I'm not sure.

54.3 Which is bigger?

1 a dash of cream; a dollop of cream	3 a head of garlic; a clove of garlic
2 a slice of bread; a hunk of bread	4 100g of butter; a knob of butter

54.4 Match words from each box to form collocations.

a bed	a drop	a flurry	of brandy	of colours	of fish
gamut	a glimmer	a pack	of hope	of hounds	of humour
a pod	a shoal	a touch	of rice	of speculation	of whales

54.5 Here are some more 'group' or 'amount' words. Complete each sentence using a word from the box. You need to use some of the words twice. Use a dictionary if necessary.

grain	pack	pad	pinch	suite	swig	torrent

1 Pass me that .... of paper, please. I need to write some thank-you letters.
2 I think his story was just a .... of lies without even a .... of truth in it.
3 The film star is staying in a .... of rooms at the Grosvenor Hotel.
4 I'd like to play patience. Have you got a .... of cards?
5 The speaker was met with a .... of abuse.
6 Sometimes Ian doesn't seem to possess even a .... of common sense.
7 Don't forget to add a .... of salt.
8 I'm so thirsty. Could I have a .... of lemonade?

55 Comparing and contrasting

A ## Comparing two places

Emily has been offered two different jobs. The jobs are **fundamentally similar** but they are in different towns – Alton and Belville. The two towns **bear** very **little resemblance to**[1] each other. Alton is a small town by the sea; Belville is **entirely different** as it is a large industrial town. Alton is a beautiful old town which attracts a lot of tourists. This is **in marked contrast to** Belville, which is rather an ugly town. There is a **wide variation** in the cost of accommodation in the two towns. Emily could rent a flat much more cheaply in Belville.

There is also **a world of difference** in the entertainment on offer in the two places. Both towns have several cinemas and theatres, but because there is a **clear distinction** between the types of people who live in each place – there are far more students and other young people in Belville – there is a **yawning gap**[2] between what the cinemas and theatres show. Belville tends to have a lot of foreign films and original new plays, and those are much more to Emily's taste. The options for eating out also **differ widely**. Although Alton is smaller, it has a lot of good restaurants, though they do tend to be rather expensive. Belville is the **exact opposite**. It has a small number of relatively inexpensive restaurants.

To sum up, Alton and Belville are in many respects **polar opposites**[3]. Emily is finding it hard to make up her mind. As soon as she decides that **the advantages** of Alton **outweigh its disadvantages**[4], then someone reminds her of the other **side of the argument**. Which of these two **strikingly different** places do you think she should decide to move to?

[1] don't look at all alike
[2] an enormous difference
[3] extreme opposites
[4] are stronger than the disadvantages

B ## Finding a balance

Tom: How's work going these days, Karl? Are you still at the bank?
Karl: Didn't you know I'd left? I decided to do something **fundamentally different** last year and retrained as a teacher.

Tom: Wow! That's a bit of a change! Your salary as a teacher surely **doesn't bear comparison with**[1] what you got as an investment banker.
Karl: Yes, but in other respects teaching **compares** very **favourably with** banking. I find it very personally rewarding – the financial advantages of banking **pale in comparison**[2].
Tom: So, what appeals to you so much about teaching?
Karl: Well, a teaching friend of mine once **drew a comparison between** teaching and gardening. Teachers tend children in much the same way as gardeners tend flowers. I love gardening, so perhaps that's why I love teaching so much!
Tom: But lots of people say it's a very stressful job these days.
Karl: Perhaps. When I first started, I found it hard to **strike the balance between** being firm and being friendly. I wanted to be my pupils' friend but I soon learnt that you can never totally **bridge the gap** between pupil and teacher.
Tom: Yes, I guess there's a **subtle distinction**[3] between being friendly and being weak.
Karl: That's right. Anyway I think I've got the balance right now and I have no regrets at all about my career change – despite the **growing disparity**[4] between what I earn now and the salaries of my ex-colleagues still at the bank.

[1] can't be compared with   [2] seem unimportant   [3] also **subtle difference**   [4] increasing difference

Exercises

55.1 **Look at A. Complete the sentences.**

1 There is a .... gap between the lives of the rich and the poor. The rich person's experience of life is entirely .... from that of someone without money.

2 Once you have read both .... of the argument, you can draw your own conclusion.

3 The two approaches are in many ways polar ....

4 There is a world of .... between your way of life and mine. Your living arrangements are, for a start, in marked .... to my own.

5 There is a .... distinction between lying and not telling the whole truth.

6 There was a .... variation between the exam marks of the stronger and the weaker candidates.

55.2 **Match the beginning of each sentence (1–8) with its ending (a–h).**

1 Harula bears very little	a difference between the cheeses from these two regions.
2 I find it hard to appreciate the subtle	
3 In my essay I attempted to draw a	b right balance between their studies and their social life.
4 My own painting doesn't bear	
5 Our results were the exact	c opposite of what we had predicted.
6 Students may find it hard to strike the	d gap between artists and scientists.
7 The conference's aim is to bridge the	e disparity between the rich and the poor.
8 There seems to be a growing	f comparison between language learning and riding a bike.
	g resemblance to her sister
	h comparison with that of a trained artist.

55.3 **Choose the correct collocation. More than one option may be possible. Use a dictionary or online corpus to help you if necessary.**

1 The two performers are *entirely / highly / strikingly* different.

2 Politicians talk a lot about how to *join / bridge / cross* the gap between rich and poor.

3 Tessa's work is OK, but it doesn't *make / work / bear* comparison with yours.

4 There is a *deep / clear / subtle* distinction between our points of view.

5 There is a *land / world / planet* of difference between our two lifestyles.

6 The two theories are *fundamentally / strikingly / widely* similar.

7 There is a(n) *growing / rising / extending* disparity between the haves and the have-nots.

8 It is important that you should also hear the other *edge / side / aspect* of the argument.

55.4 **Write sentences comparing life in the town with life in the country using the words in brackets in a collocation from this unit.**

1 (OUTWEIGH) ....

2 (FAVOURABLY) ....

3 (FUNDAMENTALLY) ....

4 (PALE) ....

5 (STRIKINGLY) ....

6 (DIFFER) ....

 Look in a good dictionary, use a search engine or the corpus at www.natcorp.ox.ac.uk to find two more collocations for: contrast, outweigh and gap.

A Adjective + noun collocations

collocation	example	meaning
a determined effort	Mike has been making **a determined effort** to save money.	a very serious and thorough effort
a concerted effort	We made **a concerted effort** to meet all our deadlines this week.	a determined effort, usually made by several people working together
a joint effort	I couldn't have done it on my own – it was truly **a joint effort**.	done by two or more people
a team effort	The manager congratulated the sales force on their magnificent **team effort**.	done by a group of people
a valiant effort	Meena has made **a valiant effort** to keep up with work despite her illness.	a brave effort in the face of great difficulty
strenuous efforts	**Strenuous efforts** were made to prevent the story from reaching the papers.	attempts requiring a lot of effort or energy
give it one's best shot	Although Kerry didn't succeed in breaking the record, he **gave it his best shot**.	make an attempt that is worthy of admiration
an abortive attempt	They made several **abortive attempts** to climb the mountain.	(formal) failed attempts
physical exertion	I'm exhausted – I'm not used to so much **physical exertion**!	hard physical effort
a hard slog	It was **a hard slog** getting my thesis finished on time but I made it!	(informal) hard work
an uphill struggle	It'll be **an uphill struggle** persuading the boss to make the changes you want.	(informal) a lot of effort with no certainty of success

B Careers advice

Note the collocations in this advertisement for training workshops.

> ### ■ CAREERS WORKSHOPS ■
>
> Our workshops **offer advice** to anyone who is thinking about a new career. We can **provide a solution** to any careers problem. Our training is based on the premise that successful career choice **requires effort**. But if you **devote energy to** making the right decisions, if you **follow our advice** and **heed**[1] **our warnings** we guarantee you will **reap the rewards**[2] of your efforts. Those who **ignore our advice** tend to find their career is **doomed to failure**[3]. So if you have a **desperate desire** to succeed, don't just **pin your hopes on**[4] good luck, come to one of our workshops. Our methods have **stood the test of time**[5]. So come on, you know it's got to be **worth a try**. Sign up for one of our workshops and you won't look back.

[1] listen to	[4] rely on
[2] be rewarded	[5] been proved successful over a long period of time
[3] sure to fail	

 ERROR WARNING You **make an effort**, NOT ~~do~~ an effort.

Exercises

56.1 Answer these questions about collocations from A.

1 'Max is not used to so much physical exertion.'
 What is Max not accustomed to – exercise or intellectual activity?
2 'Doing a degree while you're working will be a hard slog but it'll be worth it.'
 Does the speaker think it will be straightforward for their friend to do a degree?
3 'You mustn't forget that the project requires a joint effort.'
 Is the project the responsibility of one person or more?
4 'It's important that you give things your best shot.'
 Is the speaker encouraging someone to try their hardest or to spend a lot of money?
5 'In 1905 a female revolutionary made an abortive attempt to kill the heir to the throne.'
 Did the revolutionary assassinate the heir?
6 'You'll have to make a team effort if you want to win the trophy!'
 Is the speaker talking about cooperation or competition between the members of the team?

56.2 Complete this paragraph using words from the box in the appropriate form.

desire	determine	devote	doom	heed	ignore
pin	reap	require	shot	strenuous	worth

Last year I decided to set up my own online company. I received conflicting advice about doing so from different people. My friends said it was (1) .... a try and encouraged me to make a (2) .... effort to get it going. My parents said my plans were (3) .... to failure. I wish I hadn't (4) .... my parents' advice. I wouldn't have been in this mess now, had I (5) .... their warnings. I should have known that such a vague business plan was risky, but I suppose I had such a desperate (6) .... to succeed that I thought I might get away with it. It's not because I didn't give it my best (7) .... I made (8) .... efforts to get things going, (9) .... more or less all my energy to getting it started. But in the end it just (10) .... too much effort. I had been (11) .... my hopes on getting enough publicity for my site but that just never happened. So, unfortunately, it seems I will never (12) .... the rewards of my efforts.

56.3 Rewrite each sentence using the word in brackets.

1 It'll be extremely difficult to get your work finished by the deadline. (UPHILL)
2 The appeal of Shakespeare's plays has certainly lasted through the centuries. (TEST)
3 It would be sensible for you to do what he advises. (FOLLOW)
4 No parents can solve all their children's problems. (PROVIDE)
5 After a few months you will begin to benefit from all your hard work. (REAP)
6 Rob tried hard not to fall behind in the race but he just didn't have enough stamina. (VALIANT)
7 Being very active physically certainly works up an appetite. (EXERTION)
8 A lawyer would probably be the best person to advise you. (OFFER)
9 I'm very much hoping I may win a scholarship to the college. (PINNING)
10 Alex has been trying very hard to do better this term. (CONCERTED)

57 Social English

All the collocations in this unit are typical of informal English.

A Conversations

Zita: I was looking for a birthday present for my nephew but I **didn't have much luck**. You don't have any **bright ideas**, do you?

Alan: You could just give him some money or a book token perhaps?

Zita: That **thought occurred to me**, but then it looks like I haven't **gone to any trouble**.

Lisa: I really hate my sister's new boyfriend, Greg. I went out for a meal with them last night and he really **had a go at** her for being late. He **really got to her**[1].

Pat: You're being a bit hard on him. I'm sure he didn't **mean any harm**[2].

Lisa: I'm not so sure about that. Actually, I don't think I **can bear the thought of** ever having to spend time with him again.

Pat: Well, it's not you who is going out with him. I **wouldn't lose any sleep**[3] over it.

Ana: How do you feel about Nina going to work in Tasmania?

Tania: Goodness, **news travels fast!** I didn't realise anyone else knew about it yet. Well, **it came as a bit of a shock** when she first told me. But, **to be brutally honest**, now I've had time to think about it, I'm finding it a bit of **a welcome relief**.

Ana: **I know the feeling**[4]. She can be good fun but she's so sharp-tongued that I have to say I'll be **glad to see the back of**[5] her.

Paul: **Are you up for**[6] going to Sam's leaving party tonight? We're planning to **give him a** really **good send-off**[7].

Adam: I really don't think I can make it. I'm just too tired. **The simple reason** is I've **been on the go**[8] all week and I haven't had a **decent night's sleep** for ages. I just can't **face the thought of** going out tonight.

Paul: Well, that's a **feeble excuse**, if ever there was one.

Adam: I know, and I feel terrible about it because I really like him. I might invite him to my house for dinner next week instead. Would you like to come too?

Paul: Sure, I'll be up for that. **Give me a ring**[9] or **drop me an email** with the details.

[1] made her very upset	[6] would you like to
[2] intend to do or say anything wrong	[7] do something special to say goodbye
[3] wouldn't worry	[8] been very busy
[4] I feel the same	[9] phone me
[5] happy to see someone leave	

B Common errors

The *Cambridge Learner Corpus* shows that candidates for advanced English exams often make mistakes with these collocations.

example of error	correct sentence
I hope I didn't ~~bring~~ you any trouble.	I hope I didn't **cause you any trouble / put you to any trouble.**
I'm ~~very~~ looking forward to seeing you.	I'm **really / very much looking forward** to seeing you soon.
I ~~strongly~~ hope you will apologise.	I **sincerely / very much hope** you will apologise.
I'm ~~very~~ delighted by your invitation.	I'm **absolutely delighted** by your invitation.
It's a ~~big~~ pleasure to hear from you again.	It's a **great pleasure** to hear from you again.

Exercises

57.1 Choose the correct collocation to complete each short dialogue.

1 Jan: Have you decided what to do for Sophie's birthday?
   Gus: No, I'm afraid I haven't had any *decent / bright / welcome* ideas at all.
2 Liz: That wasn't a very nice thing for her to say when we were only trying to *get / make / give* her a good send-off.
   Will: I know, but I'm sure she didn't *mean / lose / drop* any harm.
3 Tom: Are you still *on / up / in* for a night out tonight?
   Sue: No, I'm afraid not. I really need to get a *big / simple / decent* night's sleep tonight.
4 Ros: Congratulations! I hear you've been promoted.
   Ana: Wow! News *goes / comes / travels* fast!
5 Flo: I wish I hadn't *had / got / given* a go at him for forgetting my birthday.
   Ed: Well, I wouldn't lose any *luck / sleep / shock* over it! He's very thick-skinned.
6 Nell: I wish I'd spent less time going out with my friends and more time revising.
   Tim: I *mean / know / have* the feeling. I made exactly the same mistake.

57.2 Correct the collocation errors in these sentences.

1 I'm very delighted with my wonderful present.
2 I'm absolutely shattered – I've been in the go all week.
3 It was a big pleasure to meet you.
4 I'm very looking forward to hearing from you soon.
5 It got as a bit of a shock when I heard that Ellen and Jim had split up.
6 To be strongly honest, I don't think he'll ever make a good teacher.
7 I didn't get much luck when I was trying to find a new dress for the party.
8 I hope I didn't bring your parents any trouble.
9 We strongly hope that you will visit us again soon.
10 The thought happened to me that he might be in some kind of trouble.
11 Please don't come to any trouble on my account!
12 Drop me a ring when you want to be picked up from the station.

57.3 Complete the crossword.

Across

1 I don't want to go there again tomorrow. I can't —— the thought of it.
2 He —— got to me with his nasty comments.
3 Oddly enough, I found it a welcome —— to be living in a much smaller flat.
4 Don't forget to drop us an —— from time to time.
5 I'm glad to be seeing the —— of my old boss.
6 The simple —— why I can't stand him is that he was very rude to my best friend.

Down

1 You can't be too tired to come out tonight. That's a really —— —— .

If you are not often in an English-speaking situation, you may find it hard to learn collocations that are typical of spoken English. English-language films can help. You can download scripts from www.simplyscripts.com. Get the script of your favourite film and note any good collocations from either the first or your favourite scene.

58 Discussing issues

A Political interviews

Interviewer: Despite the fact that you **gave repeated assurances** that you would not raise taxes, you seem to have **broken your promise** and raised five different taxes. Can you **offer an explanation** for why this happened? Haven't you **betrayed the trust** of the voters?

Politician: I **reject that charge** completely. We have **kept our** manifesto **promise** and not raised the basic rate of income tax at all.

Interviewer: Yes, but you've raised indirect taxes instead, so, in effect, you've **gone back on**[1] **your promise** of no tax increases, have you not?

Politician: No. We **made a commitment** with regard to the basic rate of income tax. And I'm happy to **reaffirm**[2] **that commitment** now. The basic rate will remain unchanged …

THESE POLITICIANS! THEY CAN NEVER **GIVE A STRAIGHT**[3] **ANSWER**! THEY'RE GREAT AT **DODGING**[4] **THE QUESTION**.

[1] not kept, or changed in some way
[2] strongly state again
[3] direct and honest
[4] avoiding

B Discussing communication

Tutor: Right. I want to **put** the following **question** to you: do you think the **channels of communication** between politicians and the people are adequate?

(The students are silent.)

Tutor: Well, let me **frame**[1] **the question** differently. Do politicians genuinely communicate directly with the public? Zoë, what do you think?

Zoë: Not really. It's just soundbites on TV, isn't it? They hardly ever meet ordinary people face-to-face. They don't mind **fielding**[2] **questions** from journalists, they're used to that, but that's not the same as **confronting the issues** directly with real people.

Tutor: Well, that's **a fair comment**. But what about politicians who have websites and write blogs? Are these better ways of **establishing communication** with people? Young people don't watch TV; they're on the web all the time.

Paul: **With all due respect**[3], I think you're **missing the point**[4], if you don't mind me saying so. The politicians can still keep their distance. They don't have to **face a grilling**[5] from journalists or anyone if they just have a web page or a blog. In some ways it's worse than media interviews.

Tutor: Fine. I **take your point**[6]. But no politician can meet everyone face-to-face, so communicating with as many people as possible using technology could be seen as more genuinely democratic, couldn't it?

Imelda: Yes, but they become less accountable. If there's a scandal, they just **issue a denial**, and when did you last hear a politican **give a full apology** for getting things wrong? They **enter into a contract** with the people and if they **breach**[7] that **contract** they should be directly accountable, and not just at election time.

Tutor: Right. Okay then. Get into groups and discuss ways in which politicians can be made more directly accountable. Okay? About ten minutes.

[1] formulate   [2] dealing with   [3] used before the speaker disagrees with or criticises the person they are addressing   [4] misunderstanding the idea someone is expressing   [5] face a lot of tough questions   [6] accept that you have a serious opinion worth considering   [7] break

Exercises

58.1 Match words from each box to form collocations and use them in the appropriate form to complete the sentences below.

reject	break	a promise	someone's trust
reaffirm	dodge	a question	a commitment
offer	betray	a charge	an explanation

1 He said he wouldn't tell anyone of my plans but he .... his .... and shared everything with his wife.
2 She was unable to .... any .... for what had happened.
3 I want to .... my .... to your scheme to help poorer families.
4 The Minister .... the .... and denied he had misled the public.
5 Why do politicians always .... the .... and never give an honest answer?
6 The Prime Minister has .... the .... of those who elected her.

58.2 Rewrite the underlined part of each sentence using the words in brackets in the appropriate form in a collocation from the opposite page.

1 The school's Director <u>reassured everyone over and over again</u> that the school was not going to close, despite reports in the press. (GIVE REPEAT)
2 Henry <u>broke his promise</u> to take part in our charity football match. (BACK)
3 Politicians rarely <u>respond directly and honestly</u> to a question. (STRAIGHT)
4 Philip <u>said very firmly that he would</u> support us. (COMMIT)
5 Thank you for <u>doing what you promised to do</u>. (KEEP)
6 The team manager <u>gave quite skilful answers to</u> a number of hostile questions from reporters after the match. (FIELD)
7 We need better <u>ways of communicating</u> with our customers. (CHANNEL)
8 I <u>accept that you have a strong argument</u> but it's a very complex problem. (TAKE)
9 He <u>said he was 100 per cent sorry</u> for his behaviour. (GIVE FULL)

58.3 Read these remarks by different people, and then answer the questions.

Simon: I didn't quite know the best way to ask him what I wanted to know.
Arlene: I took more days off than I was officially allowed and was fired from my job.
  Alex: I had to answer almost an hour of really difficult questions at the interview.
  Finn: I couldn't sign an agreement with the builder because I didn't get the bank loan.
Brona: I didn't see what was important in what the lecturer was saying, did you?

	name
1 Who faced a grilling?	
2 Who missed the point of something?	
3 Who had problems framing a question?	
4 Who breached a contract?	
5 Who didn't enter into a contract with someone?	

58.4 Make six collocations from these words and write a sentence using each.

confront	due	establish	comment	communication	denial
fair	issue	put	issue	question	respect

59 Negative situations and feelings

A Common problems and difficulties

- I had a **nasty shock** when Janelle came home yesterday with a black eye.
- Billy hit his sister in **a fit of jealousy**.
- I feel **sick with worry** / I'm **worried sick** every time Rosie goes out on her motorbike.
- Josh has come up with another **harebrained scheme** to make money. It will no doubt fail, just like the last one. [crazy plan]
- His teacher's unkind remarks have **shattered** Tom's **confidence**. [made him lose all his confidence]
- I **took exception to** my mother-in-law's unfair comments. [objected to, was annoyed by]
- The thought of having visitors to stay for a whole month **fills me with dread**. [makes me feel very upset and worried, about something in the future]
- The little boy **gave vent to his frustration** by scribbling all over the wall. [expressed his feelings of frustration, *give vent to* is only used about negative feelings]
- I tried to persuade her to go to university, but in the end I had to **admit defeat**. [accept that I would not succeed]
- If you **bottle up your feelings**, you'll only **increase your stress levels**. [don't express your feelings; make yourself feel more stressed]

B International problems

> There was an **outpouring of grief**[1] this morning when the death of King Alexander was announced. The country is still **in a state of shock** after his wife, Queen Dorina, died suddenly last month and there is a feeling that the King's own **inconsolable grief** may have **hastened his death**[2]. There is now a **threat of** civil war **hanging over** the country as much of the population has an **intense dislike** of the late King's eldest son.

[1] widespread expression of sadness caused by someone's death [2] made him die sooner

> Many reporters are today criticising the President of Grammaria for a **lapse of judgement**[3] with regard to the **disparaging remarks**[4] he made in a public speech yesterday about the government of Vocabulia. His comments have **fuelled fears**[5] that Vocabulia may retaliate with more than just words. Sources close to the President of Vocabulia said last night that their country has long experience of **suffering** rough treatment **at the hands of** Grammaria and that they had been **left with little alternative** but to take decisive action to put an end to President Tense's habit of **hurling insults** at them. **Taking a** further **sideswipe**[6] at Vocabulia this morning in an interview with morning television, President Tense said that it was a **laughable idea** that a disorganised country like Vocabulia could **pose a threat** of any real significance to the likes of Grammaria. Many suspect, however, that Grammaria may finally **be in for a shock**[7].

[3] poor judgement
[4] unpleasant comments
[5] made people feel more afraid

[6] making a critical remark about one thing while talking about something else
[7] get a nasty surprise

ERROR WARNING   We say **absolutely furious**, NOT ~~very furious~~.

Exercises

59.1 Complete the paragraph using words from A.

Jeremy is always full of (1) .... schemes. I used to try to persuade him out of them but I've long since (2) .... defeat. It only increased my stress (3) .... and it didn't make any difference to his behaviour. Now, if I (4) .... exception to any of his ideas, I just (5) .... up my feelings and let him get on with it. But, if things get really bad, I give (6) .... to my frustration by going to the gym and taking it out on the punch-bag.

59.2 Choose the correct collocation.

1 When asked about his own party's transport policies, the candidate .... a sidesweep at his opponent by mentioning the recent railstrikes.
   A made   B did   C took   D gave
2 The threat of redundancy is .... over everyone at the factory.
   A hanging   B holding   C keeping   D swinging
3 I wish he wouldn't make such unkind and .... remarks.
   A lapse   B disparaging   C inconsolable   D rough
4 I'm afraid you may be .... for a bit of a shock.
   A out   B on   C in   D up
5 Henry never says anything sensible – his ideas are all quite ....
   A laughing   B laughs   C laughter   D laughable
6 I hope you didn't .... exception to any of my comments.
   A find   B take   C make   D put

59.3 Rewrite each sentence using the word in brackets.

1 Catching a bug while he was in hospital meant the old man died sooner than he would otherwise have done. (HASTENED)
2 Cinderella was treated very badly by her wicked stepmother. (SUFFER)
3 A large number of the public expressed its grief when the film star died. (OUTPOURING)
4 The accident has made people feel more afraid with regard to safety on the railways. (FUELLED)
5 Because of their behaviour our only alternative is to boycott their goods. (LEFT)
6 It was unwise of him to act as he did. (LAPSE)
7 I was extremely worried when Dad was having his operation. (SICK)
8 It's better to give vent to your feelings. (BOTTLE)

59.4 Use a dictionary or online corpus to find two ways of completing each of these collocations – one from the unit and one more.

1 a fit of ....
2 to shatter someone's ....
3 to fill someone with ....
4 to hurl .... at someone

5 in a state of ....
6 pose a ....
7 a lapse of ....
8 an intense ....

60 Positive situations and feelings

A Good feelings

example	meaning
You should have a great **sense of achievement** at having reached the last unit of the book.	feeling of having succeeded
John has always had a very strong **sense of purpose** in his life.	feeling of having a clear aim
Kay heaved a **sigh of relief** as she saw Dick step off the plane.	happy feeling that something bad has not happened
Tamara felt a **shiver down her spine** as she heard the orchestra tuning up.	feeling of excitement (or sometimes fear)
As I stood up to speak I felt a **surge of adrenalin**.	a sudden increase in adrenalin
I had a sudden **burst of energy** and decided to spring clean the whole flat.	a feeling of being full of energy
We are all in a **state of euphoria** after our fantastic exam results.	a feeling of excited happiness
I just loved my day at the beauty spa. It was **sheer bliss**.	a feeling of calm happiness

B Interview with a film star

Interviewer: Justine, how did you feel about winning the Oscar?

Justine Fay: I can truly say that my **heart leapt** when I heard the news. Winning an Oscar has been my **lifelong ambition**, so this was a **dream come true**!

Interviewer: And how did your family feel about it?

Justine Fay: My husband is always very supportive. He had **high hopes** that I would win this time. My mother **went into raptures**[1]*! And my son literally **jumped for joy**. He's now **dead keen**[2] to become an actor himself.

Interviewer: And how would you feel about that?

Justine Fay: I've certainly **found happiness** in this profession. But it **doesn't** always **live up to** people's **expectations**[3], of course. It's not as glamorous as it's made out to be.

Interviewer: Do you think it'd **work to his advantage**[4] that both parents are in the business?

Justine Fay: Maybe. But it's more important to have talent, of course. And a lot also depends on **pure luck**, being in the right place at the right time, that sort of thing. But I'd be **cautiously optimistic** about his chances of success, I think.

Interviewer: Does the fact that your career is currently more successful than your husband's cause any tensions at home?

Justine Fay: Not at all. My husband **takes** great **delight in** any success that I have. And I have a **profound admiration** for his work. I hope one day he'll **get the recognition he deserves**. But even if he doesn't, we both know that a great many people **derive** a lot of **pleasure from**[5] his films. He receives a lot of quite moving fan mail in which people **express their admiration** for his work.

Interviewer: Thank you, Justine. It was a **great pleasure**[6] to talk to you.

[1] expressed her extreme pleasure and excitement
[2] (informal) very keen
[3] isn't as good as expected
[4] be of benefit to him
[5] (formal) find great enjoyment in
[6] NOT a ~~big~~ pleasure

* This expression is very strong and effusive and sounds a little extreme. This is appropriate for an Oscar-winning film star but you should probably take care not to over-use it yourself.

Exercises

60.1 Correct the collocation errors in these sentences.

1 The whole country seems to be in a place of euphoria after winning the World Cup.
2 I heaved a breath of relief when I heard Joe had finally passed his driving test.
3 As the starting whistle blew, a jump of adrenalin helped me get off to a good start.
4 I still always feel a shake down my spine when I set off on a long journey.
5 It was a difficult climb but we had a marvellous emotion of achievement as we stood at the top.
6 Agreeing to do a bit of overtime could walk to your advantage, you know.
7 Rick seems to have lost his idea of purpose.
8 As winter ends I always seem to feel a break of energy.
9 It was clean luck that the answer suddenly came to me in the middle of the exam.
10 I don't think those engineers ever got the cognition they deserved.

60.2 Complete each sentence using a word from the opposite page.

1 Parents .... more pleasure from their children's success than from their own.
2 I had .... hopes of this job but it hasn't .... up to my expectations.
3 I hope that all your dreams will .... true.
4 In his article the critic .... considerable admiration for the poet's early work.
5 The audience .... into raptures as the group started to play their first ever hit.
6 My .... leapt when I saw that at last I had an email from Mark.
7 My grandmother .... great delight in creating a beautiful garden.
8 We are cautiously .... that Pauline will get the job she's applied for.
9 It was a .... pleasure to meet you. I hope our paths will cross again soon.
10 The children jumped for .... when they saw their aunt at the door.

60.3 Answer these questions using a dictionary or online corpus if necessary.

1 What else can *come true* as well as a *dream*?
2 What can be *lifelong* as well as an *ambition*?
3 With what words apart from *keen*, can *dead* be used as an informal adverb to mean *extremely*?
4 With what words apart from *bliss*, can *sheer* be used as an adjective to mean *complete*?
5 What can be described as *profound* as well as *admiration*?

60.4 Answer these questions in full sentences.

1 Where do you think people are more likely to find happiness – in a relationship or a career?
2 Would you say you had a profound admiration for anyone? If so, who and why?
3 What has happened to you that can be described as a matter of pure luck?
4 Do you derive more pleasure from music or from reading?
5 When did you last experience a sense of achievement?

 As this is the final unit in the book, take this opportunity now to look back at the units you have covered and note your favourite collocations from each unit.

Key

Unit 1

1.1
1 adhere to your principles
2 arouse someone's interest
3 blond hair
4 come up with a suggestion
5 flatly contradict
6 fundamentally different
7 go on an economy drive
8 heavy rain
9 lead a seminar
10 a lick of paint
11 play the stock market
12 words of wisdom

1.2 The underlined words in these sentences can sometimes be changed in other ways but the answers given reflect collocations in B.
1 mistakes
2 wider
3 gain
4 depart from
5 create

1.3 This is the most appropriate way to complete this exercise although some other collocations are also possible, as indicated.
1 Our new family hotel is set in a **secluded** location and all the rooms have **stylish** furnishings and **breathtaking** views over the surrounding countryside.
(*Breathtaking* could also go with *location* but *secluded* could not go with *views*.)
2 Visitors will enjoy the **relaxing** atmosphere in either of our **spacious** dining rooms, both serving **delicious** food to residents and non-residents.
(*Relaxing* could also perhaps go with *dining rooms* but *spacious* could not go with *atmosphere*.)
3 We organise tours to **picturesque** surrounding villages where you'll have the opportunity to take some **stunning** photographs and sample the **mouth-watering** local cuisine.
(*Stunning* could go with *villages* but *picturesque* could not go with *photographs*.)

1.4
1 a Passengers must not <u>alight from the bus</u> while it is <u>in motion</u>. F
   b Passengers must not get off the bus while it is moving. N
2 a Let's <u>grab a bite</u> before we <u>get down to work</u>. I
   b Let's have something to eat before we start work. N
3 a SFTS has the right to bring the agreement to an end with three months' notice. N
   b SFTS <u>reserves the right</u> to <u>terminate the agreement</u> with three months' notice. F
4 a She thinks her boyfriend is planning to <u>pop the question</u> tonight. I
   b She thinks her boyfriend is planning to ask her to marry him tonight. N

1.5 The **blond-haired** boy said he had joined the English class to **make** some new friends. He also said that he wanted to learn about collocations because it would be of **great** importance in helping him to **make** fewer mistakes when writing in English.

Unit 2

2.1
1 a broad accent
2 in broad agreement
3 mitigating circumstances
4 mitigating factors
5 auburn hair
6 deliriously happy
7 a broad smile
8 a picturesque location
9 adjourn a meeting
10 a picturesque town
11 adjourn a trial
12 inclement weather

2.2 1 Melissa has quite a **broad** Scottish accent.
2 **Inclement** weather led to the cancellation of the President's garden party.
3 We were all **deliriously** happy when we heard we'd won the award.
4 Their new home was in a very **picturesque** location.
5 Because there were **mitigating** circumstances, the judge let him off with a warning.
6 I think we should **adjourn** the meeting **till/until** tomorrow.
7 She had a **broad** smile on her face when she arrived.
8 She has lovely **auburn** hair.
9 I think we're **in broad** agreement as to what should be done.

2.3 *Example answers:*

	stronger	weaker
1 extremely hot / tired / easy / expensive		✓
2 make / require / be an effort	✓	
3 cancel a class / a meeting / a match / an agreement		✓
4 deliver a letter / a warning / a baby / goods		✓
5 earn / make / scrape a living	✓	

2.4 *Possible example sentences:*
I felt deliriously happy when I passed all my exams.
I must make an effort to learn more collocations.
It's difficult nowadays to make a living as a small shopkeeper.
We had to cancel the match because of the rain.

Follow-up
Ask your teacher to check your answers if you are not confident about them.

Unit 3

3.1 The collocations are:
1 disease spreads   5 standards slip
2 evidence suggests   6 teeth chatter
3 opportunity arises   7 wind howls
4 smoke rises   8 withstand pressure

3.2 1 evidence suggests
2 wind; howling
3 withstand; pressure
4 smoke rising
5 teeth; chattering
6 standards; slipped
7 opportunity; arises
8 disease; spreading

3.3 1 pass up
2 draw up
3 take it easy for a while
4 withstand
5 snippets
6 barrage
7 a stroke of
8 spate
9 put the past behind her

3.4 *Author's answers:*
1 My husband, of course!
2 You could tell them to drive more carefully or you could say that you want to get out.
3 It depends on my mood. A gentle breeze is pleasant but a strong wind can be very exhilarating.
4 Sometimes I do. But then I have to remember to be careful not to leave my diary lying around.

3.5
1 idle	3 mounting	5 foaming	7 plain
2 vain	4 mounting	6 burst	8 miserably

Unit 4

4.1 *Possible answers:*
1 cast (as verb)   cast a light / a shadow / a look / doubt / aspersions / suspicion / votes / a spell
2 application   letter of application / to send off an application / to fill in an application form / the application of research / to have a particular application to
3 utter (as adjective)   confusion / rubbish / chaos / nonsense / waste of time / bliss
4 absolutely   absolutely silent / absolutely nothing / absolutely disgusting / absolutely delicious / absolutely loathe / absolutely adore
5 release (as verb)   a prisoner / the handbrake / gases / an album

4.2
1 cast aspersions on
2 has no relevance for/to
3 paid tribute to
4 set to work
5 rendered; speechless
6 An indeterminate number of
7 exceeded (all) our (wildest) expectations
8 I have some niggling doubts

4.3 *Author's answers:*
cast a concert (7)   cast a groan (0)   cast a play (382,000)   cast a smile (2710)
These results indicate that *cast a smile* and *cast a play* are both collocations. *Cast a smile* is much less frequent than *cast a play* because it is a more literary expression. *Cast a groan* and *cast a concert* are clearly not collocations.

4.4 Note that each time you do this you will get a different set of sentences. However you are likely to note these points:
Aspersions almost always collocates with *cast*.
Indeterminate often collocates with *number* and *age*.
Niggling often collocates with *doubt*, *problem* and *fear*.
Tribute often collocates with *pay*, but also with *great* and *fitting*.

4.5 *Author's answers:*
1 teaching – to mark homework, gifted children, to sit an exam
The one bad thing about teaching is all the homework you have to mark.
Teaching is more of a challenge if you have gifted children and children with learning difficulties in the same class.
At the end of my teacher-training course I had to sit a number of exams.
2 going to the cinema – spectacular car chase, to win an Oscar, to play the starring role
Cate Blanchett played the starring role in the last film I saw and she won an Oscar for her performance.
In all James Bond films there is at least one spectacular car chase.

3 languages – irregular verbs, feminine nouns, to extend your vocabulary
   Most irregular verbs in English are ones in everyday use.
   Romance languages, for example, distinguish between masculine and feminine nouns and this can be a major problem for students whose first language is English.
   Reading is a very good way of extending your vocabulary in any language.
4 touring round France – to catch a ferry, delicious food, historical sites
   Ferries from England to France are so frequent that there is usually no problem catching one.
   France is world-famous for its delicious food.
   I usually prefer looking at historical sites to lazing on a beach.
5 steak and salad – rare steak, to chop parsley, to crush garlic
   I prefer my steak rare.
   If you chop the parsley for the sauce, I'll crush some garlic.
6 *The Bad Mother's Handbook* – adopted daughter, to file for divorce, light reading
   Nan didn't tell anyone that Karen was her adopted daughter.
   Fewer couples filed for divorce last year than in the previous ten years.
   Light reading is particularly suitable for travelling or when you just want to relax and not think too much.

Unit 5

5.1
1 gift for languages
2 take a boat
3 grab a seat
4 turn my thoughts to
5 win the battle
6 make a difference
7 underestimate the value of
8 pending; result
9 newly qualified

5.2
to jump at the / pass up the / get the / stand a / be in with a chance
to face a challenge / to rise to the challenge / to pose a challenge / a direct challenge / a serious challenge

5.3
The correct collocations are *learn by heart* and *miss a chance*.

5.4
Author's answers:
1 Three milestones in my life that I have already passed include graduating from university, getting my first job and getting married.
2 I am fully qualified as a teacher.
3 Typical sources of income are wages or salaries, income from investments, rental income and business profits.
4 The toughest challenge I have ever faced was possibly completing my doctoral thesis on time.
5 Someone providing simultaneous translation needs to be bilingual and to have excellent powers of concentration.
6 Personal letters, photos and old diaries have sentimental value for me.

5.5
1 Make
2 Get
3 commit
4 made
5 do
6 avoid
7 Make
8 possible
9 made
Ideally you would tick all the ideas, as they are all good ways of improving your knowledge and use of collocations.

Unit 6

6.1 1 I feel <u>dead tired</u> all the time. (I)
I feel very/extremely tired all the time.
2 We were all <u>bored stupid</u> by the poetry reading. (I)
We were all very/extremely/utterly bored by the poetry reading.
3 Currency exchange <u>offices are located</u> in the arrivals lounge. (F)
There are exchange offices in the arrival lounge.
4 She <u>conducted a study</u> of single-parent family units. (F)
She did a study of single-parent families.
5 She <u>did her degree</u> in London and found work there in 2001. (N)
6 I just got the latest software so my computer is <u>bang up-to-date</u>. (I)
I have just bought the latest software and so my computer is fully up-to-date.
7 <u>Affix</u> a passport-size <u>photograph</u> to the application form. (F)
Stick a passport photo on the application form.
8 Jake <u>asked</u> his tutor <u>for an extension to complete his dissertation</u>. (N)

You may find it useful to look up some of these expressions in a good dictionary to see what else they collocate with. Paperwork, for example, can be bang up-to-date but a car is unlikely to be described as such.

6.2 1 This is <u>breaking news</u> here on Global TV Extra. J
2 These are the songs that are <u>climbing the charts</u> this week. E
3 There are <u>tons of good reasons</u> for not studying law. IC
4 Visitors must <u>keep to the designated areas</u> at all times. N
5 In any such case, customers shall <u>forfeit the right</u> to compensation. L
6 <u>Fuel consumption</u> may vary according to model and <u>road conditions</u>. T
7 I'll <u>give you a ring</u> after dinner. IC
8 The Minister will tour Asia in a <u>bid to win support</u> for the plan. J
9 Joss Engold stars in the <u>latest blockbuster</u> from Star Studios. E
10 A microchip is a <u>miniaturised electronic circuit</u>. T
11 Please <u>restrict your use</u> of the fitness machines to 20 minutes. N
12 A witness may be asked to <u>testify</u> for a second time. L

6.3 1 do
2 running
3 come
4 take
5 getting
6 feel
7 write
8 clear

6.4 1 presented   2 elevated   3 exhibiting   4 complained   5 inability

Unit 7

7.1 1 The presidential visit **kept everyone on their toes**.
2 Rosetta **shouldered the blame** for the failure of the project.
3 I don't think Greg will ever win Rosie's heart; it's time he **faced the facts**.
4 The company had done so well that year that it agreed to **foot the bill** for a staff night out.
5 I'm glad I'm not **heading** this team.
6 Carola **has an eye for** a bargain.

7.2   1 A decrease in savings is likely to go hand in hand with inflation as people will have less money available for saving.
2 If a relationship hits the rocks, it is the end of that relationship.
3 If you say someone is hopping mad, you mean that they are very angry.
4 No, not necessarily. If you run into difficulties or trouble, it just means that you encounter them or have them. The verb *run* here doesn't have any associations with speed.
5 You'd call a magazine dealing with celebrity gossip light reading. A weighty tome would only be used to refer to a book that is long and has difficult content – unless it is being used ironically, of course. So you might joke to a friend who is reading a celebrity magazine, 'I can see you're reading your usual weighty tome!'
6 If you talk about facing the facts, the facts are likely to be unpleasant.

7.3   1a Jill got the job very easily.
1b Jill got the job – but we don't know whether it was easy for her to get it or not.

2a Pat is in charge of the project team.
2b Pat is supporting the project team / giving the project team her support.

3a Dad very quickly drew the wrong conclusion.
3b Dad drew the wrong conclusion – but we don't know whether he did so quickly or not.

4a Rod left the room feeling happy and carefree.
4b Rod left the room feeling sad and despondent.

5a I've got no chance of winning at all.
5b I've got a very small chance of winning.

7.4   1 driving
2 eye
3 burden
4 slim
5 weighty
6 heading

7.5   1 The metaphor here is based on the word *run*. An athlete literally runs in a race. But if he metaphorically runs into trouble that simply means that he has a problem. The problem might not be connected with running in any way.
2 The metaphor is based on the connection between being fat and dieting. Diet pills are intended to help people lose weight but if they have a fat chance of success, they are unlikely to succeed.
3 The play on words is based on the idea of ballet dancers literally dancing on their toes and the figurative meaning of the expression *keep someone on their toes* which is to keep someone energetic and concentrated.
4 The play on words connects the word *foot*, used here metaphorically to mean pay, with its literal meaning of the part of the body where we wear shoes.
5 The play on words is based on the fact that *hop* is a verb closely associated with the movement of rabbits (and frogs). The new legislation must be something that makes rabbit owners angry e.g. a tax on owning rabbits.

Unit 8

8.1   blatantly obvious   stinking rich
downright rude   thoroughly ashamed
spotlessly clean   wildly inaccurate

8.2   1 stinking rich   4 spotlessly clean
2 blatantly obvious   5 wildly inaccurate
3 downright rude   6 thoroughly ashamed

8.3
1. wildly exaggerated
2. highly recommended
3. dead easy
4. loosely based on
5. faintly/mildly ridiculous
6. completely/totally/entirely dependent
7. thoroughly enjoyed
8. mildly surprised
9. absolutely delighted
10. slightly different

8.4
1. greatly appreciate
2. utterly ridiculous
3. terribly/extremely/incredibly difficult
4. awfully/extremely/incredibly sweet
5. deeply/slightly offensive
6. awfully/terribly/extremely/incredibly lonely
7. totally/entirely/completely separate
8. a highly educated
9. awfully/terribly/incredibly/extremely busy
10. terribly/incredibly/extremely expensive

8.5
1. Correct
2. Incorrect. We say *greatly appreciated*.
3. Incorrect. We say *strongly influenced*.
4. Correct

Unit 9

9.1
1. Correct
2. Correct
3. The company director **made** a formal apology for his earlier comments.
4. The manager had to make a number of changes to office procedures in order to **make** all the improvements he had planned for the company.
5. My sister **made** all the arrangements for the party.

9.2
1 habit	6 offer
2 room	7 discovery
3 enemies	8 attempt
4 success	9 stand
5 acquaintance	10 calculations

9.3
1. The Green Party plans to **stage** a major protest against the government's new farming policy. (more formal)
2. Tessa helped me to **run up** some lovely cushion covers for my new flat. (less formal)
3. I regret to inform you that several clients have **lodged** complaints about your conduct. (more formal)
4. You won't **create** a good first impression if you arrive late for your interview. (more formal)
5. It won't take me long to **rustle up** a meal for the children. (less formal)
6. Do you expect your business to **turn in** a profit this year? (less formal)

9.4
1. At the meeting the chairman made a rather interesting proposal.
2. I hope we can make an/our escape soon as I'm terribly tired.
3. I'm reading a fascinating book about how new words and phrases are coined to express new social and technical needs.
4. We changed the layout of the hall to create a more relaxed atmosphere for the yoga class.

5 I made several attempts to phone the company at the weekend.
6 Kim made a very positive contribution to the discussion.
7 The service was poor but I wouldn't go so far as to lodge a formal complaint.
8 I first made Roger's acquaintance on a train.

Unit 10

10.1
1 speaking	6 told
2 told	7 say
3 saying	8 talk
4 talking	9 speaking
5 speak	

10.2
1 notified
2 impart its wisdom
3 protested his innocence
4 professed ignorance
5 divulge his sources
6 pronounced him
7 declared Magda Karlson the winner of
8 disseminate information

10.3
1 Do you think I managed to **get** the message across in my speech?
2 Needless to say, he didn't **say** a word to his parents about what had happened.
3 You can't chew gum and **speak** properly at the same time.
4 He refused to **give** his reasons for turning down our invitation.
5 She was devastated when we **broke** the news to her.
6 Correct
7 I really like this documentary maker, he **talks** a lot of sense.
8 At the beginning of your dissertation you must **state** your goals clearly.

10.4
1 protestation(s) (The noun *protest* is not accurate here because it carries a meaning of opposition. *Protestation*, however, means a declaration, which echoes the meaning of protest in the collocation *protest one's innocence*, meaning to declare one's innocence.)
2 statement
3 dissemination
4 notification
5 declaration

10.5 *Possible answers:*
1 declare **war on**, declare **independence**, declare **support for**
2 impart **bad news**, impart **facts**, impart **a secret**
3 divulge **information**, divulge **secrets**, divulge **confidential details**

Unit 11

11.1 1 for   2 up with   3 up   4 to   5 up to   6 by   7 down   8 in with

11.2
1 didn't live up to	5 abide by
2 come up with	6 adhere to
3 jot down	7 fit in with
4 take up	8 filed for

11.3 1 dip into them   2 adhere to them   3 keep it up   4 see them off

11.4
1 Everyone **burst** into laughter when she told the story.
2 We had a run along the beach to work **up** an appetite before lunch.
3 The police have said they intend to **come** down heavily on anyone carrying an offensive weapon at the match.

4 Do you think you could free **up** some time to have a quick meeting this afternoon?
5 The police acted on a **tip**-off and managed to avert a possible disaster. (A *rip-off* is a colloquial word meaning something that is not worth what you paid for it, e.g. That meal was an absolute rip-off.)
6 I hope the party will live **up** to your expectations.
7 We sat on our hotel balcony, soaking **up** the atmosphere of the carnival.
8 Tanya quickly saw **off** her opponent in the semi-final and now goes on to the final.

11.5 *Possible answers:*
1 I'll **keep it up** by watching English-language TV and reading news items on the Internet.
2 The last Bond film didn't **live up to my expectations**.
3 I might be tempted to **dip into my savings** for a special holiday.
4 I'd try to **come up with an alternative** means of transport.
5 I'd do my best to **fit in with the plans** they had already made.
6 I sometimes find it very hard to **adhere to my principles**.

Unit 12

12.1
1 My husband and I do a job share.
2 Circulate the report to all members of staff.
3 Kazuki has been happier since he went part-time.
4 I hope it won't be necessary to lay off many of our staff.
5 It's not easy to make a living as an actor.
6 Meeting people is the best aspect of the job.
7 Marian was the last person to join the staff in our company.
8 Anna will be going on maternity leave next month.
9 Try to build up a good network of contacts.
10 We've had a ridiculous volume of work this month.

12.2 1 number 2 holds 3 offer 4 change 5 open 6 take up 7 right 8 take

12.3
1 The recession meant that the company had to **lay off some workers/staff** or **lay some workers/staff off.**
2 Your family should really **take priority over** your work.
3 Nita soon **moved up the ladder** at work.
4 Bill hates his new boss so much that I think he'll soon **hand in his resignation**.
5 Vic earns **a good living** as a freelance journalist.
6 I need to **put together my CV** before I apply for jobs.
7 My father always wanted to **practise medicine** in a rural community.

12.4 George makes a **living** as a sports reporter on a local newspaper but he is under **considerable / a lot of** pressure at work at the moment. He's had far too much work to **do** recently. He's been put on a fast-**track** scheme for promotion and they're really pushing him. It's so hard that he's thinking of handing **in** his resignation and going **freelance**. It wouldn't be easy but I'm sure he'd soon **carve** a niche for himself as a sports journalist.

Unit 13

13.1
1 to pencil a meeting in	5 to fit the job description
2 a daunting task	6 wrongfully dismissed
3 to master new skills	7 to lose your livelihood
4 to take up references	8 professional misconduct

13.2
1 land	4 sweated
2 fitted (US English: fit)	5 were / would be
3 running	6 take

13.3 1 stay the course   4 relieved of his duties
         2 get the sack   5 take industrial action / stage a strike
         3 a living wage   6 narrow the list down

13.4 *Author's answers:*
1 I suppose that copying materials and collating pages could be called menial work.
2 I certainly hope that it will.
3 As someone who does a lot of freelance work, I work a lot of unsocial hours. I get up early to work at my computer, for example. But it is my own choice and not imposed on me by an employer, so I don't mind it. The plus side is that I can have a long lunch with a friend whenever I want to.
4 When I was working at a language school, there was quite a high turnover of staff as teachers often used to go off and work in different countries.
5 When I was teaching in a language school, I often did overtime – taking students on excursions and so on. It was paid.
6 No, I haven't. I feel superstitious about it. I worry that if I pretend to be ill then I will soon become ill in reality.
7 I haven't taken industrial action but I think I might consider it if colleagues were being wrongly treated.
8 Yes, it is. Getting a book ready for publication is very much a team effort.
9 As a freelancer I sometimes have a heavy workload and sometimes I don't. It can be quite difficult to spread my work in a balanced way.

Unit 14

14.1 1 Opinions are **divided** on the issue of single-sex schools and there are sound arguments on both sides of the case.
2 I believe that the government will win another term in office but my girlfriend takes a different **view**. [or … has a different opinion.]
3 I **honestly/really** think that you'd be making a serious mistake if you took that job.
4 I don't believe it's a foregone **conclusion** that the larger company will win the contract.
5 People are gradually **becoming** aware of the problem of climate change.
6 You should bear in **mind** that your visitors will be tired after their long flight.
7 I've got a **rough** idea of what I want to say in my essay but I haven't planned it properly yet.
8 Increasing numbers of people today subscribe to the theory that small is beautiful.

14.2 1 laterally   2 error   3 grasped   4 pass   5 poor   6 firm

14.3 1 It's unwise to **jump to conclusions** about people's motives.
2 **It's common knowledge** that Ellie has been taking money from the till.
3 I agreed to help him (though it was) **against my better judgement**.
4 I'm afraid your decisions show **a lack of judgement**.
5 We have to decide when to have the party. Can you **give it some thought**?
6 I think you are **judging him too harshly**. Remember he's only 18.
7 Surprisingly, there's a **widespread belief** that left-handed people are more intelligent.

14.4 1 a fertile land / egg / soil / environment / mind / area
2 to fuel resentment / a feeling of … / a heating system / a vehicle (the verb is used mainly in the passive when referring to vehicles) / a debate / desire / gossip
3 to wrestle with a decision / your conscience (Note that this verb collocates with only a small number of words.)
4 a nagging fear / voice / pain / sense / feeling

14.5 The common collocations are *personal conviction* and *harshly treated*.

Unit 15

15.1
1 True
2 False. A company wants to meet its targets.
3 True
4 True
5 False. A company has failed if it has to call in the receivers.
6 False. A company will feel more secure with wider profit margins.

15.2
1	receivers	5	line
2	points	6	production
3	books	7	dividends
4	sense	8	profits

15.3
1 The company is pleased to report a **substantial** increase in profits over the last quarter.
2 The new health and safety committee is to be **chaired** by a retired doctor.
3 There is increasingly **fierce** competition between airline companies. (Competition can also be described as *intense* or *stiff*.)
4 The company's exports to Japan **saw/experienced/showed** considerable growth over the last decade.
5 The sales figures for March show a **slight** decrease on those for February.
6 Our sales in the domestic market are certain to **see/experience/show** a rise next year.
7 Last year sales were three times **greater** in Europe than in Australia.
8 We feel that this proposal **makes** considerable business sense. (Notice that although you *do* business, something *makes* business sense.)
9 Although we need to reduce our costs, it's important we **maintain** the quality that our reputation is built on.
10 Business leaders hope new government policies will **stimulate** growth (or be a stimulus to growth).

15.4
1 The Managing Director of a company might call an emergency meeting when there is some kind of crisis affecting the company – a strike, for example, or a major increase in the cost of raw materials or fuel.
2 A sports car company is likely to have young people in their twenties as their target market.
3 Shareholders would be pleased if their company announced record profits because it would be likely to increase the value of their investment and to lead to higher dividends.
4 Students and governments set themselves objectives.
5 A business would have to allocate part of its budget to staff, research and development and raw materials, for example.
6 A company might try to stimulate growth in demand for its products by increasing its advertising.

Unit 16

16.1
1 Have you ever made a **complaint** to the management about the food in a restaurant?
2 I hate **going** shopping on Saturdays as the town is so crowded then.
3 If you want your shopping delivered, you can **place** your order with us online or by phone.
4 We **carried out/did** a large-scale customer survey before developing our new product range.
5 **Online** shopping is proving increasingly popular.
6 I was surprised by the **poor** quality of the acting in that film we saw last night.

16.2
1	value	6	fuss
2	satisfied	7	handled
3	healthy	8	conform
4	prompt	9	elsewhere
5	hold	10	come

16.3 1 regular   5 providing
        2 refund   6 top
        3 take   7 grounds
        4 custom

16.4

```
¹P U ²R P O S E
      E
     ³G R O U N D S
      U
⁴F U L L
      A
     ⁵S T A N D A R D
      I
    ⁶H O N O U R
      N
⁷D I S C O U N T
```

Unit 17

17.1 1 You graduate from university.
       2 mature students
       3 (prestigious) seats of learning
       4 distinguished scholars or leading authorities (in their fields)
       5 gifted children
       6 straight A students

17.2 1 We were all very impressed by the student's mental agility.
       2 My grandmother is very intelligent but she's had little formal education.
       3 I've never found it easy to learn scientific formulae by heart.
       4 I'd love to study medicine there but it's very hard to get a place.
       5 For the first year Shakespeare exam we had to read six set texts.
       6 I am so proud of you for managing to get full marks.
       7 Your work is not too bad but there is certainly still room for improvement.
       8 Your little girl has shown herself to be a very quick learner.
       9 The test has been designed to enable pupils to demonstrate their ability.
      10 I hope to study there but may not be able to meet the entry requirements.

17.3 1 truant   4 natural   7 attend
       2 wanders   5 marked   8 requirements
       3 shows   6 win   9 enrol

17.4 *Author's answers:*
       1 English, maths and science.
       2 The universities of Oxford and Cambridge.
       3 Yes. I once signed up for a Spanish evening class but only went to two lessons.
       4 I'd love to read History of Art.
       5 The academic year begins in September and ends in July.
       6 Different universities and departments have different entry requirements and you have to fulfil whatever their specific requirements are.

17.5 *Possible answers:*
       1 power   2 club   3 support   4 work record

Unit 18

18.1
1 undertake
2 presented
3 reviews
4 provided
5 indicates
6 test
7 covers
8 tackles
9 puts

18.2
1 The research ethics are described in the university's research manual.
2 You need to make an in-depth critique of the arguments.
3 You need to do background reading.
4 You do the analysis in order to find out whether the data support your hypothesis. (remember: try to avoid saying *prove* a hypothesis)
5 All the interviewees were people who had first-hand knowledge of the situation.
6 It is impossible to give a full explanation of the decline of agriculture in the 1960s.

18.3 Order of events:
1 Select a topic.
2 Form a working hypothesis.
3 Make the case for studying the topic in the introduction.
4 Write a critical analysis of previous studies.
5 Lay out your results in tables and diagrams.
6 Submit your report.

18.4
1 The **thrust** of Torsten's argument is that public transport can never replace the private car.
2 Economists **formulated** a new theory of inflation in the late 1980s.
3 It is important that we should **confront** the issue of climate change immediately.
4 In her essay, she put forward a **vigorous** defence of the European Union constitution.
5 I shall not attempt to give an **exhaustive** account of population growth in this essay.
6 The article does not back **up** its conclusions with enough convincing evidence.

Unit 19

19.1 1 surprise   2 throw   3 dined   4 appearance   5 sprung   6 special   7 night

19.2 1 made   2 flying   3 stick to   4 calls   5 find   6 quality   7 social
8 pay   9 played

19.3
1 We could go clubbing later. (more informal)
2 The restaurant has a convivial atmosphere. (more formal)
3 London is playing host to the Olympics in 2012. (more formal)
4 Her life is a social whirl. (more formal)
5 I have to attend a formal function on Thursday. (more formal)
6 We invite you to join the festivities at the opening of the Arts Festival. (more formal)
7 Grapsley Park is the perfect venue for an outdoor concert. (more formal)

19.4 *Author's answers:*
1 eating out
2 plain food, as long as it's cooked properly
3 a barbecue with friends
4 I like both, but giving a dinner party can be a lot of work.
5 I much prefer playing the host.
6 definitely a whirlwind visit! Guests are always best when they don't stay long!

Unit 20

20.1
1 It can be hard to carry **on** a serious conversation in a noisy room.
2 He finds it very difficult to open his **heart** and talk about his feelings to anyone.
3 I don't like discussing things with people who always want to **win** any argument.
4 My mother always used to tell me not to **spread** unkind rumours.
5 I usually find it better not to get **drawn** into an argument with Paul.
6 We had a very enjoyable time just sitting in the park enjoying some **idle** chatter.
7 I managed to resist all his attempts to engage me **in** conversation.
8 I've never talked to him much – we've done no more than **exchange** pleasantries.

20.2
1 lost	5 bring
2 broached	6 drop
3 take	7 tough
4 strong	8 hold

20.3
1 juicy gossip	5 four-letter word
2 broad generalisations	6 tough question
3 exchange news	7 rash promise
4 take seriously	8 opening gambit

20.4
1 Please drop the subject immediately.
2 Sam has a habit of making empty promises.
3 You must take the lab's safety regulations seriously.
4 It's better not to overstate your case.
5 Could we please change the subject?
6 Did you hear the rumours (that were) flying around about your boss last year?
7 There is rather a lot of bad/foul/strong language in the play. (*Foul* is the strongest of these alternatives.)
8 Such broad generalisations tend to be rather meaningless.
9 His opening gambit took me by surprise.
10 The children bombarded me with questions about my trip.

Unit 21

21.1
1 I	5 C
2 E	6 A. Note that the expression *to go to the polls* is often used, particularly in newspapers, to mean take part in an election.
3 B	
4 F. Note the collocation *to heal a rift*, meaning that a harmonious relationship has been re-established following a break due to a serious disagreement.	7 G
	8 D

21.2
1 delivered; speech   2 broker; agreement   3 impose; censorship
4 prime-time television   5 held; conference   6 act; go-between   7 reach agreement

21.3
1 The President has finally bowed to public pressure to hold a referendum.
2 Early this morning the Eco-democratic Party proclaimed victory in the election. (*announced its victory* would also be possible)
3 The police detective discovered the clue which led to the recovery of the stolen jewels.
4 The police will not call off the search until the child has been found.
5 We were on holiday when the recent political troubles broke out.
6 The police are carrying out a nationwide search (or a countrywide search) for the missing boy.
7 The two parties will try to negotiate a settlement today.
8 Today thousands of students held a demonstration / held demonstrations against the increase in fees.

21.4
1 In the first sentence, the outcome of the rally will show whether the army is strong or not. In the second sentence, the rally is proof of the army's strength.
2 The clues in the first sentence are more important than those in the second.
3 The reward for the cat in the second sentence is large.
4 The verb *deliver* suggests either a more formal situation for the speech itself or a more formal context for reporting about the speech than is suggested by *make*.
5 In the first sentence, the countries are going to talk for the first time.
In the second sentence they have made an agreement.

Follow-up
Possible collocations:
    to hold a meeting / a conversation / an election
    to broker a deal / a ceasefire
    to reach / come to an agreement
    a sizeable / narrow / large / vast majority

Unit 22

22.1
1 The Committee, with one **dissenting** voice, voted to take a firm **stance** on the issue.
2 It was only a **throwaway** comment but it has **excited** a lot of speculation.
3 As new evidence **emerges** of government involvement in the scandal, people are beginning to question the Prime Minister's public **pronouncements** on the affair.
4 The prince refused **point-blank** to provide a **detailed** account of his actions that night.
5 The Minister was accused of **misleading** the electorate when he said that very few migrant workers had been **given** leave to stay in the country.

22.2
1 disorderly	3 explanation	5 flatly	7 disclosures
2 clarify	4 statement	6 permission	8 re-opened

22.3
1 vociferous opponent
2 gauge (public/people's) reaction
3 passionate entreaty
4 regular updates
5 air their grievances
6 took issue
7 declined to comment
8 critically ill
9 abject apology

Unit 23

23.1
1 This year's National Day festival celebrates 50 years of independence.
2 In this region we have a rich tradition of poetry, music and dance.
3 A group of children performed a traditional dance from the region.
4 This year's festival represents a break with tradition, as it will be held in May.
5 The tradition of carol singing dates back hundreds of years.
6 The people are determined to uphold the tradition, despite opposition.
7 The town holds its annual festival in spring.
8 Our village has a proud tradition of giving food to older villagers every new year.

23.2
1 All the men wore traditional **dress** consisting of green jackets and white trousers.
2 The festival **marks** the beginning of the Celtic summer.
3 The festival is part of the region's cultural **heritage**.
4 Hundreds of people, locals and tourists, join **in** the festivities.
5 The annual 'Day of the Horse' **falls** on 30 March this year.
6 Everyone in the village was in **festive** mood as the annual celebrations began.
7 The average age at which couples tie the **knot** is rising.
8 This region has a **rich** tradition of folk singing and dancing.
9 Getting joined **in** matrimony is a significant reason for celebration.
10 The area is famous for observing a number of age-old/long-standing traditions.

23.3 1 Erik
2 Evan
3 Alicia
4 Monica
5 Brona

23.4 1 (b) married
2 wedded bliss
3 the knot
4 *Toast* used uncountably means bread made brown and crisp by heating it. *Making a toast* (countable) means offering an expression of good wishes or respect for someone which involves holding up and then drinking from a glass after a short speech.
5 pre-wedding nerves (one can also say *pre-wedding jitters*)
6 be joined in matrimony
7 to make a toast / to toast someone
8 informal

Unit 24

24.1 1 These vitamins have been **clinically** proven to protect the body from winter viruses.
2 Our **tasty** snacks cost only 24p.
3 Enjoy a weekend of **sheer** luxury at the Highlands Health Hotel.
4 We manage a number of **exclusive** restaurants in Paris and New York.
5 Our new shampoo will subtly bring out the **natural** highlights in your hair.
6 Our lipsticks come in a range of **long-lasting** colours.
7 We guarantee you will be impressed by the **unrivalled** service provided by all our hotels.
8 Our new concealer will make the **fine** lines around your eyes disappear.

24.2 1 I don't believe those ads that claim their creams have anti-ageing properties.
2 While working in Austria I ate so many lovely cakes that I piled on the pounds.
3 Why not have a bowl of soup or a banana if you're feeling a bit peckish.
4 We guarantee that you will see instant results with our luxury hand cream.
5 You should use this shampoo to revive your sun-damaged hair.
6 Sometimes I wish it were really possible to banish wrinkles.
7 The hotel gives all its guests the chance to experience gracious living.
8 We were invited to a banquet, where they entertained us in grand style.
9 At the airport she bought herself a couple of glossy magazines.
10 This part of town is famous for its classy hotels and exclusive restaurants.

24.3
| 1 range | 3 back | 5 set | 7 labels | 9 popular |
| 2 hit | 4 launched | 6 high | 8 season's | 10 victim |

24.4 *Possible answers:*
1 luxury cream / restaurant / hotel / travel
2 excruciatingly uncomfortable / painful / embarrassing / boring / funny
3 flawless complexion / performance / design
4 unrivalled service / collection / style
5 launch a new collection / an attack / a new service / a boat
6 exclusive restaurant / offer / story / club / part of town

Unit 25

25.1
| 1 tailed | 3 diverted | 5 disrupted |
| 2 down | 4 building up | 6 keep; bear |

25.2
  1 heavy/dense traffic
  2 eased off / died down (Although both of these are possible, the meaning is not exactly the same. *Eased off* simply means became less, whereas *died down* means to become less and eventually disappear to nothing or almost nothing.)
  3 a valid/current driving licence (*Valid* and *current* in this context have almost the same meaning. They both mean that it is a licence that fulfils all the legal conditions. However, *current* puts the emphasis on the time element of the licence – licences and other official documents expire after a fixed period of time.)
  4 Lengthy delays
  5 Bear left
  6 a manual car
  7 grind the gears
  8 hailed as a major development

25.3

1 reverse		3 advantage		5 change		7 took
2 set		4 development		6 valid / current		8 heavy

25.4
  1 a right-hand drive car
  2 move sideways
  3 my driving test
  4 was (soon) hailed as a major development
  5 The key advantage of
  6 There were lengthy/long delays
  7 Traffic was severely disrupted
  8 got stuck in traffic
  9 the oncoming traffic

Unit 26

26.1 1 beaten; sights   2 unexplored   3 an intrepid   4 trekking; arduous   5 sense

26.2

1 feet	4 low-cost	7 peeled	10 hopelessly
2 unexplored	5 standby	8 face	11 party
3 stretch	6 epic	9 conditions	12 has

26.3
  1 The first leg of the journey was straightforward.
  2 My budget didn't stretch to travelling first class / to first-class travel.
  3 Arriving at our base camp boosted our spirits. / Our spirits were boosted when we arrived at our base camp.
  4 There will be sunny spells in most areas today.
  5 We had a stopover in Singapore on our way to Australia.
  6 Jack has always had a thirst for adventure.
  7 Grandmother's spirits are high today.
  8 The movement of the ship lulled me to sleep.

26.4 *Possible collocations*:
  1 arduous task / climb
  2 a mountain / a remote / a lonely wilderness
  3 uncharted waters / seas / lands

Unit 27

27.1 1 summon up 2 extreme 3 took 4 acquire 5 jump 6 hang

27.2
  1 push   6 shape
  2 whale; keep   7 card
  3 chance   8 kick
  4 latest; pitch   9 missed; awarded
  5 stands; victory   10 challenge

27.3
  1 I'd jump at the chance to meet Johnny Depp, wouldn't you?
  2 The spectators stood and clapped as the teams took the field.
  3 You should only attempt this climb if you are pretty fit.
  4 The crowd went wild at the end of the match.
  5 We had a whale of a time in Australia.
  6 I decided to take up the challenge of starting my own business.
  7 The little boy soon got the hang of riding his bike without stabilisers.
  8 The team captain felt dreadful when he scored an own goal.

27.4
  1 latest   2 convincing   3 performance   4 defence   5 blinder

Unit 28

28.1
  1 unveil a plan   5 drum up a lot of support
  2 stick to a schedule   6 cover every eventuality
  3 make something a reality
  4 leave it to someone's discretion

28.2
  1 on   2 up   3 plan   4 exercise   5 long-term   6 option

28.3
  1 consideration   4 factor
  2 groundwork; launch   5 suggestion
  3 outright   6 change

28.4
  1 Final preparations for the music festival are now **underway**.
  2 I was very upset when they rejected my suggestions **out of hand**.
  3 The company came **up** with the idea of encouraging customers to recycle packaging.
  4 I don't think you will find it easy to **put** your ideas into practice.
  5 He declared his **outright** opposition to the plan.
  6 **Constructive** criticism is always welcome, but negative criticism is not.

28.5

```
            ³M ⁴A
 ¹P ²R  A  C  ⁵T  I  C  ⁶E
  L  E  K  T  O        A
  A  A  E     Y        G
  N  C                 E
     H                 R
```

Unit 29

29.1
  1 star-studded   3 originality   5 role   7 series   9 spectacularly
  2 lasting   4 display   6 accomplished 8 experiment 10 fire

29.2
  The options that are NOT possible are:
  1 high   4 burst   7 wrote
  2 starring   5 highly
  3 spectacularly   6 consummate

29.3
  1 professional   3 reviews   5 disaster   7 attention
  2 up   4 events   6 experiment   8 suspense

29.5
  an unmitigated disaster
  a dismal failure

Unit 30

30.1
1 satisfy requirements
2 have an obligation
3 arrive at an agreement
4 carry out a risk assessment
5 pass a new law
6 bring in regulations
7 adhere to standards
8 exercise authority

Other quite common collocations using these words are:
meet requirements
satisfy conditions

30.2
1 flout
2 adhere
3 sought; granted
4 comply with the law
5 satisfy; being in breach of

30.3
1 positions
2 cut through
3 introduce
4 tightening
5 faceless
6 approve

30.4

```
¹R U L E S
 I
²S A T I S F Y
 K
³D A N G E R
 S
 S
⁴E X E R C I S E
 S
⁵E S S E N T I A L
 M
⁶B R E A C H
 N
⁷O B T A I N E D
```

30.5 *Possible answers:*
1 satisfy someone's desires
2 have a duty
3 arrive at a decision
4 carry out an experiment
5 meet someone's needs
6 address an issue
7 bring in a law
8 adhere to the rules

Unit 31

31.1   1 Tomas   2 Sylvia   3 Ulla   4 Marcos   5 Gerard

31.2
1 offshore
2 run (we also say *run out*)
3 vital
4 eco-friendly
5 dire (we could also say *disastrous* or *devastating*)
6 offset

31.3
1 Food miles
2 Renewable energy
3 widespread flooding
4 irreversible climate change
5 find a solution to
6 our carbon footprint

7 Offshore wind farms
8 the disposal of household waste

31.4 1 Temperatures **soared** during the summer months and reached a record high.
2 We must change our **ways** before it is too late.
3 They now have a **solar** heating system in their house; it's very economical.
4 The desert experiences **searing** heat during the day but is cold at night. (Note: we say **searing heat** or **soaring temperatures,** but we do NOT say ~~searing~~ temperatures or ~~soaring~~ heat.)
5 The weather **patterns** have changed in recent years: winters are milder, summers are hotter.
6 He has one of those **hybrid** cars which alternates between petrol and battery power.
7 The government must **introduce** green taxes so people who damage the environment pay more.
8 Vehicle **emissions** are the main source of pollution in big cities.
9 We need to find alternative energy **sources** for private homes.

Unit 32

32.1 1 the country; the city
2 the city; the country
3 the country; the city
4 the country; the city
5 the city; the country

32.2 1 The first sentence refers to cars and other traffic on the roads, whereas the second sentence refers to shoppers and other pedestrians on the pavements.
2 The first sentence means that the speaker lives in the centre of town, whereas the second sentence is talking about other people who live in quiet, residential and well-off suburbs.
3 The first sentence means that he lives in a very quiet, traditional place where nothing much happens, whereas the second sentence means that she lives in a very busy, active city centre.
4 The first sentence means the speaker loves living in the city, whereas in the second one, the speaker loves living in the country.

32.3 city life, urban living
long opening hours, open all hours
rustic charm, rural idyll
in the back of beyond, in the middle of nowhere

32.4 1 quiet backwater
2 in the back of beyond / in the middle of nowhere
3 urban regeneration
4 a tree-planting scheme
5 a desirable place to live
6 residential dwellings

32.5 1 derelict buildings   4 urban regeneration
2 busy roads / congested roads   5 the rural idyll
3 a bustling city centre   6 long opening hours / open all hours

32.6 *Possible answers:*
1 flock to the countryside / unspoilt countryside / rolling countryside / surrounding countryside / protect the countryside
2 a rural landscape / a barren landscape / dominate the landscape / a watercolour landscape / a landscape painter / a rugged landscape / an urban landscape
3 a fishing village / a mountain village / outlying villages / surrounding villages / a picturesque village / the global village / a coastal village / a remote village / a neighbouring village

Author's answers:
1 Sports programmes bore me rigid.
2 I think I might consider life in a remote country village in Britain to be a rural idyll for a couple of weeks but then I would probably miss the facilites of a big town.
3 No, the public transport system where I live is not reliable at all. The buses are very infrequent and they often arrive late or not at all.
4 No, I can't think of any derelict buildings where I live. Land with derelict buildings on it tends to be quickly redeveloped.
5 There are some small shops, a post box, a school, and a doctor's surgery.

Unit 33

33.1
1 make a payment
2 supplement my income
3 spend a fortune
4 borrow heavily
5 stay afloat

33.2

to arrange an overdraft	to get into debt
a bad debt	a hefty debt / overdraft
to be in debt	the national debt
to clear a debt	to pay off a debt / an overdraft
deep in debt	debt-ridden
overdraft facility	to run up a debt / an overdraft
to get an overdraft	an unauthorised overdraft

Other possible collocations:
to repay a debt / to owe a debt (of gratitude) / a debt mounts up
an overdraft limit / to reduce your overdraft / a sizeable overdraft

33.3
1 The firm has huge debts and has had to borrow $10 million. The new Chief Executive has introduced cost-cutting **measures**.
2 When I left university I had no **outstanding** debts, unlike most of my friends, who owed thousands of pounds.
3 The manager falsified company **records** and stole money from her employer.
4 I had no **source** of income, so I had to get a job, and quickly.
5 We **put** down a deposit on a new car last week.
6 She **defaulted** on her loan repayment and had to sell her business.
7 Many people don't trust online banking because they are afraid of **identity** theft.
8 If we don't cut **down** on luxuries, we're going to find ourselves in serious debt.
9 There are special offers for students who **open** a current account at the university bank.
10 You will pay a lot of interest if you go over your **agreed** credit limit.

33.4
1 The metaphor is that of a boat which must keep/stay afloat (otherwise it will sink under water).
2 You're expected to pay it back.
3 (c). To write off a loan would mean to accept that it will never be paid.
4 (a)
5 credit-card fraud

33.5 1 falsifying 2 fraudulent 3 payment 4 theft 5 interest-free

Unit 34

34.1
1 The government is finding it very difficult to curb inflation.
2 The country is suffering because of the current economic climate.
3 Although heavy industry is in decline, service industries are thriving.
4 The CEO is anxious to safeguard his company's interests.
5 New machinery has enabled the factory to increase its output.
6 The tax authorities plan to tackle the issue of undeclared earnings.
7 The budget plan explains how we intend to allocate our various resources.
8 We must tackle and solve the problems caused by social exclusion.

34.2

Own guidance	Previous rival government
build on success	leave inflation unchecked
extend opportunity	levy heavy taxes
meet with success	poor value for money
safely steer the economy	rampant inflation
steady growth	rising unemployment
thriving industry	thriving black economy
uninterrupted growth	

34.3
1 long
2 extend
3 undeclared
4 rising
5 stimulating
6 plummeting
7 public
8 push up
9 raise
10 introduce

34.4
1 public; private
2 undeclared
3 long; short
4 Falling
5 raising; pushed up; plummet
6 extend; stimulate
7 stunt
8 introduce

Unit 35

35.1
1 address 2 provide 3 broke down 4 break 5 made 6 incite

35.2
1 for human habitation
2 sanitary conditions
3 underage drinking
4 antisocial behaviour
5 public disorder
6 for good / for change

35.3
1 Poor people often have to claim benefits in order to survive financially.
2 The city council introduced a neighbourhood watch scheme.
3 The government took some draconian measures to prevent public disorder.
4 All governments need to address the issues of global poverty and disease.
5 The authorities had to provide shelter and food to the earthquake victims.
6 As the discontent grew, riots erupted in all the major cities.

35.4
1 The violence threatened **the social fabric**.
2 The Minister said it was time for a **fresh drive** to cut crime.
3 Customs officials found some **illegal substances** in the passenger's luggage.
4 The **run-down areas** of the city are often dangerous at night.
5 We hope our new organisation will be a **force for political change**.
6 He proposed a **novel solution** to address the issue of social inequality.
7 **Dysfunctional families** are a difficult problem for social workers.
8 The union representative **made a plea** for the workers to stand firm.
9 There were scenes of **public disorder** on the streets last night.
10 It is very difficult for young people to find **affordable housing**.

Unit 36

36.1 1 If you switch off your computer without shutting it **down** properly, you may lose data.
  2 I didn't expect everything to run **smoothly** in my new job but I didn't imagine it would be quite so difficult as it was.
  3 Alex had some technical problems **installing** his new computer equipment.
  4 The company is famous for its **cutting-edge** design.
  5 If they'd serviced their machines regularly, they wouldn't have had to halt **production**.
  6 Vic dreams of making a discovery that would help to push **back** the frontiers of science.
  7 Scientists usually **publish** their findings in academic journals.
  8 There was a power **cut** this morning. The power went off at ten and it wasn't **restored** till midday.
  9 Urs loves pure research but his brother is more interested in the application of research to practical projects and in **harnessing** new technology for commercial ends.
  10 They carried out **research** over a ten-year period and finally published their **findings** this month.

36.2 1 He's swiping a card.   3 She's using SATNAV.
  2 She's entering her PIN number.   4 He's switching channels by TV remote control.

36.3 1 High-definition TV (HD TV), flat screen TV and remote controls
  2 It's used for storing music (files).
  3 The systems might crash.
  4 No, online banking is now available at most banks.
  5 A wireless hotspot
  6 Switch channels
  7 Download a new ringtone
  8 They suffer from wear and tear.

36.4 1 (a) the small screen (b) the big screen (also the silver screen)
  2 online dictionary / education / course / magazine
  3 remote mountain village / past / possibility / manner

Unit 37

37.1 enjoy good health   gentle exercise
  reduce your stress levels   build up your resistance
  do plenty of exercise   do sport
  go on a diet   watch what you eat

37.2 1 diet
  2 dose. A dose of medicine/penicillin is a measured amount of it, while a dose of flu is an experience of flu (*dose* in this second sense would only be used about an unpleasant experience).
  3 build up
  4 disease
  5 cold
  6 course

37.3 1 j   6 c
  2 b   7 f
  3 h   8 d
  4 a   9 g
  5 e   10 i

37.4

1 side effects	5 taking an overdose
2 untimely death (*premature* is also possible but does not sound right after *very*)	6 exceed the recommended dose
3 shake it off	7 have an operation
4 poor health	8 watch what you eat
	9 make a full recovery

Unit 38

38.1
1 **Soaring crime rates** have been recorded in the last twelve months.
2 Why should young criminals **escape punishment** for crimes just because of their age?
3 The lawyers **contested the verdict of the court**.
4 The judge **dismissed** the case because he felt the evidence was **unreliable**.
5 John Jones **denied all knowledge of** the robbery.
6 The judge **adjourned** the trial **until** next month.

38.2

1 good	4 kept in prison for the full amount of time
2 go to prison	5 invented
3 kept in prison	

38.3
1 He was put **on** trial for murder.
2 He was later remanded **in** custody.
3 The witness appeared **in** court for the first time today.
4 The murderer was soon brought **to** justice.
5 The case against Mr Sharp was proved **beyond** reasonable doubt.

38.4

1 miscarriages	4 unanimous	7 justice
2 extenuating	5 denied	8 adjourned
3 appeared	6 awarded	9 minor

38.5
find guilty, find not guilty (Note that a *guilty verdict* and a *not guilty verdict* are also possible collocations.)
give evidence, give a sentence (usually used in passive – be given a sentence)
stand trial, face trial
unreliable witness, unreliable evidence
contest a verdict, overturn a verdict

Possible sentences using the collocations:
He was found guilty of theft, but found not guilty of murder.
The witness gave evidence which resulted in the accused being given a five-year sentence.
She was facing trial for murder, but escaped from prison and never actually stood trial for the offence.
It was an example of unreliable evidence from an unreliable witness.
The verdict was contested, and was subsequently overturned.

Follow-up
Here are some examples of collocations found from a search on the website suggested. Note that each search throws up 50 different sentences and so it is possible that you may have found some quite different examples.

deliver a verdict	an expert witness	bitter custody battle
return a verdict of	a witness statement	keep in custody
reach a verdict	witness evidence	hold in custody
record a verdict	a vital witness	discharge from custody
verdict of accidental death	struggle for custody	be released from custody
a key witness	take into custody	an interim custody order
bear witness to	custody officer	in police custody
to witness atrocities	provide safe custody	

Unit 39

39.1 1 SPATE 3 STRIKE(S) 5 POWER
2 VIOLENCE 4 CAUGHT 6 CEASEFIRE

39.2 *Possible answers:*
1 The UN's aim is to restore peace in an area where there has clearly been a lot of fighting.
2 They have managed to get both sides to agree to a ceasefire.
3 The ceasefire is due to come into effect from midnight the following day.
4 There have been hostilities for ten years.
5 No, it has been getting worse. It has been escalating.
6 The two sides have clearly been deadly/bitter enemies for a long time.

39.3 1 lift the blockade 5 launch a counter-attack
2 surgical strikes 6 create instability
3 fragile peace 7 collateral damage
4 go on the offensive 8 suffer casualties

39.4 1 The two countries have been engaged in **hostilities** for a long time.
2 The ceasefire **comes** into effect today and all hope it will bring **stability** to the area again.
3 The government has promised to **withdraw** its troops next year.
4 There is an **uneasy** truce between the two sides at the moment.
5 When peace is **restored**, we shall be able to **disband** the army.
6 The newspaper reported that the enemy had **suffered** a defeat despite the fact that they had **deployed** large numbers of troops to the area.
7 They accused us of **stockpiling** weapons and of preparing to launch **an unprovoked** attack.
8 Some argue that the nuclear deterrent has prevented violence from **escalating**.

Unit 40

40.1 1 childhood 2 stand 3 Forging 4 lifelong 5 circle 6 long-term

40.2 1 casual 3 social 5 stable 7 firm/close 9 cordial
2 bad 4 close 6 complete 8 moral 10 friendly

40.3 1 life
2 sprang
3 won
4 provided me with
5 heal
6 took
7 broke down
8 close/firm

40.4 1 We should have a **heart-to-heart** chat to resolve our differences.
2 She **came** under attack from some colleagues at work who didn't like her.
3 If you **abuse** someone's trust you deserve to lose their friendship.
4 We tried hard to **make** the relationship work but failed.
5 I think you need to **put** some distance between yourself and Eduardo.

Unit 41

41.1 newborn baby spoilt brat child prodigy juvenile delinquent disaffected youth
(Other possible collocations are: *spoilt baby, spoilt child, delinquent youth*.)

41.2   1 child prodigy   3 juvenile delinquent   5 disaffected youth
        2 newborn babies   4 spoilt brat

41.3   1 It is all too easy to **take** your close friends and your family for granted.
        2 Liz's got four children and she's just bought herself a sports car. Do you think she's going **through** some kind of midlife crisis?
        3 My sister **had** a baby boy last month.
        4 You'll spoil your daughter if you keep on **pandering** to her every whim.
        5 My parents are vegetarians, so I **respect** their wishes and don't eat meat in their house.
        6 Sorry. I must be having a **senior** moment. I just can't remember your name!
        7 Jacqui insists she has seen the **error** of her ways.
        8 Don't worry about your daughter leaving home. She won't **come** to any harm.
        9 Make sure you don't let the child out of your **sight**.

41.4   1 Leaving home means going to live in another place, and leaving the house is what you do when you go out of your front door every day.
        2 A hazy memory is vague, not clear or distinct, and a distinct memory is very clear.
        3 A grumpy old man is one who is bad-tempered and complains a lot, and a dear old man is one who is kind and good-natured.
        4 An occasional twinge is a pain that happens from time to time, and a sudden twinge is a pain that happens unexpectedly.
        5 Something becomes a habit but a person develops a habit.
        6 If you fall into a pattern, that pattern gradually develops, whereas if you fit into a pattern, the pattern has already been established by someone else and you adapt to it.

41.5   *The collocations that are impossible (or at least very unlikely) are:*
        1 go   4 problem   7 an increase
        2 firm   5 perfect   8 sensitive
        3 talk   6 wake up

Unit 42

42.1   1 False. It could include members of his/her family, but it also includes his/her immediate colleagues and/or friends.
        2 False. A lavish lifestyle is one that is very extravagant and luxurious, but it is not necessarily one that occasionally breaks the law.
        3 False. When someone goes into rehab, they want to lose an addiction, usually to alcohol or drugs.
        4 False. The highest bidder is the person who is prepared to pay most for something.
        5 True
        6 True
        7 False. A kiss and tell story is one where *one person* talks to the press about a romantic or sexual relationship they had with a famous person.
        8 False. A prenuptial agreement is made before a couple marry.
        9 True
       10 False. It suggests that the interviewee spoke only to one journalist or newspaper.

42.2   1 rise   5 highly
        2 ambition (could also be *dream*)   6 reveal
        3 heaped   7 enjoyed/had
        4 nomination   8 made

42.3   1 A messy one.   6 An award.
        2 An exclusive one.   7 A pre nuptial one.
        3 A very significant one.   8 The highest.
        4 Her achievements.   9 A fairy-tale one.
        5 Her story.   10 Glowing ones.

42.4 1 an in-depth interview 3 a significant impact
2 a meteoric rise to fame 4 a lavish lifestyle

Unit 43

43.1 1 a slippery customer 5 take the flak
2 mindless violence 6 poison the atmosphere
3 shirk one's responsibilities 7 hold in contempt
4 pick a fight 8 a disruptive influence

43.2 1 bone idle 4 out of order / a downright disgrace
2 poisoning the atmosphere 5 minor niggles
3 trust Glyn an inch 6 a nasty piece of work

43.3 1 betray 4 pick 7 cloud 10 have
2 hold 5 rests 8 play
3 have 6 belittle 9 stoop

43.4 1 mindless 3 disruptive 5 achievement(s)
2 glaring 4 disgrace 6 nagging

Unit 44

44.1 1 keen interest 4 paramount importance
2 honing; skills 5 pursue; interest
3 meet; challenge 6 accumulate; experience

44.2 1 Paul has an encyclopaedic knowledge of African history.
2 Karen has very good interpersonal skills / has excellent people skills.
3 Eric accumulated considerable experience of farming / on farms when he was in Canada.
4 Toyah has an excellent teaching qualification but she lacks classroom experience.
5 I trust Dr Robinson implicitly.
6 This job will offer you the perfect opportunity to hone your computer/computing skills.
7 I have every confidence in your ability to / that you will be able to complete the course.
8 It was Duncan's financial acumen that led to his promotion.

44.3 I am happy to **act** as a referee for James McBride, who has applied for a teaching post at
your language school. I **have** every confidence in Mr McBride's abilities as a teacher. He
spent last summer working at the school where I am Principal and he was a **much/greatly**
appreciated member of our staff. He was very successful in **establishing/developing** a
good relationship with both students and staff. He **is highly educated / has a good level of
education** with a particularly **extensive/comprehensive** knowledge of English literature. He
combines **good** teaching qualifications with **considerable** experience of teaching students
at all levels of English. He also has **advanced/good** computer skills, which should certainly
prove useful in a technologically advanced school such as yours.

44.4 1 revealed 3 meet 5 perform
2 wholeheartedly 4 provide 6 highly

44.5 financial / business / political acumen
highly valued / placed / prized
perform a task / an operation / a song

Unit 45

45.1

blank expression
gruff exterior
striking resemblance
cool reception
stubborn streak
bubbly personality

1 striking resemblance
2 bubbly personality
3 blank expression
4 stubborn streak
5 gruff exterior
6 cool reception

45.2 Sentences 3, 4, 6 and 8 are complimentary.

45.3
1 bears a striking resemblance to
2 boosting your confidence
3 forthright manner
4 strong points
5 has admirable qualities
6 bursting with energy

45.4
1 perfectly
2 hostility
3 unacceptable
4 characteristics
5 thinly
6 reception

Unit 46

46.1
1 Living in such a confined space is difficult with three kids.
2 The piano took up a lot of room, so we sold it.
3 This office is better than the cramped conditions I used to work in.
4 We're moving because we're short of space where we're living at the moment.
5 We demolished an old outhouse to leave room for a bigger kitchen and utility room.
6 The attic is a waste of space, so we're going to convert it into a study.

46.2
1 a lasting contribution to
2 (vacant) parking spaces
3 dim and distant memory
4 ample room
5 the vast expanse

46.3
1 A decade has elapsed
2 foreseeable future
3 a bygone era
4 go down in history
5 over the course of time
6 not-so-distant future

46.4

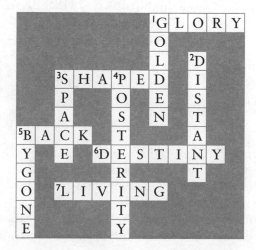

Unit 47

47.1 1 Kevin   2 Joe   3 Fabrice's boss   4 Ilona   5 Zara

47.2
1 gave
2 make
3 utter
4 travels
5 let
6 descended
7 faltered
8 lost
9 slurred

47.3
1 I could hear a slight **trace** of an Irish accent in her voice.
2 Paolo was met with a **stony** silence as everyone tried to absorb the bad news.
3 The old woman let **out** a cry of anger when she heard the result of the trial.
4 She has a **broad** American accent, even though she was not born there.
5 I could hear **hoots** of laughter coming from the next room.
6 The voices were **muffled,** so I could not make out what anyone was saying.
7 Silence **reigned** in the classroom as the pupils were all hard at work.
8 Speak up. I hate it when you mutter something under your **breath.**

47.4
1 distant
2 incessant (also constant)
3 soft (also quiet)
4 dull
5 deathly
6 clap (Note that the phrase *a murmur of thunder* in the original sentence would be a very unusual combination of words in English.)

Unit 48

48.1 1 feasible alternatives   2 viable options   3 the easy option   4 a step by step approach

48.2
adopt a method
concentrate the mind
enlist help
immense asset
instantly recall
perfect a technique
perfectly simple
remarkable ease
simple rule
take the time

48.3
1 perfected
2 simplicity
3 ease
4 hard work
5 degree of accuracy
6 break
7 taking the
8 complexities

48.4 1 C   2 D   3 A   4 B   5 D

Unit 49

49.1
1 adverse weather conditions
2 a complete disaster
3 a constant struggle
4 widespread flooding
5 grave danger
6 a state of confusion
7 catastrophic results
8 high risk
9 a severe blow
10 a complete disaster

49.2
1 tackle
2 struck
3 spot
4 respond
5 carries
6 hindering
7 face
8 fighting
9 poses

49.3 1 d   2 c   3 f   4 b   5 a   6 e

49.4
1 We are **having/experiencing** a number of problems with our new car.
2 Some problems **arose/occurred** when we tried to follow your instructions.
3 Somehow our society must **find** a solution to the problem of child poverty.
4 A difficulty has **arisen** with regard to a member of our project team.
5 Even advanced students sometimes **make** mistakes with this type of collocation.
6 I've always **had/experienced** a lot of difficulties with English spelling.

49.5 *Possible answers:*

encounter	resistance	tackle	an issue	pose	a question
	problems		an opponent		a problem

Unit 50

50.1
1 We had a bumper crop of apples from our trees last year.
2 A substantial amount of their income comes from the apartments they rent out.
3 I feel confident that a substantial/significant/good/fair number of people will vote for Mac.
4 Jill's room at college is a good size.
5 We have a finite number of tickets, so we're offering them on a first-come-first-served basis.
6 I was terrifed by the sheer size of the dog.
7 My new colleague is still an unknown quantity.
8 There were a fair few / a fair number of careless mistakes in your homework.

50.2
1 majority	3 fees	5 patience	7 amount
2 overdose	4 proportions	6 crop	8 few/number

50.3
1 unbounded enthusiasm   5 fair few
2 bumper crop   6 endless supply
3 astronomical fees   7 inordinate amount
4 infinite patience   8 sheer quantity

50.4

	minority	majority	amount	number	percentage	quantity	importance	significance
small	✓		✓	✓	✓	✓		
little							✓	✓
large	✓	✓	✓	✓	✓	✓		
great							✓	✓
big								
high				✓				
wide								

50.5
1 infinite wisdom / variety / number
2 epic film / journey / struggle
3 overwhelming urge / desire / need
4 endless arguments / possibilities
5 massive house / scale / heart attack

Unit 51

51.1
1 a) to change beyond recognition
   b) to implement planned changes
2 a) major   b) minor   c) major   d) minor   e) major
3 a) The town remains unchanged.
   b) Over the years many changes have taken place in the school.
4 Yes.
5 It's usually easier for a young person than an elderly person to adapt to changing circumstances.
6 The fact that they went out.

51.2

1 show/showed
2 times
3 turned
4 undergoing
5 wildly
6 increase
7 made
8 recognition
9 dramatically
10 implement

51.3

1 There is room for improvement in your coursework assignment.
2 There was a sudden shift in public attitudes towards the issue of capital punishment.
3 Several changes in our management structure took place last year.
4 There have been sweeping changes to the school programme since I was a pupil here.
5 Some quite significant changes came about last year.
6 Penny is a changed woman since she got the job she wanted.
7 My life turned / was turned upside-down when I lost my job.
8 It'd make a change to stay in a hotel rather than go camping this summer.

Unit 52

52.1
1 abandon   2 lull   3 bring   4 called

52.2

1 I'm afraid it was me burning the toast that set off the smoke alarm.
2 As soon as she saw her mother the little girl broke into a run.
3 Because of the President's visit, they've closed off the area.
4 I didn't manage to fall asleep until dawn was breaking.
5 I hope they won't decide to terminate the contract.
6 The missing child was found, so the police called off their search.
7 The school is planning to instigate some anti-bullying measures.
8 We were halfway up the mountain when the rain set in.

52.3

1 SINGER CLEARS UP CONFUSION ABOUT LYRICS
2 ARMY QUELLS UNREST ON BORDER
3 NEW REPUBLIC BREAKS DIPLOMATIC RELATIONS WITH NEIGHBOURS
4 PEACE PROCESS TALKS COLLAPSE
5 VIOLENCE SPARKS FEARS OF FURTHER UNREST
6 STAR DISPELS RUMOURS OF DIVORCE
7 STADIUM FINALLY NEARS COMPLETION
8 MINISTER ALLAYS FEARS OF TAX INCREASE

52.4

1 opening
2 enter
3 allay
4 stop
5 breaks
6 dispel
7 quell
8 completion

Unit 53

53.1

1 I think that computers will eventually render books obsolete.
2 The preliminary meeting set the wheels of the new project in motion.
3 Her mother calling her sister the 'pretty one' bred a lot of resentment.
4 I always suspected the new tax law would spell disaster for the economy.
5 I'm sure that your hard work will produce a positive result.
6 The boss's decision to cut wages provoked an outcry from the staff.
7 The way he behaved last night planted doubts in my mind about his honesty.
8 The Minister's absence has prompted speculation that he is unwell.

9 The uncertainty of the situation is driving us crazy.

10 The floods last week wrought havoc in low-lying areas.

53.2
1 demanded	4 compelling	7 desired
2 dire	5 contributing	8 wrought/wreaked
3 face	6 reason	9 plant

53.3
1 The dust from the building site next door is nearly driving me crazy.

2 It will take them a long time to establish the cause of the accident.

3 If we set things in motion now, your visa should be ready next week.

4 The customer survey which the company carried out produced some surprising results.

53.4
1 The desired effect of any medication is to cure an infection or disease, or treat its symptoms.

2 A knock-on effect might or might not be welcomed as it can be either positive or negative.

3 Root cause. The *root cause* means the original source of the problem and the *primary cause* is the main cause amongst several possible causes.

4 It probably takes about five minutes before you feel the full effect of a dental injection.

5 Some people would argue that television has had some ill effects on society – it may, for example, have encouraged people to read less and to talk to their families less in the evenings.

6 a video or audio cassette player

Unit 54

54.1
1 birds (flock of birds) – swarm of bees/flies

2 wasps (swarm of wasps) – herd of zebras/cattle

3 sardines (shoal of sardines) – flock of sheep/birds

4 fish (shoal of fish) – pod of whales/dolphins

5 elephants (herd of elephants) – tribe of baboons/monkeys

6 lions (pride of lions) – pack of wolves/dogs

54.2
1 flurry	6 gamut
2 dash	7 swarm (could also be an army or a colony of ants)
3 flurry	8 flicker
4 stroke	9 glimmer
5 drop; sprinkling	

54.3
1 a dollop of cream	3 a head of garlic
2 a hunk of bread	4 100g of butter

54.4
a bed of rice	gamut of colours	a pod of whales
a drop of brandy	a glimmer of hope	a shoal of fish
a flurry of speculation	a pack of hounds	a touch of humour

54.5
1 pad or pack (a pad of paper is paper glued together at the top intended for hand-writing, while a pack of paper refers to the loose sheets of paper sold together for printing)

2 pack; grain

3 suite

4 pack

5 torrent

6 grain

7 pinch

8 swig

Unit 55

55.1 1 yawning; different   3 opposites   5 clear
2 sides   4 difference; contrast   6 wide

55.2 1 g   2 a   3 f   4 h   5 c   6 b   7 d   8 e

55.3 1 entirely / strikingly
2 bridge
3 bear
4 clear / subtle
5 world
6 fundamentally / strikingly
7 growing
8 side

55.4 *Possible answers:*
1 I think the advantages of living in the country far outweigh the disadvantages.
2 Life in the country compares very favourably with life in the town.
3 Social relationships in the country are fundamentally different from those in the town.
4 The pleasures of town life pale in comparison with the pleasures of country living.
5 Unfortunately, public transport in the country is strikingly different from the transport services available in the city.
6 Entertainment and sports facilities available in the town and in the country differ widely.

Follow up
Here are some possible collocations:

in stark contrast	outweigh the benefits	a gap between her teeth
in sharp contrast	outweigh the risks	the generation gap
to contrast dramatically	a gap in the market	

Unit 56

56.1 1 Exercise – this is made clear by the word *physical*.
2 No, the speaker thinks it will be difficult – this is made clear by the phrase *hard slog*.
3 It's the responsibility of two or more people – this is made clear by the word *joint*.
4 To try their hardest – this is shown by the use of *give things your best shot*.
5 No, she didn't – this is made clear by the word *abortive*.
6 Cooperation – this is made clear by the word *team*.

56.2 1 worth   5 heeded   9 devoting
2 determined   6 desire   10 required
3 doomed   7 shot   11 pinning
4 ignored   8 strenuous   12 reap

56.3 1 It'll be an uphill struggle to get your work finished by the deadline.
2 The appeal of Shakespeare's plays has certainly stood the test of time.
3 It would be sensible for you to follow his advice.
4 No parents can provide a solution to/for all their children's problems.
5 After a few months you will begin to reap the rewards of all your hard work.
6 Rob made a valiant effort not to fall behind in the race but he just didn't have enough stamina.
7 (Hard) physical exertion certainly works up an appetite.
8 A lawyer would probably be the best person to offer you advice.
9 I'm pinning my hopes on winning a scholarship to the college.
10 Alex has been making a concerted effort to do better this term.

Unit 57

57.1 1 bright 2 give; mean 3 up; decent 4 travels 5 had; sleep 6 know

57.2
1 I'm **really/absolutely** delighted with my wonderful present.
2 I'm absolutely shattered – I've been **on** the go all week.
3 It was a **great** pleasure to meet you.
4 I'm **really / very much** looking forward to hearing from you soon.
5 It **came** as a bit of a shock when I heard that Ellen and Jim had split up.
6 To be **brutally** honest, I don't think he'll ever make a good teacher.
7 I didn't **have** much luck when I was trying to find a new dress for the party.
8 I hope I didn't **cause** your parents any trouble. Or I hope I didn't **put** your parents **to** any trouble.
9 We **sincerely / very much** hope that you will visit us again soon.
10 The thought **occurred** to me that he might be in some kind of trouble.
11 Please don't **go** to any trouble on my account!
12 **Give** me a ring when you want to be picked up from the station.

57.3

Crossword:
1 FACE
2 REALLY
3 RELIEF
4 EMAIL
5 BACK
6 REASON
Down: FEEBLE, REALLY/EXCUSE, BACKUP, REASONE

Unit 58

58.1
1 broke; promise
2 offer; explanation
3 reaffirm; commitment
4 rejected; charge
5 dodge; question
6 betrayed; trust

58.2
1 gave repeated assurances
2 went back on his promise
3 give a straight answer
4 made a (firm) commitment to
5 keeping your promise
6 fielded
7 channels of communication
8 I take your point
9 He gave a full apology

58.3 1 Alex 2 Brona 3 Simon 4 Arlene 5 Finn

58.4 *Collocations in possible sentences:*
We all have to **confront the issue** of climate change.
With all **due respect**, I think that your comments are very short-sighted.
The police are trying to **establish communication** with the terrorists in the building.
I accept what you say. It's a **fair comment**.
The politician / film star / footballer **issued a denial** after reports in the newspapers that he/she was having an affair.

The lecturer **put** an interesting **question** to the class about the reasons for antisocial behaviour.

Unit 59

59.1 1 harebrained   2 admitted   3 levels   4 take   5 bottle   6 vent

59.2 1 C   2 A   3 B   4 C   5 D   6 B

59.3 1 Catching a bug while he was in hospital hastened the old man's death / the death of the old man.
2 Cinderella suffered (very rough treatment) at the hands of her wicked stepmother.
3 There was a public outpouring of grief when the film star died.
4 The accident has fuelled fears about / with regard to safety on the railways.
5 Because of their behaviour we are left with little/no alternative but to boycott their goods.
6 It was a lapse of judgement for him to act as he did.
7 I was sick with worry / worried sick when Dad was having his operation.
8 It's better not to bottle up your feelings.

59.4 1 a fit of jealousy / temper / rage
2 to shatter someone's confidence / illusions / dreams
3 to fill someone with dread / joy / foreboding
4 to hurl insults / abuse / stones at someone
5 in a state of shock / euphoria / emergency
6 pose a threat / problem / challenge / question
7 a lapse of judgement / time / concentration
8 an intense dislike / fear / loathing

Unit 60

60.1 1 The whole country seems to be in a **state** of euphoria after winning the World Cup.
2 I heaved a **sigh** of relief when I heard Joe had finally passed his driving test.
3 As the starting whistle blew, a **surge** of adrenalin helped me get off to a good start.
4 I still always feel a **shiver** down my spine when I set off on a long journey.
5 It was a difficult climb but we had a marvellous **sense** of achievement **as** we stood at the top.
6 Agreeing to do a bit of overtime could **work** to your advantage, you know.
7 Rick seems to have lost his **sense** of purpose.
8 As winter ends I always seem to feel a **burst** of energy.
9 It was **pure** luck that the answer suddenly came to me in the middle of the exam.
10 I don't think those engineers ever got the **recognition** they deserved.

60.2 1 derive   6 heart
2 high; lived   7 takes/took
3 come   8 optimistic
4 expressed   9 great
5 went   10 joy

60.3 *Possible answers:*
1 a hope or a wish
2 a habit or a dream
3 easy, certain or jealous
4 luck, willpower, nonsense or coincidence
5 an effect, a hope or a change (but not something concrete like, say, a swimming pool)

60.4 *Author's answers:*
1 I think that most people are more likely to find long-lasting happiness in a relationship than a career – though you can find plenty of happiness in a career too, of course.

2 I have profound admiration for a twelve-year-old girl I know who takes most of the responsibility for looking after her seriously disabled mother and who always appears cheerful.

3 Getting my first writing commission was a matter of pure luck, of bumping into someone at the right moment.

4 I enjoy both, but I think I derive more pleasure from reading.

5 I last experienced a sense of achievement when I finished writing the units for this book.

Index

probe a ~ 6
soaring ~ rates 38
go through a midlife crisis 41
critical analysis 18
critically ill 22, 37
criticism
constructive ~ 28
mounting ~ 3
in-depth critique 18
bumper crop 50
caught in the crossfire 39
crowded street 32
cry
let out a ~ 47
strangled ~ 47
cultural heritage 23
curb inflation 34
current
~ driving licence 25
~ economic climate 34
open a ~ account 33
run up curtains 9
custodial sentence 38
remand in custody 38
take your custom elsewhere 16
customer
regular ~ 16
satisfied ~ 16
slippery ~ 43
cut noun
power ~ 36
cut verb
~ through red tape 30
cut down on luxuries 33
cutting-edge design 36
put together a CV 12
break the cycle 35
collateral damage 39
award damages 38
damaging disclosure 22
perform a dance 23
danger
grave ~ 49
minimise ~ 30
dash of cream 54
tradition dates back to 23
daunting task 13
dawn breaks 52
dazzling
~ display 29
~ smile 45
dead
~ easy 8
~ keen 60
pronounce someone ~ 10

deal with the complexities 48
death
hasten someone's ~ 59
premature ~ 37
untimely ~ 37
deathly hush 47
re-open a debate 22
debt
clear a ~ 33
get into ~ 33
outstanding ~ 33
run up a huge ~ 33
write off a ~ 33
decades elapse 46
decent night's sleep 57
the deciding factor 28
decision
abide by a ~ 11
reach the ~ 28
declare
~ independence 21
~ outright hostility 28
~ outright opposition 28
~ someone the winner 10
decline noun
~ in demand 15
experience a ~ 15
see a ~ 15
show a ~ 15
decline verb
~ to comment 22
decrease
show a ~ 51
slight ~ 15
substantial ~ 15
deeply offensive 8
default on repayments 33
defeat
admit ~ 59
humiliating ~ 21
defence
break through the ~ 27
spring to someone's ~ 40
vigorous ~ 18
amazing degree of accuracy 48
lengthy delays 25
take delight in 60
absolutely delighted 8, 57
juvenile delinquent 41
deliriously happy 2
deliver a speech 21
demand noun
decline in ~ 15
satisfy a ~ 15

demand verb
~ an explanation 53
demonstrate an ability 17
hold a demonstration 21
issue a denial 58
dense traffic 25
deny all knowledge 38
depart from a pattern 1
dependent
completely ~ 8
entirely ~ 8
totally ~ 8
deploy troops 39
put down a deposit 33
derelict building 32
derive pleasure from 60
silence descends 47
fit the job description 13
get the recognition you
deserve 60
design
cutting-edge ~ 36
eco-friendly ~ 31
designer label 24
desirable place to live 32
desperate desire 56
desired effect 53
clear your desk 13
desperate desire 56
shape your destiny 46
detailed account 22
determined effort 56
develop a good relationship 44
hail as a major development 25
devote energy to 56
traffic dies down 25
diet
go on a ~ 37
stick to a ~ 19
differ widely 55
difference
make a ~ 5
subtle ~ 55
world of ~ 55
different
completely ~ 8
entirely ~ 8, 55
explore ~ ways 48
fundamentally ~ 1
slightly ~ 8
strikingly ~ 55
totally ~ 8
difficult
handle a ~ situation 44
~ to pin down 5

~ something some thought 14
~ vent to your frustration 59
given
   be ~ leave 22
   be ~ a sentence 38
   be ~ a yellow card 27
be glad to see the back of 57
full glare of publicity 42
raise your glasses 23
glimmer
   ~ of hope 54
   ~ of interest 54
   ~ of light 54
   ~ of understanding 54
restore to its former glory 46
glossy magazine 24
glowing
   ~ review 29
   ~ tribute 42
go *noun*
   be on the ~ 57
go *verb*
   ~ clubbing 19
   ~ on a diet 37
   ~ on an economy drive 1
   ~ freelance 12
   ~ hand in hand with 7
   ~ out for a meal 19
   ~ through a midlife crisis 41
   ~ on the offensive 39
   ~ part-time 12
   ~ through a phase 41
   ~ into production 15
   ~ into raptures 60
   ~ into rehab 42
   ~ shopping 16
   ~ on strike 13
   ~ trekking 26
   ~ wild 27
   not ~ to any trouble 57
go back on a promise 58
go down in history 46
act as a go-between 21
goal
   score an own ~ 27
   state a ~ 10
it goes without saying 10
golden era 46
good
   ~ behaviour 38
   ~ computer skills 44
   ~ few 50
   ~ knowledge 44
   ~ level of education 44

~ number (of) 50
~ size 50
create a ~ impression 9
develop a ~ relationship 44
earn a ~ living 12
enjoy ~ health 37
establish a ~ relationship 44
force for ~ 35
give someone a ~ send off 57
with ~ qualifications 44
really ~ 6
well ~ 6
juicy gossip 20
have got the chance 5
grab
   ~ a seat 5
   ~ a snack 6
gracious living 24
graduate from university 17
grand style 24
sheer epic grandeur 26
grant permission 30
take for granted 41
grasp the importance of 14
grave danger 49
great
   ~ pleasure 57, 60
   ~ significance 50
   enjoy ~ success 42
   have ~ success 42
   (of) ~ importance 1, 50
   place ~ value on 5
greater
   exercise ~ control over 28
   exports are five times ~ than
   imports 15
greatly
   ~ appreciate 8
   ~ influence 8
introduce green taxes 31
grief
   inconsolable ~ 59
   outpouring of ~ 59
air a grievance 22
face a grilling 58
grind the gears 25
cover a lot of ground 18
grounds for complaint 16
necessary groundwork 28
growing disparity 55
growth
   experience a ~ 15
   see a ~ 15
   show a ~ 15

steady ~ 34
stimulate ~ 15, 34
uninterrupted economic ~ 34
gruff
   ~ exterior 45
   ~ voice 47
grumpy old man 41
guilty
   find ~ 38
   find not ~ 38
habit
   become a ~ 41
   make a ~ of 9
unfit for human habitation 35
hail
   ~ as a major development 25
   ~ a taxi 32
hair
   auburn ~ 2
   blond ~ 1
   sun-damaged ~ 24
halt *noun*
   bring to a ~ 52
   call a ~ to 52
halt *verb*
   ~ production 36
hand *noun*
   go ~ in hand with 7
   reject out of ~ 28
hand *verb*
   ~ in assignments 6
   ~ in your resignation 12
handle
   ~ a complaint 16
   ~ a difficult situation 44
set of handlebars 25
suffer at the hands of 59
get the hang of 27
threat hangs over 59
find happiness 60
happy
   blissfully ~ 1
   deliriously ~ 2
hard
   ~ slog 56
   sounds like ~ work 48
harebrained scheme 59
harm
   not come to any ~ 41
   not mean any ~ 57
harmful to the environment 31
harness technology 36
judge someone harshly 14
hasten someone's death 59

have
~ absolutely no idea 6
~ an attitude problem 43
~ a baby 41
~ a barbecue 19
~ (got) the chance 5
~ a change of heart 12
~ difficulties 49
~ an effect on 53
~ every confidence in 44
~ an experience 27
~ an eye for 7
~ great success 42
~ a knock-on effect 53
~ an obligation 30
~ an operation 37
~ a party 9
~ a quality 45
~ relevance to 4
~ no respect for 43
~ a snack 6
~ a special charm 26
~ a stopover 26
~ a whale of a time 27
~ a word with 6
not ~ much luck 57
wreak havoc 53
hazy memory 41
head a team 7
heal the rift 40
health
be in poor ~ 37
enjoy good ~ 37
risk to public ~ 31
healthy competition 16
heap praise on 42
heart
~ leaps 60
have a change of ~ 12
learn by ~ 17
massive ~ attack 37
open your ~ to 20
with a light ~ 7
heart-to-heart chat 40
searing heat 31
solar heating 31
heavily
~ influenced 29
borrow ~ 33
come down ~ on 11
heavy
~ book 7
~ burden 7
~ rain 1
~ responsibility 7

~ traffic 25
~ workload 13
hectic pace of life 32
heed a warning 56
enlist help 48
herd
~ of cattle 54
~ of elephants 54
cultural heritage 23
high
~ hopes 60
~ percentage 50
~ risk 49
~ turnover of staff 13
hit the ~ street 24
spirits are ~ 26
high-definition TV 36
high-street fashion 24
highest
~ accolade 42
~ bidder 42
natural highlights 24
highly
~ educated 8, 44
~ praised 42
~ recommend 29
~ recommended 8
~ unlikely 8
~ valued 44
speak very ~ of 10
think ~ of 29
hike in prices 15
hinder progress 49
broad hint 2
go down in history 46
hit
~ the high street 24
~ the rocks 7
get hitched 23
hold noun
put someone on ~ 16
hold verb
~ someone's attention 29
~ someone/something in
contempt 43
~ a conversation 20
~ a demonstration 21
~ a festival 23
~ a press conference 21
~ a position 12
home
leave ~ 41
second ~ 41
there's no place like ~ 1
hone your skills 44

brutally honest 57
honestly think 14
honour a commitment 16
hoots of laughter 47
hope noun
flicker of ~ 54
glimmer of ~ 54
vain ~ 3
hope verb
sincerely ~ 57
very much ~ 57
hopelessly lost 26
hopes
high ~ 60
pin your ~ on 56
hopping mad 7
play host to 19
engage in hostilities 39
hostility
declare outright ~ 28
open ~ 45
wireless hotspot 36
pack of hounds 54
hours
long opening ~ 32
open all ~ 32
unsocial ~ 13
disposal of household waste 31
affordable housing 35
run up a huge debt 33
hugely popular look 24
unfit for human habitation 35
humiliating defeat 21
touch of humour 54
hunk of bread 54
overcome a hurdle 49
hurl insults 59
deathly hush 47
husky voice 47
hybrid car 31
hypothesis
supports the ~ 18
working ~ 18
idea
bright ~ 57
come up with an ~ 28
have absolutely no ~ 6
haven't the foggiest ~ 6
laughable ~ 59
rough ~ 14
toy with an ~ 28
adhere to ideals 11
identity theft 33

idle
~ chatter 20
~ threat 3
bone ~ 43
rural idyll 32
profess ignorance 10
ignore someone's advice 56
ill
~ effects 53
critically ~ 22, 37
illegal substance 35
rare illness 37
imagination
fertile ~ 14
fire someone's ~ 29
immense asset 48
impact
significant ~ 42
withstand the ~ 3
impart
~ knowledge 10
~ wisdom 10
change imperceptibly 51
implement
~ a change 51
~ a plan 28
trust someone implicitly 44
importance
grasp the ~ of 14
(of) great ~ 1, 50
of paramount ~ 44
imports
exports are five times greater
than ~ 15
impose censorship 21
impression
create an ~ 9
create a bad ~ 9
create a good ~ 9
indelible ~ 29
lasting ~ 29
improvement
marked ~ 17
modest ~ 51
room for ~ 17, 51
show an ~ 51
make improvements 9
in-depth
~ critique 18
~ interview 42
wildly inaccurate 8
incessant noise 47
not trust an inch 43
incite violence 35

inclement weather 2
income
source of ~ 5, 33
supplement your ~ 33
inconsolable grief 59
increase noun
modest ~ 51
show an ~ 51
slight ~ 15
substantial ~ 15
increase verb
~ dramatically 51
~ output 34
~ significantly 51
~ your stress levels 59
indelible impressions 29
declare independence 21
indeterminate number 4
research indicates 18
indigenous people 26
take industrial action 13
thriving industry 34
infectious disease 37
infinite patience 50
inflation
curb ~ 34
rampant ~ 34
influence noun
disruptive ~ 43
influence verb
greatly ~ 8
strongly ~ 8
influenced
heavily ~ 29
strongly ~ 29
dig out info about a crime 6
information
disseminate ~ 10
item of ~ 48
snippet of ~ 3
infringe the regulations 30
show initiative 17
inner city 32
protest innocence 10
inordinate amount 50
create instability 39
install equipment 36
instantly recall 48
instigate measures 52
insults
barrage of ~ 3
hurl ~ 59
intense dislike 59
intensely personal 3

interest
arouse someone's ~ 1
awaken your ~ 29
flicker of ~ 54
glimmer of ~ 54
keen ~ 44
raise ~ rates 34
interest-free overdraft 33
interests
promote ~ 15
pursue your ~ 44
safeguard someone's ~ 34
interpersonal skills 44
interview
exclusive ~ 42
in-depth ~ 42
intrepid explorer 26
introduce
~ green taxes 31
~ a levy 34
~ a neighbourhood watch
scheme 35
~ new legislation 30
~ regulations 30
see off an intruder 11
invest in the long-term 34
investigate a crime 6
investigation
conduct an ~ into a crime 6
subject to police ~ 6
touch of irony 54
irreversible climate change 31
issue noun
address an ~ 35
confront an ~ 58
tackle the ~ 18
take ~ with 22
issue verb
~ a denial 58
~ a statement 22
confront issues 18
get itchy feet 26
item of information 48
simplicity itself 48
fit of jealousy 59
job
aspects of the ~ 12
fit the ~ description 13
land a ~ 13
walk straight into a ~ 7
do a job-share 12
join
~ in the festivities 19, 23
~ the staff 12

light *noun*
  cast ~ on a situation 7
  glimmer of ~ 54
like
  sounds ~ hard work 48
  there's no place ~ home 1
agreed credit limit 33
push yourself to the limits 27
affect the bottom line 15
fine lines 24
pride of lions 54
list
  draw up a ~ 3
  narrow the ~ down 13
literature review 18
little
  be left with ~ alternative 59
  bear ~ resemblance to 55
  precious ~ chance 27
live
  ~ a comfortable life 41
  desirable place to ~ 32
live up to expectations 11, 60
lose your livelihood 13
living
  ~ wage 13
  earn a good ~ 12
  gracious ~ 24
  make a ~ 12
  urban ~ 32
  within ~ memory 46
loan
  call in a ~ 33
  pay back a ~ 33
picturesque location 2
swarm of locusts 54
lodge a complaint 9
long opening hours 32
long-lasting colour 24
long-standing tradition 23
long-term
  ~ relationship 40
  ~ solution 28
  invest in the ~ 34
look *noun*
  new season's ~ 24
  hugely popular ~ 24
look *verb*
  ~ your age 45
  ~ into a crime 6
  really ~ forward to 57
  very much ~ forward to 57
loosely based on 8
widespread looting 49

lose
  ~ an argument 20
  ~ your livelihood 13
  ~ your voice 47
  not ~ any sleep over 57
hopelessly lost 26
lot
  cover a ~ of ground 18
  take up a ~ of room 46
  take up a ~ of space 46
  talk a ~ of sense 10
  under a ~ of pressure 12
give a loud laugh 47
low-cost airline 26
low-income family 35
luck
  not have much ~ 57
  pure ~ 60
  stroke of ~ 3, 54, 60
lull *noun*
  ~ in the conversation 52
  ~ in the fighting 52
lull *verb*
  ~ someone to sleep 26
cut down on luxuries 33
luxury
  ~ cream 24
  sheer ~ 24
hopping mad 7
glossy magazine 24
maintain quality 15
hail as a major development 25
majority
  overwhelming ~ 50
  secure a ~ 21
  slim ~ 21
make
  ~ someone's acquaintance 9
  ~ an apology 9
  ~ arrangements 9
  ~ an attempt 9
  ~ calculations 9
  ~ the case for 18
  ~ changes 51
  ~ a commitment 58
  ~ a complaint 16
  ~ a contribution 9
  ~ a difference 5
  ~ a discovery 9
  ~ an effort 56
  ~ enemies 9
  ~ an escape 9
  ~ friends 1
  ~ a full recovery 37
  ~ a habit of 9

  ~ improvements 9
  ~ a living 12
  ~ mistakes 1, 49
  ~ an offer 9
  ~ a payment 33
  ~ plans 28
  ~ a plea 35
  ~ a proposal 9
  ~ a relationship work 40
  ~ room for 9
  ~ a sound 47
  ~ sound business sense 15
  ~ a stand against 9
  ~ a success of 9, 42
  ~ some suggestions 9
  ~ someone welcome 19
  it would ~ a change 51
man
  changed ~ 51
  grumpy old ~ 41
manageable chunk 48
manner
  abrasive ~ 45
  forthright ~ 45
manual car 25
narrow profit margins 15
marked
  ~ improvement 17
  in ~ contrast to 55
market
  play the stock ~ 1
  target ~ 15
marks *noun*
  full ~ 17
  gain ~ 1
marks *verb*
  event ~ 23
  festival ~ 23
massive
  ~ heart attack 37
  ~ overdose 50
master new skills 13
call off a match 52
maternity leave 12
be joined in matrimony 23
weighty matters 7
mature student 17
meal
  go out for a ~ 19
  rustle up a ~ 9
not mean any harm 57
cost-cutting measure 33
measures
  draconian ~ 35
  instigate ~ 52

announce record profits 15
falsify records 33
recovery
~ of money 21
make a full ~ 37
modest ~ 51
recycle waste 31
cut through red tape 30
reduce
~ your carbon footprint 31
~ your stress level 37
act as a referee 44
provide a reference for 44
take up references 13
full refund 16
refuse point-blank 22
urban regeneration 32
regime topples 21
regular
~ customer 16
~ update 22
regulations
conform to safety ~ 16
infringe the ~ 30
introduce ~ 30
go into rehab 42
silence reigns 47
reject
~ a charge 58
~ out of hand 28
flatly ~ 22
rekindle memories 41
relations
break diplomatic ~ 52
cordial ~ 40
relationship
~ breaks down 40
develop a good ~ 44
establish a good ~ 44
long-term ~ 40
make a ~ work 40
stable ~ 40
relationships
forge new ~ 40
platonic ~ 40
release a CD 29
have relevance to 4
reliable
~ public transport 32
~ source 5
relief
provide ~ 35
sigh of ~ 60
welcome ~ 57
relieve someone of their duties 13

relish a challenge 49
remain
~ on friendly terms 40
~ unchanged 51
remand in custody 38
disparaging remark 59
with remarkable ease 48
opening remarks 52
remote *adjective*
by ~ control 36
remote *verb*
~ access your email 36
render
~ obsolete 53
~ speechless 4
renewable energy 31
default on repayments 33
give repeated assurances 58
submit a report 18
reputation
a considerable ~ 29
a well-deserved ~ 29
request an extension 6
require effort 56
requirements
meet the entry ~ 17
satisfy the ~ 30
research
~ ethics 18
~ indicates 18
do ~ 9, 18
publish ~ 36
select a ~ topic 18
resemblance
bear little ~ to 55
bear a striking ~ to 45
breed resentment 53
residential dwellings 32
resign from office 21
hand in your resignation 12
build up resistance 37
allocate resources 34
respect *noun*
gain ~ 5
have no ~ for 43
with all due ~ 58
respect *verb*
~ someone's wishes 41
respond
~ to an emergency 49
~ well to treatment 37
pending the response 5
shirk responsibilities 43

responsibility
heavy ~ 7
take on ~ 13
exclusive restaurant 24
restore
~ to its former glory 46
~ peace 39
~ power 36
the blame rests with 43
produce a result 53
results
catastrophic ~ 49
lay out the ~ 18
pending the ~ 5
reveal
~ a secret 42
~ a talent 44
get into reverse 25
review
glowing ~ 29
literature ~ 18
undergo a revival 51
substantial reward 21
reap the rewards 56
bed of rice 54
rich
~ source 5
~ tradition 23
stinking ~ 8
ridiculous
faintly ~ 8
utterly ~ 8
heal the rift 40
get your priorities right 12
right-hand-drive car 25
bored rigid 32
give someone a ring 57
download a ringtone 36
riot erupts 35
rise
experience a ~ 15
see a ~ 15
show a ~ 15
meteoric ~ to fame 42
rising unemployment 34
risk
~ to public health 31
carry a ~ 49
carry out a ~ assessment 30
high ~ 49
minimise a ~ 49
congested road 32
hit the rocks 7
cast in the role of 29

shatter someone's confidence 59
flock of sheep 54
sheer
~ epic grandeur 26
~ luxury 24
~ quantity 50
~ size 50
provide shelter 35
shift
dramatic ~ 51
sudden ~ 51
shirk responsibilities 43
shiver down your spine 60
shoal
~ of fish 54
~ of sardines 54
shock
be in for a ~ 59
come as a bit of a ~ 57
nasty ~ 59
in a state of ~ 59
shopping
do the ~ 16
go ~ 16
online ~ 16
short of space 46
give it your best shot 56
shoulder the blame 7
broad shoulders 2
show *noun*
~ of unity 21
show *verb*
~ a decline 15
~ a decrease 51
~ a downward trend 51
~ a fall 15
~ a growth 15
~ an improvement 51
~ an increase 51
~ initiative 17
~ a rise 15
~ an upward trend 51
shut down a computer 36
sick
~ with worry 59
worried ~ 59
throw a sickie 13
side
~ effects 37
the other ~ of the argument 55
take a sideswipe 59
move sideways 25
sigh of relief 60
let someone out of your sight 41
do the sights 26

sign up for a course 17
great significance 50
significant
~ amount (of) 50
~ impact 42
~ number (of) 50
~ quantity (of) 50
increase significantly 51
silence
~ descends 47
~ reigns 47
meet with a stony ~ 47
fundamentally similar 55
simple
~ reason 57
~ rule 48
~ truth 3
simplicity itself 48
simultaneous
~ equation 5
provide ~ translation 5
sincerely hope 57
situation
cast light on a ~ 7
handle a difficult ~ 44
size
good ~ 50
sheer ~ 50
skills
advanced computer ~ 44
good computer ~ 44
hone your ~ 44
interpersonal ~ 44
master new ~ 13
sleep
decent night's ~ 57
not lose any ~ over 57
lull someone to ~ 26
slight
~ change of plan 28
~ decrease 15
~ increase 15
slightly
~ different 8
~ offensive 8
slim
~ chance 7
~ majority 21
standards slip 3
slippery customer 43
hard slog 56
slur your words 47
small
~ amount 50
~ minority 50

~ number 50
~ percentage 50
~ quantity 50
smile
broad ~ 2
dazzling ~ 45
friendly ~ 45
warm ~ 45
run smoothly 36
snack
grab a ~ 6
have a ~ 6
tasty snacks 24
snippet of information 3
flurry of snow 54
soak up atmosphere 11
soaring crime rates 38
temperature soars 31
social
~ exclusion 34
~ fabric 35
~ network 40
~ whirl 19
soft whisper 47
solar heating 31
solution
find a ~ 31
long-term ~ 28
novel ~ 35
provide a ~ 56
song
break into ~ 52
burst into ~ 3
sound *adjective*
make ~ business sense 15
sound *noun*
~ travels 47
make a ~ 47
sounds like hard work 48
source
~ of amusement 5
~ of entertainment 5
~ of fun 5
~ of funding 5
~ of income 5, 33
alternative energy ~ 31
cheap ~ 5
divulge a ~ 10
reliable ~ 5
rich ~ 5
valuable ~ 5
sources close to 42

unanimous verdict 38
unbounded enthusiasm 50
remain unchanged 51
leave unchecked 34
excruciatingly uncomfortable 24
undeclared earnings 34
underage drinking 35
underestimate the value of 5
undergo
   ~ a revival 51
   ~ a transformation 51
glimmer of understanding 54
undertake a study 18
preparations are underway 28
undivided attention 41
uneasy truce 39
rising unemployment 34
unexplored wilderness 26
unfit for human habitation 35
uninterrupted economic
growth 34
unique selling point 15
show of unity 21
university
   graduate from ~ 17
   read a subject at ~ 17
unknown quantity 50
highly unlikely 8
unmitigated disaster 29
unpaid overtime 13
unprovoked attack 39
unreliable
   ~ evidence 38
   ~ witness 38
quell unrest 52
unrivalled service 24
unsocial hours 13
untimely death 37
unveil a plan 28
regular update 22
uphill struggle 56
uphold a tradition 23
life is turned upside-down 51
show an upward trend 51
urban
   ~ living 32
   ~ regeneration 32
use SATNAV 36
not utter a word 47
utterly
   ~ absurd 8
   ~ ridiculous 8
vacant parking space 46
vain hope 3
valiant effort 56

valid driving licence 25
valuable source 5
value
   ~ for money 16, 34
   assess something's ~ 5
   novelty ~ 5
   place great ~ on 5
   practical ~ 5
   sentimental ~ 5, 41
   underestimate the ~ of 5
highly valued 44
wide variation 55
wide variety 50
vast expanse 46
vehicle emissions 31
give vent to your frustration 59
perfect venue 19
verdict
   contest a ~ 38
   overturn a ~ 38
   unanimous ~ 38
viable option 48
fashion victim 24
victory
   convincing ~ 27
   proclaim a ~ 21
take the view that 14
vigorous defence 18
picturesque village 1
violence
   ~ erupts 39
   ~ escalates 39
   incite ~ 35
   mindless ~ 43
visit
   flying ~ 19
   pay someone a ~ 19
   whirlwind ~ 19
vital
   ~ clue 21
   absolutely ~ 31
vociferous opponent 22
voice
   ~ falters 47
   booming ~ 47
   dissenting ~ 22
   gruff ~ 47
   husky ~ 47
   lose your ~ 47
   muffled ~ 47
   raise your ~ 47
volume of work 12
living wage 13
walk straight into a job 7
within walking distance 32

attention wanders 17
warm smile 45
heed a warning 56
waste
   ~ of space 46
   disposal of household ~ 31
   dump ~ 31
   recycle ~ 31
   toxic ~ 31
watch *noun*
   introduce a neighbourhood ~
   scheme 35
watch *verb*
   ~ what you eat 37
concentration wavers 17
way
   in a straightforward ~ 48
   take the easy ~ out 48
   take something the wrong ~ 40
ways
   change your ~ 31
   explore different ~ 48
   see the error of your ~ 41
stockpile weapons 39
wear
   ~ and tear 36
   ~ traditional dress 23
weather
   ~ patterns 31
   adverse ~ conditions 49
   face severe ~ conditions 26
   inclement ~ 2
wedded bliss 23
fairytale wedding 42
weighty
   ~ matters 7
   ~ problems 7
   ~ tome 7
welcome
   ~ relief 57
   make someone ~ 19
well
   ~ good 6
   ~ qualified 44
   respond ~ to treatment 37
a well-deserved reputation 29
have a whale of a time 27
whales
   pod of ~ 54
   school of ~ 54
what
   ~'s in fashion 24
   watch ~ you eat 37
set the wheels in motion 53
take it easy for a while 3